Messy Play in the Early Years

Combining a rich theoretical foundation with practical tips, advice and case studies, *Messy Play in the Early Years* provides an informative and practical exploration of the unique qualities, characteristics and learning possibilities of messy play.

Packed with valuable insights from research and theory, along with practitioners' experiences, this accessible book will bolster readers' understanding and appreciation of messy play and demonstrate how a range of material engagements can enhance young children's development and learning. Exploring an array of resources and a broad spectrum of approaches, including adult- and child-led inquiry, chapters consider how the specific sensory qualities of materials encourage problem-solving, scientific thinking, creativity, self-regulation and self-expression as children discover and make sense of new phenomena. With examples of international practice and reflective questions throughout, the book highlights a variety of approaches to meeting differing time, space and budgetary needs, simplifies preparation and planning, and empowers practitioners and children to understand and use messy play effectively.

An essential guidebook to supporting an engaging and rewarding journey into messy play, *Messy Play in the Early Years* will be an invaluable resource for early years students, practitioners and parents looking to understand and enhance children's learning possibilities.

Sue Gascoyne is an early years consultant, trainer and founder of Play to Z Ltd, an award-winning sensory resources and equipment company. Sue is also a Creative Arts and Play Therapist working in primary schools to support children with emotional and behavioural problems.

I loved reading this well-considered and thoroughly researched book. Sue Gascoyne gifts us with an accessible guidebook for travelling a really interesting journey through 'the landscape of messy play'. Pulling together many ways of thinking to broaden how we look at messy play, it makes sense of this deeply significant sensory engagement – and transforms our ideas about what 'messy' really means.

Through a lively combination of theoretical ideas with careful observations indoors and outdoors, we can see so much more of what children are really doing, feeling and thinking in their engagements with materials. We also come to realise that 'materials' are a great deal more than passive, non-active 'stuff', making the case for just how much materials matter in the lives of young children.

Jan White, *Professor of Practice, University of Wales Trinity St David, UK*

This is an important book on an area of play which is often neglected within the literature on play. It is highly informative, supported with wonderful photographs of children engaging in the reality of messy play. It dispels many commonly held myths regarding this type of play whilst providing a theoretical underpinning which enables practitioners and students to justify their messy play provision. It offers a wealth of ideas for creating and evaluating messy play environments and materials and provides guidance for the adult role when engaging in this type of play. It is a valuable resource for both students starting out on their early years' journey, as well as practitioners wishing to develop their play practice.

Karen McInnes, *Head of Learning, Teaching and Research, Norland, UK*

Drawing on her considerable expertise as a play therapist Sue Gascoyne shares a new understanding of the role of messy play as a protagonist in children's play. Guaranteed to make the reader question their own understanding and interpretations of children's material engagements, this book encourages them to reflect on their practice and challenges practitioners to make changes in their work practices. Sue offers readers a new lens which will help them recognise the significance for children of the world around them as a place where joy, wonder and curiosity combine to inspire young children. This accessible, thought provoking and stimulating book was a joy to read.

Menna Godfrey, *Lead practitioner in a private kindergarten, UK*

As a life-long believer in messy play for creativity, curiosity, growth and development, I am delighted to recommend this book for parents, teachers, clinicians and nursery workers. Too often children are told 'don't make a mess', 'be sure to clear up', 'don't spill', 'that was a clean dress!', which immediately stunts their expression, and makes them wary of crossing borders! This remarkable book gives us the why's and wherefore's of messy play, and ways of putting it into practice. It describes a myriad of techniques in an accessible way. It has my heart-felt support and recommendation.

Sue Jennings, *Professor of Play, European Federation of Dramatherapy, UK*

Messy Play in the Early Years

Supporting Learning through Material Engagements

Sue Gascoyne

Routledge
Taylor & Francis Group
LONDON AND NEW YORK

First published 2019
by Routledge
2 Park Square, Milton Park, Abingdon, Oxon OX14 4RN

and by Routledge
52 Vanderbilt Avenue, New York, NY 10017

Routledge is an imprint of the Taylor & Francis Group, an informa business

© 2019 Sue Gascoyne

The right of Sue Gascoyne to be identified as author of this work has been asserted by her in accordance with sections 77 and 78 of the Copyright, Designs and Patents Act 1988.

All rights reserved. No part of this book may be reprinted or reproduced or utilised in any form or by any electronic, mechanical, or other means, now known or hereafter invented, including photocopying and recording, or in any information storage or retrieval system, without permission in writing from the publishers.

Trademark notice: Product or corporate names may be trademarks or registered trademarks, and are used only for identification and explanation without intent to infringe.

British Library Cataloguing in Publication Data
A catalogue record for this book is available from the British Library

Library of Congress Cataloging in Publication Data
Names: Gascoyne, Sue, author.
Title: Messy play in the early years / Sue Gascoyne.
Description: Abingdon, Oxon ; New York, NY : Routledge, 2019.
Identifiers: LCCN 2018033538 (print) | LCCN 2018044901 (ebook) | ISBN 9781351234702 (eb) | ISBN 9780815377122 (hb) | ISBN 9780815377146 (pb) | ISBN 9781351234702 (ebk)
Subjects: LCSH: Play. | Early childhood education.
Classification: LCC LB1137 (ebook) | LCC LB1137 .G38 2019 (print) | DDC 372.21—dc23
LC record available at https://lccn.loc.gov/2018033538

ISBN: 978-0-8153-7712-2 (hbk)
ISBN: 978-0-8153-7714-6 (pbk)
ISBN: 978-1-351-23470-2 (ebk)

Typeset in Bembo
by Florence Production Ltd, Stoodleigh, Devon, UK

Printed and bound in Great Britain by
TJ International Ltd, Padstow, Cornwall

Dedication

In loving memory of my mum.

Thanks for everything mum. I hope you won't mind sharing this dedication with a little boy who touched my heart in my own messy play adventure.

For baby James' dad, James Wallace.

Contents

Acknowledgements — *viii*
List of figures and tables — *ix*

1. Introducing messy play and material engagements — 1
2. Messy play and its theoretical roots — 14
3. Investigating and quantifying messy play — 40
4. Patterns in messy play use — 64
5. Planning enabling messy play environments — 94
6. Creating enabling environments for messy play — 122
7. Material encounters and inquiry-based learning — 151
8. Agency and messy play — 177
9. Misadventure or mess adventures? — 199

References — *201*
Index — *208*

Acknowledgements

A huge thank you to all the children, practitioners and parents from Cheeky Monkeys Colchester and Earls Colne, Myerside Parent and Toddlers Group, Nannas Day Nursery, Rainbow Trekkers and Splat Messy Play, whose generous insights and wonderful material encounters have richly embellished and breathed life into the pages of this book. For Samuel Armstrong, Nikita Baldwin, Abi Barton, Hayley Chart, Anjali Rajan Dileep, Heidi Griggs, Menna Godfrey, Sylvia Kind, Ben Kingston-Hughes, Lynne Latham, Karen O'Neill and Fiona Smith for sharing their experiences and nuggets of learning so freely and without whose contribution this book would be infinitely poorer. To Menna Godfrey and Catherine House for their valued and inciteful sounding boards and Emma and Gemma for keeping me topped up with treats! Thanks to my husband Dan for helping me turn my vision into a reality and to my children, Freya and Zach, who have inspired and taught me so much and without whom my own messy play journey would never have started.

Figures and tables

Figures

1.1	'Love and hate' – extremes of messy play	9
1.2	A framework for considering messy play engagements	10
1.3	Dynamite or rock – understanding children's and adults' messy play needs and concerns	11
2.1	The messy play triangle and its theoretical context	15
2.2	The context for messy play	16
3.1	Benefits of messy play	49
3.2	The emotional affordance of materials	56
3.3	Stages in messy play use	58
4.1	Key messy play themes	65
4.2	An array of messy play materials	66
4.3	How messy play materials are used	67
6.1	A framework for planning messy play encounters	123
6.2	Messy play experiences are limited only by the imagination	126
6.3	A sliding scale of messy play interactions	127
7.1	Foundations for inquiries	155

Tables

2.1	Four stages of sensory interaction (Grace, 2018)	32
3.1	Types of messy play resources	41
3.2	Attention restoration qualities and messy play	46
3.3	Stages of messy play interactions	61
7.1	Ingredients of inquiry-based learning	156

7.2	Messy play and phases of scientific thinking	161
7.3	Possibilities and porridge oats	165
7.4	Possibilities and tea making	169
7.5	Possibilities and playdough making	170

1 Introducing messy play and material engagements

> Most practitioners instinctively know that messy play is good, even if it fills some with dread or can only be tolerated if 'not in my home!' Love it or hate it, 'material engagements'[1] are a key ingredient of the early years landscape and this book aims to increase understanding and provide confidence in the true learning and development value of messy play.

My own interest in messy play started fourteen years ago when my daughter was a toddler. I'd given her cooked couscous to play with only to be interrupted by a work call. The resulting mess, smeared gunge over the kitchen floor, table and chairs, taught me a valuable lesson about attentive parenting, not to mention appropriate equipment, as those fabric chairs were never the same again! Even then, exhausted from clearing up the aftermath and having galvanised a phobia of messy play in my husband, I knew that my daughter's explorations had been worthwhile, despite the mess!

Since then I have shared a journey of discovery of messy play with my own children and an array of families, practitioners and children in childcare and therapeutic settings. As my adventure has progressed I have found myself returning time and again to the uniquely special qualities of messy play and my mission to understand the what, why and how of this revered and reviled play, so that we can better appreciate and support children's interactions. In this book I hope to shine a torch on those very questions, taking the reader on a journey of discovery about messy play.

Messy play myths

We'll start by exploring and, hopefully dispelling, some common myths so we can illuminate what messy play is, and what it is not.

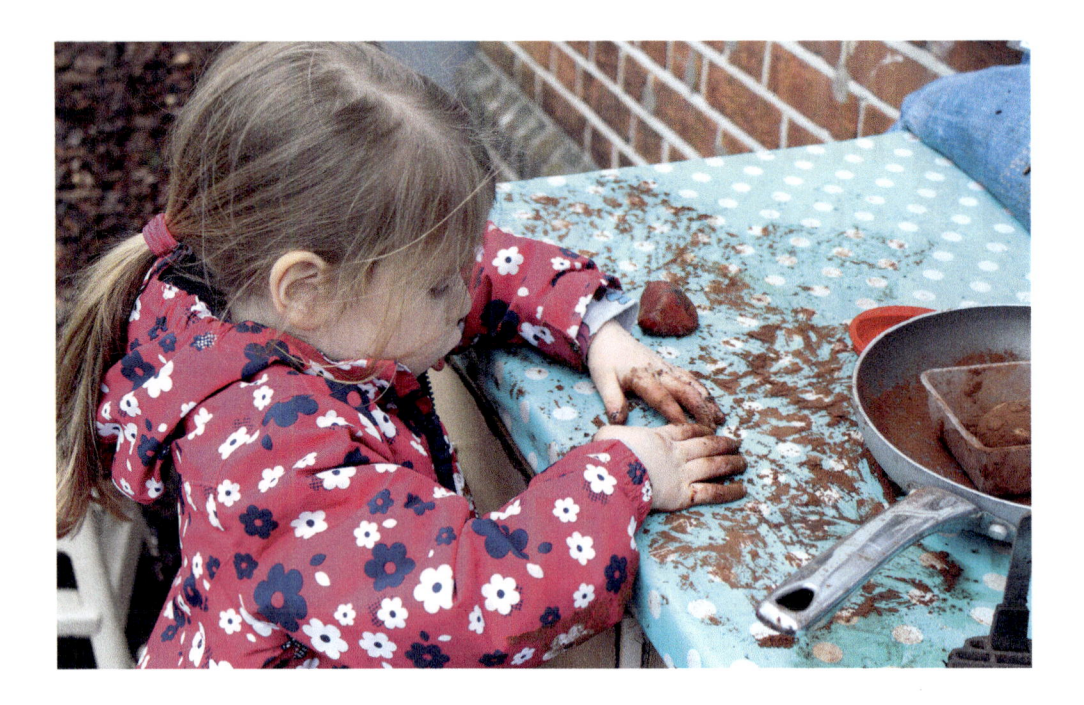

Myth 1 – 'Messy play is really messy'

When we think of messy play we tend to picture super-messy resources like mud and gloop.[2] Although messy play encounters like my couscous misadventure can undoubtedly be untidy, this is not their purpose, but rather a product of children's material engagements, thinking and need for immersion (Chapter 2). As will be evident when we focus on the spectrum of materials in Chapter 4, messy play resources can be classified according to their wet, dry or sticky texture and composition, each of which will impact upon the specific qualities of the resources being explored and how they are used.

Stretched budgets and a desire to look afresh at messy play have informed the emphasis upon low- and no-cost natural resources and early years staples in this book. While specialist messy play materials have a limited presence, most things are capable of being used for messy play, making resources infinitely varied and limited only by the imagination.

Myth 2 – 'Messy play is just for very young children'

While a focus on the youngest children is welcome and we know from countless reports just how important quality early years experiences are to children's life potential, that doesn't mean that older children can't benefit too:

> I remember one time we started mud-sliding down a small hill after a particularly heavy rainstorm and a group of 8-to-11-year olds all joined in. This was an inner-city

> adventure playground with no provision for wellies or wet weather gear so [we] were all in ordinary clothes. About twenty children and staff took part and they had completely covered backsides and legs. One 15-year-old, 'Tommy', spent his time teasing the children who were covered in mud. . . . He stood alone watching the other younger children (and me) sliding down the hill, occasionally grunting insults at us. [When] someone shouted that tuckshop was open. . . . every child ran as fast as they could into the building and queued-up. Tommy didn't follow. About 10 minutes later the door to the project was flung open and Tommy walked in. He was so covered in mud you could barely see clothing and face. The smile on his face could be seen though. He had waited until everyone else had gone inside and then repeatedly slid down the hill on his front!
>
> (Ben Kingston-Hughes, 2018)

As we shall discover in Chapter 2, some older children may have missed out on valuable opportunities to experience the world in a sensory and whole-bodied way in their formative years. For these children, accessing paint or another media through an intermediary brush will never be as satisfying as smearing and squelching it in their hands. Only once they have enjoyed experiencing it in an active, sensory and embodied way (Jennings, 2011), will they discover, as if a young child 'What is this material like?', can they start to explore 'What can I do with it?' and 'What can it become?'.

In Chapter 5 I introduce the value of material engagements for increasing children's and adults' mindfulness. But the value of material engagements doesn't end there. No matter how playful we are as adults, we can always benefit from an injection of awe, wonder and curiosity. The surprising qualities of messy play (explored in Chapter 3) challenge our assumptions, reminding us of what it's like to experience the world as a 'sensory being' (Grace, 2018). Unencumbered by worries, we're able to enjoy the sheer sensory experience in the moment. For some adults, messy play brings with it those rare moments of freedom and release that come from being playful.

International festivals such as Thailand's New Year Songkran festival revel in this sensory freedom, as young and old wield buckets and water guns and you can expect to be soaked for days on end! If you've partaken in Spain's La Tomatina festival with its people and buildings caked in plum tomatoes, or India's dazzling Holi Festival, where for one day only, adults throw handfuls of vibrant paint on anyone and everyone who happens to pass by, then it's easy to be struck by their similarities to messy play. The resulting scene of swirling colours or tomato pulp has more than a nod to messy engagements and adult participants get a taste of the thrill and liberation of material encounters!

> **Reflection**
>
> Try to experience immersion in a messy encounter, be it being buried in sand on the beach, getting soaked through in the rain, body-sliding in mud or cocooning yourself in shredded paper or leaves. Savour the moment and notice any heightened sensory awareness or emotions.

Myth 3 – 'Messy play is noisy, energetic and just good fun'

Messy play can be exciting and fun, providing endless possibilities, but it can also be enriching and satisfying, captivating and incredibly calming. These two extremes were evident in a survey of 35 practitioners (Gascoyne, 2018a), which identified sensory stimulation; fun; and calming and soothing (as well as communication and self-expression) as the most commonly cited benefits of messy play. Some children may find messy play encounters frustrating, others repulsive yet strangely compelling. For a child with sensory processing difficulties, touching certain substances may make finger play with gloop the antithesis of fun. As we shall discover on our journey through the landscape of messy play, experiences are infinitely varied, shaped by:

- the messy play materials,
- individual child and context,
- physical and emotional environment,

- the adult's approach and
- quality of adult/child relationship.

So, to pigeon-hole messy play as 'just good fun' would be to miss out on its potential to deliver so much more. With an artificial split sometimes suggested between real learning and play, it's worth emphasising that just because children find messy play fun, it doesn't mean they won't distil learning. Indeed, messy play effortlessly delivers a wealth of cross-curricular learning opportunities, rooted in real discoveries, as will become apparent throughout this book. It was even reputedly a forbidden pursuit in at least one serial killer's childhood[3] – a chilling indicator perhaps of its wider benefits.

Myth 4 – 'Messy Play is all about the end product'

With some books suggesting the creation of animals and pictures as legitimate messy play outcomes, you'd be forgiven for thinking that an end product is a natural conclusion. In fact, it was this focus on making something that was a key motivator for writing this book and offering an alternative approach! Definitions of messy play are limited but Duffy (2007) suggests that it should be about the process rather than an end product and this is something with which I wholeheartedly agree. An adult-initiated activity such as exploring paint with the objective of creating a picture is not messy play. However, the emergence of an end product doesn't rule out messy play. Agency is key. If the child chooses to create a product from, during or as a natural extension to, their material explorations then this is a valid outcome. The subtle differences are helpfully illuminated in the following three examples:

- **Cheesy puff** – An 8-year-old was exploring a mixture of sand and dried couscous (I'd learnt my lesson about using cooked couscous!). She added a maize packing 'peanut' to the mix and frustration quickly turned to delight as she discovered that the sandy mixture had stuck to its exterior so that it resembled a well-known cheesy snack!

- **Butterfly print** – A 7-year-old experimented with adding different-coloured paint to a box, using their hands to spread, splat and smear the paint over its insides. When he had finished he firmly planted his hands on a piece of A4 paper, squishing and moving them to remove the excess paint. He then folded the sodden paper in half, carefully opening to reveal a butterfly-like print. He got several pieces of paper to make prints of the design, each one getting slightly fainter. Exclaiming what 'a beautiful butterfly' he marvelled at these with evident satisfaction.

- **Make a sparkly snowman** – 'Stretch the snow gak[4] into snowman shapes ... Decorate with ... buttons and pipe cleaners. Photograph the snowmen and use the photos for Christmas cards' (Featherstone, 2016: 34).

Our understanding of messy play will shape a multitude of factors, from what we provide and how, to the quality of children's experience.

> **Reflection**
>
> Discuss each of these snapshots of play and compare against Duffy's (2007) definition of messy play provided on page 7. Decide which represents messy play, providing reasons for your answers.

Myth 5 – 'Messy play should be carefully planned and purposeful'

As with most myths they tend to contain a nugget of truth. Preparation is of course invaluable (although no guarantee) for stress-free material engagements but this should not become an excuse for avoiding spontaneity. Many of the encounters described in this book were unplanned, and in my opinion all the richer for their authenticity and surprise. Successful preparation takes several forms, from the obvious task of preparing the resources and physical environment, to preparing children, colleagues and parents, to ensure an enabling emotional environment too, as we shall discover in Chapter 5.

It's important to be transparent about where the balance of power lies and to what extent children really are agents of their own messy play explorations rather than simply protagonists of our vision and plans, a theme which we will explore further in Chapter 8. Beckerleg (2009) urges adults to have a clear plan when introducing messy play interventions, and while this is essential when working with children with sensory processing difficulties for whom some experiences may cause pain or discomfort, as we shall discover in Chapter 6 this may not be the best approach for mainstream explorations.

Messy materials provide plentiful opportunities for cognitive disequilibrium (Piaget's concept for when thinking must change to incorporate new information). Like the toddler who was surprised by the lack of an imprint in sand (Chapter 7); the boy who expected objects to sink in Gelli Baff/Play[5] (see page 54); or the 4 and 5-year-olds that discovered they'd created an amazing mud-slide simply because a child fell and then slid down it (Chapter 7), each of these children's encounters and learning would be the poorer if the result of a carefully orchestrated process rather than an 'aha moment' (Gopnik, 2000). The unusual sensory qualities of messy play resources and surprising ways of 'behaving' challenge children to problem-solve, understand, discover and make sense of phenomena. And it is this process of 'messing about' with resources which Hawkins (1974) considered to be invaluable for older children's understanding of properties and science (which we will explore further in Chapter 7).

Of course, spontaneity does not mean a lack of purposefulness, nor is it the preserve of children. As was apparent in the wonderfully unplanned episode of mud-sliding on page 2, messy play can deliver outstanding benefits, far exceeding any 'planned for' curricular objectives.

What is messy play?

Having dispelled some common myths, it's time to unpick what messy play is! While the words messy play probably conjure up sand, water, paint, playdough, gloop, clay, shredded paper, shaving foam or mud, as the spread of resources introduced in Chapter 4 shows, most things have the potential to be used for material engagements, be it fabric, a collection of natural treasures or even paper. According to Duffy (2007: 1), messy play involves:

> Children using all their senses in the process of exploration, especially the sense of touch; offering . . . plenty of opportunity to mould and manipulate materials; and not having a focus on making or producing something.

This is certainly true of the mud-sliding episode described! Much more than simply about mess and materials, its context and value as a thinking tool are equally important. Although a staple in UK early childhood provision, there has been limited research into the theoretical underpinning and value of messy play. We know that sensory stimulation is a key part of how young children learn about themselves and the world around them (as we shall explore in Chapter 2), and material encounters provide a particularly rich vein for cognitive disequilibrium, as well as providing an insight into the child's understanding of the world. Messy play is part of children's 'need for close contact with different substances, for creative experiments that involve learning through chaos' (Szekely, 2015: 42) and it is this sense of chaos that gives children opportunities to explore containment, control and transformation, as well as testing adult's resolve!

A word about the term 'messy play'

While discussing messy play in a training session some practitioners shared their discomfort with its negative associations. You only have to look at the *Oxford English Dictionary* definition to see that they have a point! Mess is defined as:

i) A dirty or untidy state of things.

ii) A thing or collection of things causing a dirty or untidy state.

iii) A person who is dirty or untidy.

iv) Used euphemistically to refer to the excrement of a domestic animal.

v) A situation that is confused and full of problems.

vi) A person whose life is confused and full of problems.

vii) A portion of semi-liquid food.

Many of these definitions concern 'a dirty or untidy state of things', associating mess with 'disorder, disarray, clutter, shambles, muddle, mishmash, chaos, confusion and disorganisation'.

Perhaps concerns about hygiene and safety explain some adults' reticence to certain types of messy play, with shaving foam potentially more appealing than mud.[6] Alternative definitions relate to 'a situation that is confused and full of problems' for which the words 'dilemma, difficulty, predicament, confusion, trouble, mire and plight' are suggested. While messy play can and does involve many of these, particularly confusion, challenge and at times chaos, rather than being negatives, these qualities are fundamental to its challenge and appeal.

Given extremes like those set out in Figure 1.1 (Childcare Expo seminar; Gascoyne 2018b) it's little wonder that messy play divides opinion and, depending upon your perspective, conjures up extremes of joyful release or dread. As a trip to the seaside reveals, mess provokes wide-ranging reactions:

> Like the child who complained 'Mum, I've got sand in my shoes' and the parent who flatly responded, 'We're at the beach and there's sand, so get over it!'

Or

> The child that tentatively showed their elderly caregiver a mud-caked hand, only to be immediately told, 'We'll have to get some water to wash it.' As the child looked at the now drying grey veneer there was a sense of intrigue at the strange tightening feeling as clay dries, and a moment of uncertainty, much like a child who has fallen and looks to the adult's reaction to decide whether to laugh or cry. In that adult's response this child's reaction to the mud was forged as a negative. They set off in search of water to wash of the 'mud' (but not sand). Ironic perhaps given the grey powdery mud had by now been replaced with sand-caked hands from digging!

With tactile defensiveness (a difficulty in touching certain textures) and resistance to getting messy increasingly prevalent, sensitive approaches and tools such as those suggested in Chapter 5 help children (and adults) experience the wonder of mess.

Children's play is frequently likened to the work of a scientist, rightfully so as the similarities are clear, but this is not one-way as Newton likened his own investigations to 'a boy playing on the seashore' (Gelb, 1995: 15). While it may be tempting to picture messy play explorations as an eccentric professor, whose focus insulates them from the social niceties of clearing up, this fails to recognise that children's engagements with materials aren't simply a subconscious bi-product of being focussed on something else, but a tool for thinking, experimentation and discovery. There is a danger that we judge the external appearance of mess, chaos and disorder, rather than recognising children's systematic, ordered and purposeful investigation and underlying sophisticated thinking. Comparable to judging Newton by his overflowing waste paper bin rather than his theories that forever changed our understanding of the world, if

Figure 1.1 'Love and hate' – extremes of messy play

we are too focussed on the appearance of disarray and mess we may miss the signs of a genius at work.

A distinction should be drawn between the internal thought process of the child and the external manifestation of their messy explorations, a cautionary reminder about making assumptions about children's play (an issue which we will return to in Chapter 8). With materials reframed as not just resources for shaping children's thinking but resources for thinking *with* (Pacini-Ketchabaw, Kind & Kocher, 2017), the importance of messy play is elevated to much more than simply fun.

Autonomy, Relatedness and Competence

The playful adults on that epic mud-slide weren't afraid to get covered in mud, but even if we don't engage directly with resources, that doesn't mean that we're not instrumental in shaping the success, or otherwise, of children's material engagements. Deci and Ryan's Self-Determination Theory (SDT; Deci & Ryan, 2000) identifies three psychological needs which shape and underpin children's and adults' daily interactions. As well as helping adults understand their pivotal role in supporting appropriate child behaviours, as Figure 1.2 demonstrates, they also provide a useful framework for considering messy play.

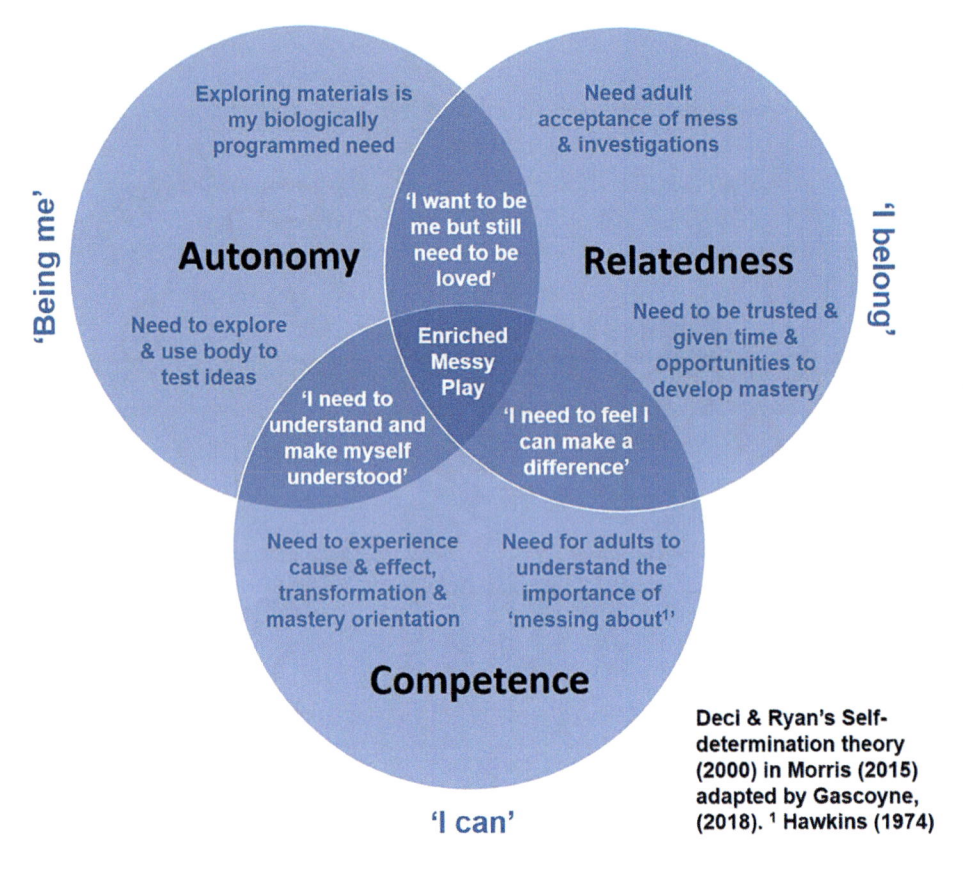

Figure 1.2 A framework for considering messy play engagements

'Being me'

Autonomy
- Exploring materials is my biologically programmed need
- Need to explore & use body to test ideas

Relatedness — 'I belong'
- Need adult acceptance of mess & investigations
- Need to be trusted & given time & opportunities to develop mastery

'I want to be me but still need to be loved'

Enriched Messy Play

'I need to understand and make myself understood'

'I need to feel I can make a difference'

Competence — 'I can'
- Need to experience cause & effect, transformation & mastery orientation
- Need for adults to understand the importance of 'messing about[1]'

Deci & Ryan's Self-determination theory (2000) in Morris (2015) adapted by Gascoyne, (2018). [1] Hawkins (1974)

Autonomy – Often erroneously associated with an individual making their own choices, in fact **autonomy** can only happen with structure and consistent boundaries. Typically provided by the adult or environment, these limits satisfy human beings' fundamental need for safety and a sense of predictability. Termed 'security of exploration' by Grossmann et al (2008, in Whipple, Bernier & Mageau, 2009: 221), this is essential for enabling childen to 'explore and find out about the world' (Morris, 2015: 53).

Relatedness – Developing secure attachments (or **relatedness**) in infancy is strongly associated with positive wellbeing and behaviour and applicable to practitioners as much as children. As we will explore further in Chapter 2, **relatedness** is multi-layered, applying to children's caregivers, the resources and environments which they encounter and their understanding of self. Central to this psychological need is the child's understanding of the world and others and their connectivity to these. Encounters with objects and environments involve children thinking 'What does this thing do?' and 'What can I do with it?' revealing the inter-relations at the heart of material engagements.

Competence – Defined as 'feeling that one can make an impact on situations or events' (Morris, 2015: 88), **competence** is linked to predictability and control, bringing us full circle to the importance of appropriate structure, predictability and boundaries in children's lives. **Competence** develops when children feel they can make a difference. Messy play resources capitalise on this with their rich potential for cause-and-effect investigations and children's ability to transform resources, providing a sense of agency and mastery.

Messy play encounters introduce a wealth of opportunities for children to develop a sense of **relatedness**, both with the natural or man-made environment, and to practitioners and peers. As a child mixes different-coloured paints to create a new colour, they develop their **relatedness** to the smooth liquid and experience the essence of agency as they see the impact of their actions upon the paint. This **autonomy** brings with it **competence** and mastery orientation in achieving a self-set goal, or the sheer joy of discovering what it's like to be caked in paint or mud!

Understanding children's need to feel **autonomous**, **competent** and belong is immensely helpful in supporting messy play interactions, as a child's experience of **Autonomy**, **Relatedness** and **Competence** (referred to as **ARC** in this book) will contribute to their sense of fulfilment and lens on life. Adults also have their own set of **ARC** needs, which given messy play extremes, can sometimes feel like they're in conflict with children's! With mess equated in some adults' and children's minds as being naughty, a disparaging or despairing look or tone can quickly convey what the adult really feels about messy play. Conversely, a child's self-expression through mess can feel scarily uncontained for adults, like my episode with cooked couscous!

As Figure 1.3 shows, children's subconscious concerns about messy play are potentially numerous. Adults too may have an unspoken agenda and all these factors and more will shape children's and adult's shared (positive or negative) experiences of messy play. When applied both to the adult and child I believe that **ARC** holds the key for successful material engagements, a recurring theme throughout this book.

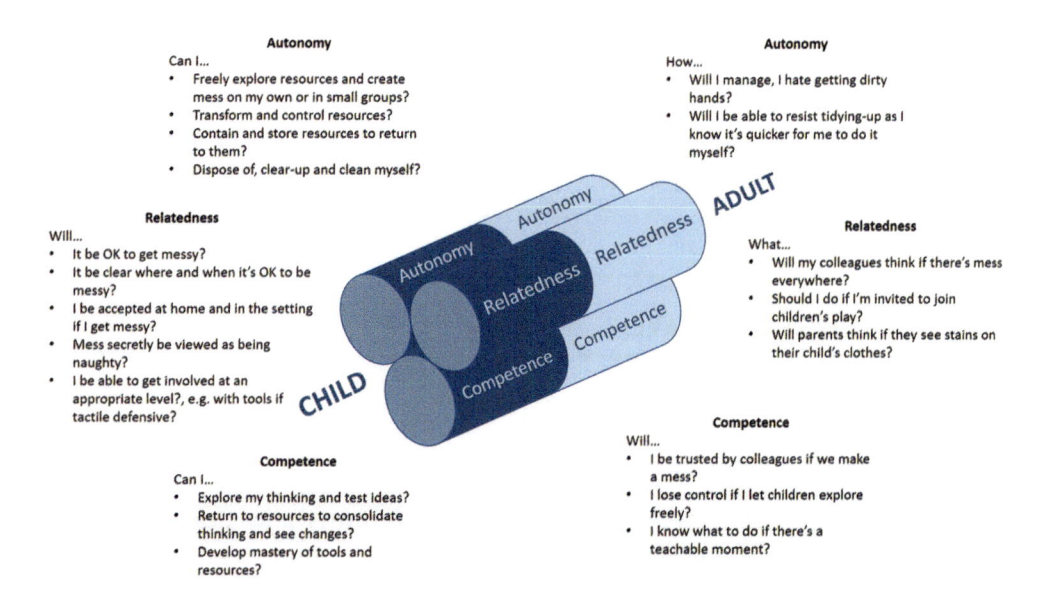

CHILD

Autonomy
Can I...
- Freely explore resources and create mess on my own or in small groups?
- Transform and control resources?
- Contain and store resources to return to them?
- Dispose of, clear-up and clean myself?

Relatedness
Will...
- It be OK to get messy?
- It be clear where and when it's OK to be messy?
- I be accepted at home and in the setting if I get messy?
- Mess secretly be viewed as being naughty?
- I be able to get involved at an appropriate level?, e.g. with tools if tactile defensive?

Competence
Can I...
- Explore my thinking and test ideas?
- Return to resources to consolidate thinking and see changes?
- Develop mastery of tools and resources?

ADULT

Autonomy
How...
- Will I manage, I hate getting dirty hands?
- Will I be able to resist tidying-up as I know it's quicker for me to do it myself?

Relatedness
What...
- Will my colleagues think if there's mess everywhere?
- Should I do if I'm invited to join children's play?
- Will parents think if they see stains on their child's clothes?

Competence
Will...
- I be trusted by colleagues if we make a mess?
- I lose control if I let children explore freely?
- I know what to do if there's a teachable moment?

Figure 1.3 Dynamite or rock – Understanding children's and adults' messy play needs and concerns

Reframing messy play as material engagements

With the words messy play so loaded in some cultures and meaningless in others, this begs the question whether this book should be reinforcing the use of the term messy play, or ditching this in favour of material engagements? In the end I have opted to use both, in the hope that this imbues messy play with the intentional learning potentialities of material engagements, giving it the recognition it deserves.

Navigating around this book

Like any good travel guide, my aim is to illuminate the potential, through words and images, without taking away the magic of self-discovery. Nuggets of research and theory are included to add weight and reason, while vignettes of messy play (shaded in blue) provide rich colour and vibrancy. Crammed with practical examples and ideas, the reflective activities (shaded in green) serve as potted training sessions, helping to ensure you get the most from your own messy play journey. Chapter summaries at the beginning and ends serve as both route-planner and memory-jogger for readers.

If you're expecting a book packed with recipes and messy play activities, then sadly this is likely to disappoint. A wealth of useful website links are highlighted to supplement Pinterest, which is jam-packed with enough recipes and messy play activity ideas to fill several books. Neither does this book present a 'one-size-fits-all' approach, but rather a guidebook for your messy play adventure, highlighting sights and sounds, tips and potential approaches to suit time and differing needs. You are about to embark on a journey which will hopefully change your experience of messy play. Like any serious explorer, a process of preparation and self-reflection will be key to ensuring that you get the most out of it, so be sure to use the prompts in green to guide you through this process. Above all I hope this book is an opportunity to gain a fresh perspective on material engagements and a clearer lens on children's infinite propensity for finding joy, wonder and curiosity in the world around them.

IN THIS CHAPTER WE HAVE:

- Outlined the myths surrounding messy play.
- Discussed what messy play is and isn't.
- Introduced the framework of **Autonomy, Relatedness and Competence (ARC)**, a guiding framework for planning and considering material engagements.
- Set out the structure and reader's expectations for the remainder of the book.

Notes

1 Material engagements are children's exploration, investigation and application of wide-ranging materials, from natural treasures to gloop, and all manner of materials in between.
2 Gloop is made by mixing water with cornflour or corn starch. It is called oobleck in some countries, after *Bartholomew and the Oobleck* (Dr Seus, 1949).
3 Ruth West was reputedly not allowed to get messy as a child.
4 Several DIY recipes include Borax, the use of which is not recommended as this can cause irritation and burns. All resources featured in this book have been safety tested, but you should check allergies and be sure of their suitability for the specific child before using. Borax-free recipes are available online for slime and other messy play mixtures.
5 To avoid repetition of these brand names, the term Gelli will be used throughout the remainder of the book to represent Gelli Baff or Gelli Play. This should not be confused with the American spelling of jelly.
6 This may also link with Hyan's finding in classrooms that young children's curiosity was 'dampened by adult responses that reflected biophobic views', i.e., seeing nature as frightening (Ramsey, 2015: 125).

2 Messy play and its theoretical roots

> Fundamental to adults appreciating and valuing messy play is an understanding of why it is so beneficial. In part this can be found by looking backwards to the theoretical underpinnings of this early years staple, but also forwards, to our rapidly evolving understanding of neuroscience and how children learn through active sensory exploration of materials.

It's just mess – why bother with theory?

If you're the type of learner that devours theory for the rich insights it provides into children's play and learning, then I hope this chapter provides both the breadth and depth of coverage necessary to inform your reflective practice. If, on the other hand, your tendency is to skim the theory, to move onto the 'practical bits', then my intention has been to infuse this chapter with practical relevance so that it adds a meaningful context and depth to children's play. Understanding the theoretical underpinnings and benefits of messy play is key to elevating its status in the early years and, given the extremes of opinions that messy play tends to elicit, may prove essential for changing hearts and minds. As adults supporting children's earliest material engagements, we have an opportunity not just to enrich children's lives while in our care, but also influence parents and carers to give messy play a chance at home. Judging by comments like *'Don't do it! Not at home'*[1] we've clearly got our work cut out!

Any good travel guide includes a map with which readers can pinpoint their position and decide which sights to take in. Like the areas of a city, Figure 2.1 maps out the different theoretical influences on messy play, from our growing understanding of the importance of attachment, sensory stimulation and movement for children's learning, to the vital contribution made by the natural environment. This chapter draws from the historical legacy of how adults can best support children's curiosity, self-esteem and active learning, culminating in a focus on neuroscience. It could easily take a book alone to cover each theory or movement, so by necessity entries are limited, brief and focussed only on illuminating the underpinnings of messy play.

Reflection

Take a minute to jot down which theories and theorists you feel are most relevant to messy play. A knowledge of these, together with any that you might not have considered, will help you convince others of its benefits and historical roots.

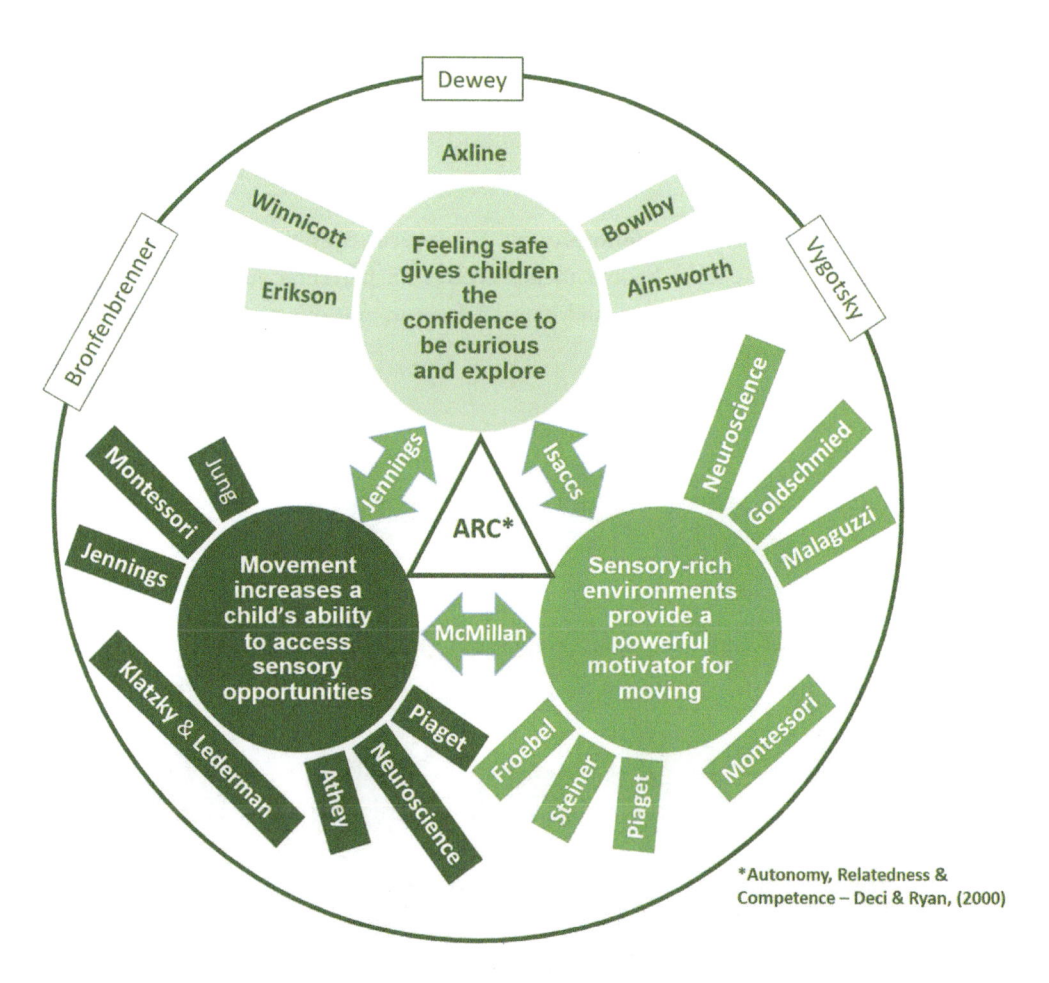

Figure 2.1 The messy play triangle and its theoretical context

Children learn best when able to freely enjoy plentiful and varied **sensory experiences** in a **whole-bodied** way. This is only possible when a child feels sufficiently **safe and secure** to curiously explore the environment around them. Picture the broad base of Maslow's hierarchy of needs and it is evident that only when basic safety, warmth, nurture and nourishment needs are met, can children thrive unencumbered by their reptilian brain 'fight or flight' responses.

16 Messy play and its theoretical roots

In an ideal world each of these three components – safe attachment, sensory stimulation and whole-bodied movement – blends into a rich and seamless recipe for childhood.

It is only when something goes awry in this triangle of learning that we become consciously aware of the need for specialist provision. One reason a book like this is needed is because children's lives have become increasingly disconnected from the natural environment and the wellbeing, sensory and active engagement which it provides. Throughout this chapter these three interconnected themes will be explored, drawing from the historical theories and movements of child development and the insights that neuroscience brings to our understanding of messy play. For each theory or approach, some key features are listed before their relevance to messy play is explored.

The child's environment

An apt starting point is **Urie Bronfenbrenner's Ecological Systems Model** (1917–2005). As Figure 2.2 shows, this lesser-known theory centres on the child and myriad of family, relational, cultural, historical, financial and political systems, that directly and indirectly affect the child, their parents and caregivers.

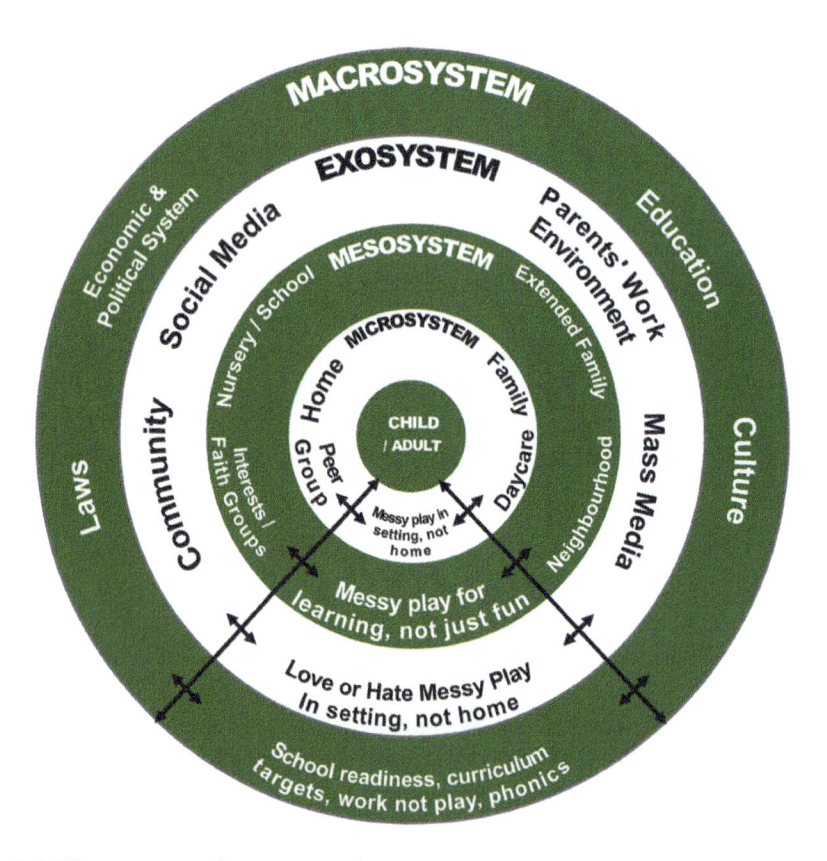

Figure 2.2 The context for messy play

- The child (or adult) is at the centre of a series of concentric systems, each exerting an influence on the other.

- Harmonious relationships within and between systems positively affect the child's development, while conflict and disagreement negatively affect the child.

RELEVANCE

The quality of the physical and emotional early childhood microsystem is the product of countless conscious and subconscious decisions by parents and practitioners, each of whom will be affected by their own influences. So, a school readiness political focus at the Macroscale may influence a practitioner's or parent's views of the value of play-based approaches to learning. Similarly, the parent and practitioner's childhood experiences of material encounters, or connection to social media,[2] will either support or limit a child's access to and enjoyment of messy play. Every decision, from if and how practitioners position chairs and tables, 'the choice of objects with which the children play or work' (Tudge et al, 2017: 53) to decoration of the room, will be shaped by the encircling systems and influence the child's Microsystem.

A difference in parents' valuing and provision of messy play at home may introduce anxiety about mess for children and adults in the setting. Attuned practitioners can draw from children's 'funds of knowledge', essentially knowledge from the child's home, family and interests (Moll et al, 1992), to bridge the gap and limit concerns about mess. Staff can also share their knowledge to reassure parents and influence messy play interactions at home, as occurred in one setting during an experiment (described in Chapter 5), offering children just yellow powder paint:

> Throughout this inquiry we shared our ideas with parents mainly through end of session conversations (explaining why some of their children looked jaundiced!), newsletters [and] an evening meeting for parents [sharing] images of children engaging with the materials and discussing the deep levels of involvement.
>
> (Menna Godfrey, 2018)

The emotional environment

Stages of development

Erik Erikson (1902–1994) introduced the idea of life being made up of several stages[3] of development:

- Trust and mistrust – birth to 1 year
- **Autonomy** and shame – 2 to 3 years
- Initiative and guilt – 4 to 5 years.

Depending upon the child's experiences at each of these stages, a series of strengths or weaknesses will emerge.

RELEVANCE

With the potential for messy play to trigger strong and often negative emotions like shame, doubt and guilt in adults, the relevance of this to material encounters is clear. An adult's reaction to mess, be it mud-sodden clothes, a paint-splattered floor or gloop-covered body, will determine whether a child perceives and stores these memories as positive experiences or sources of shame, disappointment and guilt. As we will explore further in Chapter 8, this will later shape their views of messy play as an adult.

A secure foundation in their first year enables infants to develop a strong sense of self and positive lens on the world, both essential for exploration. For Erikson the focus on **autonomy** in the second year of life presents the challenge of supporting young children's developing sense of independence, while also maintaining the adult's **autonomy**. This is a delicate balancing act, particularly when it comes to messy play, and a theme featuring prominently throughout this book. Erickson's third stage typically occurs at 3 to 5 years and is characterised by the child's increasing assertion of their ideas and interests. When positively supported, these develop into a sense of self and ability to take initiative, but if subjected to criticism (as is feasible with messy play), guilt may emerge.

> **Reflection**
>
> Pick a time when you will be free from interruptions. If you feel awkward try to persevere, as this will benefit the children that you support.
>
> Think about a type of messy play resource with which you have a strong negative reaction. It could be sand, clay, gloop or shaving foam, or a very specific resource like brown playdough. Close your eyes to picture the resource, noticing how you feel. Has your heart-rate changed or are you feeling more anxious? Spend a few minutes sitting with this uncomfortable feeling, picturing the moment, perhaps when an adult responded negatively to something you'd created, or a time when you were perhaps rebuked for making a mess, ruining something or wasting food or time. When you're ready, imagine what you might say to a child whom you support and empathetically say this to yourself.

A strong foundation of attachment

John Bowlby (1907–1990) and **Mary Ainsworth's** (1913–1999) insights into young children's need for secure attachment have changed childcare practice globally:

- Secure attachment from primary caregivers is essential for children's wellbeing, curiosity, self-esteem and 'abilities to and availability for learning' (Brooks, 2014 in RNIB, 2014: 8).
- Children with sensory processing difficulties are particularly vulnerable to learning delays, as sensory attachment may be impaired, and adults may feel unable to connect with the child.

Donald Winnicott's (1896–1971) practical views on parenting and recognition that adults don't always get things right has lots to commend it!

- The relationship between the infant and their mother/caregiver is seen as vital, acting as a 'mirror' to the child (Phillips, 2007: 101).
- Through 'attentive presence' and complete acceptance the child experiences wellbeing and self-regulation, irrespective of anguish or frustration caused, linking with Axline's principles below.

RELEVANCE

Attachment is particularly relevant to messy play as for some children (and adults) it can be scary, and therefore anchorage by a sensitive practitioner is essential for participation. Like the 19-month-old boy sat on his key person's lap, who with time and support was able to dab his toes in paint (Chapter 6). Children are skilled at reading body language, sensing the difference between genuine acceptance and lip-service masking anger and shame. A pragmatist, Winnicott recognised adults' limitations to always respond warmly to children's provocations, throwing us a lifeline which has served me well as a therapist and parent! He describes the importance of the child/adult relationship being able to survive negatives, and the sense of worth and resilience that this gives children.

Reflection

Think about a time when you have felt frustrated by a child wilfully ignoring your requests and the resulting mess. How did you respond? Were you able to stay calm and in an 'adult role' (Neurolinguistic Programming) or did you resort to blame? Think about what could have been done differently to avoid or manage this situation and achieve heightened levels of awareness and acceptance for the child.

The physical environment

If Erikson, Winnicott and Bowlby have helped shape our understanding of the emotional environment and children's needs, Froebel, Montessori, Piaget and Malaguzzi were advocates for the importance of sensory-rich physical environments. An emphasis upon sensory stimulation and a connection with the environment are certainly not new. Many early educationalists intuitively understood the importance of natural environments, which is why plentiful and varied sensory experiences are essential for children's cognitive and physical development.

A sensory-rich environment

As well as introducing the idea of **Gifts** (educational materials) and **Occupations** (activities), which we will explore on page 27, **Friedrick Froebel's** (1782–1852) kindergarten revolutionised views of childhood, enshrining the importance of open-ended, child-initiated play. **Rudolf Steiner** (1861–1925) also recognised the value of a sensory environment and its abundant store cupboard of natural materials:

- Open-ended resources such as wood, stones, shells, twigs, feathers and leaves were offered in the belief that 'the objects of play should be as simple as possible so that the child can clothe them with his own natural powers of fantasy' (Mickleburgh, 2010: 22).

Like Steiner, **Maria Montessori** (1870–1952) understood the value of experiential and sensory experiences for young children:

- A process of 'tak[ing] in stimuli from the environment through their senses and movement' and 'absorb[ing] imprints into . . . everyday experiences' (Povell. 2017: 23).

- Recognising the power of resources to 'educate the senses', she claimed this 'offers the child a key to guide his exploration of the world' (Mooney, 2000: 27).

The senses and movement also featured heavily for **Jean Piaget** (1896–1980):

- In the first two years of life, children primarily learn about themselves and their surrounding environment using their body, movement and senses, termed the Sensorimotor stage.

- In the Pre/Concrete/Formal Operational phases, language acquisition and physical exploration support the development of logical thinking.

RELEVANCE

Material engagements are ideal for supporting young children as their sensory and open-ended qualities invite touch and physical engagement. In the Pre, Concrete and Formal Operations stages too, encounters with messy resources give children sensations like cold, slimy and soft, underpinning language and supporting the development of children's thinking as they test ideas; discover cause-and-effect, such as when mixing a liquid with a solid; and how different substances behave. Increased material engagements bring opportunities for discombobulating moments, like the sold/liquid qualities of custard powder and gloop, which challenge and refine thinking.

Movement and the senses

With children's levels of movement and access to the environment at a frightening low in many urban communities, adults over-estimating the duration and vigorousness of physical activity (Sallis et al, 1996, cited in Bell, 1997: 133), and prisoners in the UK typically accessing the outdoor environment for longer than children (Swift, 2016), the importance of opportunities for whole-bodied movement has never been greater.

Active discovery

- **Montessori** viewed 'mind and movement [as] parts of the same entity' (Lillard, 2005: 40 in Povell, 2017: 23), arguing that children should be allowed to 'move about freely, as opposed to being trapped like butterflies on a board' (Povell, 2017: 23), a view also held by the Pikler movement (Marlen, 2014).

- Children learn through active discovery, rather than passive reception (Gettman, 1987: 17), a fact since proven by the discovery of the haptic sense, a combination of tactile and kinaesthetic senses, which increases sensory feedback and is now being capitalised upon in smart phones.

- Both **Montessori** and **Jung** recognised that 'the way to the brain, is through the hands' (Jung, 1959) Indeed, it is by touching things, primarily with their hands, that children discover about themselves and the world around them. With a disproportionate part of the human brain dedicated to processing sensory and motor feedback from the hands and mouth, it is clear why these are the preferred exploratory tools of very young children!

- Far from haphazard, a series of subconscious exploratory hand movements furnish the brain with information about the shape, texture, temperature and weight of objects, essential for categorising information (**Lederman & Klatzky**, 1987).

- Children also manifest and test their thinking and categorisation physically through repeated and evolving patterns of behaviour, termed schemas (**James Mark Baldwin**, 1894, **Piaget**, 1962, **Chris Athey**, 2007), such as immersing hands in mud or gloop as part of an enveloping schema.

Embodiment, projection, role

With the body seen as the 'primary means of learning', **Sue Jennings** (1990) suggests three stages of interactions which occur in enabling environments:

- **Embodiment** – babies and young children become immersed in and experience materials physically through movement and their senses.

- **Projection** – children discover what resources can do and how they can be used.

- **Role** – older children use resources imaginatively.

When children have ample sensory opportunities to explore and the attentive presence of an adult, they naturally move from one stage to the next (like the Pikler approach), without the need for prompting or hurrying. However, if a child misses an earlier stage they will need to plug these gaps later.

RELEVANCE

If you contrast an adult interacting with paint with that of a young child, we see that children are genetically programmed to explore in a whole-bodied sensorial way. Mouthing is inevitable, so be sure to provide child-safe resources like natural yoghurt (see Chapter 5), edible playdough or water to minimise the need to limit this natural response. Messy play is ideal for the **Embodiment stage**, as a child presses their palm into, squishes between their fingers, dabs with their toes or smears themselves with paint; climbs into a tray of sand or shredded paper to experience immersion; or jumps in a puddle. Material encounters like those described throughout this book, introduce plentiful and varied exploration with the hands, furnishing the brain with information. As children experiment with materials, testing their ideas from earlier encounters and handling (**Projection stage**), they explore cause-and-effect, such as 'what happens when I draw a finger through a shallow tray of gloop?', and notice and discover patterns and surprises. After ample exploration, they may use mixed-up concoctions of sand or other media imaginatively to create pretend meals (the **Role stage**).

An older child unable to resist the temptation of touching or immersing themselves in resources is likely to be at the **Embodiment stage**. Like this 6-year-old Keralan boy exploring playdough ingredients, who unlike the other children following the adult's instructions:

> was doing it his way. He was enjoying sitting with the children, mixing the flour, adding colours to it, making a paste out of it. He was not making any shapes despite my repeated instructions.... He was concentrating completely on what he was doing, barely interested in what others were doing. And, he was the one who had the most mess on his clothes and hands. He was not worried about the damage the colours and the mixture were doing to his clothes and body.
>
> (Anjali Rajan)

Discovering playdough for the first time it's no wonder that he didn't want to follow instructions, but simply wanted to enjoy his own explorations and discovery. With children's lives increasingly structured with 'reduced space for life' (Marti, in Jewell, 1999) and exposure to the natural environment substituted by fantasy worlds, older children (and adults) need opportunities to experience material encounters free from judgement and shame.

> While setting up a session at an activity centre with treasure baskets and trays of sand for the children to freely explore, 'a 3-year-old boy appears at the door looking at the [resources]. His mother ... quickly says, "You're too old for it". The boy stays lingering at the door, so I invite him to play. His mother agrees.... For the next hour he plays intently ...' (Gascoyne, 2012: 145) exploring the objects, scooping sand, problem-solving, communicating and 'cooking dinner' for his mum.

This child knew what he wanted and needed to do, and his engagement with the materials, transporting and enveloping the sand (schemas), noticing of patterns and similarities, and creative re-purposing were entirely age-appropriate.

The natural environment – in and outdoors

Bringing nature indoors with natural treasures

Tomkins and Tunnicliffe's (2007) research on **Nature Tables** (displays of interesting and unusual natural objects) gives an insight into the types of features which offer the greatest appeal to children. This includes items:

- With a 'novel nature or appearance,

- Aesthetic attributes,

- That display some responsiveness, and

- Which engage with their previous experience, or elicit 'affective feeling' (Papatheodorou, 2009).

Developed by **Elinor Goldschmied**, a **Treasure Basket** (Goldschmied & Jackson, 1994) is a collection of natural and household treasures, picked for their sensory and aesthetic qualities. Its aim was to give babies access to a world of learning but it has since been extended by Gascoyne (2012) for use with older children. As they manipulate the objects and discover what they are, what they can do and what they can become, they learn about themselves and the world.

- When offered with open-ended resources like sand or water as part of the **Sensory Play Continuum** (Gascoyne, 2009), the potential for problem-solving and discovery increases.

- Like open-ended movable resources such as **Heuristic Play** (Goldschmied & Jackson, 1994) and **Simon Nicholson's Loose Parts Play**, more commonly associated with outdoors, they give children agency as there is no right way of being used.

A cornerstone of **Reggio Emilia** Pre-schools is the belief that young children's natural and sensorial perception should be nurtured and encouraged not just within their surroundings but by them (**Rinaldi**, 2006). Established by **Loris Malaguzzi** (1920–1994), this international movement recognises the importance of providing opportunities for sensorial experiences because the environment:

- Is the third teacher (Fraser & Gestwicki, 2002), hence the importance of the arrangement of space and optimisation of natural light.

- 'Is a fully participating element' in education (Malaguzzi, 1997: 40, cited in Thornton & Brunton, 2015: 53).

- Is also a central component of the Material Encounters project in Canada, introduced in Chapter 6, documenting children's in-depth explorations with materials (Pacini-Ketchabaw et al, 2017).

RELEVANCE

Although messy play materials or even sand are not typically associated with Reggio Emilia settings, the value of natural resources and transformational processes, like growth and decay, are well understood. When planning material encounters it is important to bear in mind the importance of how things look and are presented (an area which we unpick in Chapters 5 and 6). Novel objects and situations are powerful motivators for material engagements, like the appeal of gloop, Gelli or water beads. Such opportunities need to be balanced with the familiar, to give children adequate stability and confidence to explore. By juxtaposing open-ended resources like sand with children's fascination for objects, it increases appeal and 'affordance', essentially what an environment or resource can offer or provide (Gibson, 1979). We return to this topic in Chapter 4 when we consider children's use of messy play materials.

Taking children outdoors

The outdoors environment doesn't simply contribute to physical development but gives children the opportunity 'to experience, explore and experiment with an alternative environment' (Arnold, 2003, cited in Papatheodorou, 2009: 8). With **Montessori's** belief that children absorb that which surrounds them, the way this is arranged is vitally important.

- The Open Air Nursery established by **Rachel** and **Margaret McMillan** (1859/60–1917/31) recognised that children achieve their full potential through first-hand experience and active learning, stressing the importance of free play (Running Past, 2018).

- This strongly resonates with the pedagogical approaches of **Forest Schools** and **Nature Kindergartens**, which encourage exploration, investigation and taking risks outdoors in tandem with a heightened sensory and environmental awareness.

- **Mud kitchens** (see White & Edwards, 2012 and page 92) are increasingly popular, giving messy investigations and creations a focus outdoors.

RELEVANCE

A rich, varied and constantly changing natural environment supports children's learning and development, providing ample reasons to explore mud, stones, twigs and puddles, as well as re-purposing and transforming these 'loose parts'. Material encounters like these position children, no matter how young, as 'discoverers' (Tomkins & Tunnicliffe, 2007), challenging children who are unsure of textures and properties, and adult's assessment of risks and clothing, both familiar quandaries for messy play.

Adults' role in supporting children's material encounters

So far, we have focussed on the emotional and physical environments. Our attention now turns to adults' crucial role in shaping these to either support or limit children's messy encounters.

Adults as 'directors of the environment'[4]

Understanding the importance of carefully selecting or creating resources is a common theme:

- According to **Dewey**, 'children make connections based upon the objects within their environment and the degree to which they are supported in the exploration of those objects' (Cunningham & Breault, 2017: 152).

- **Froebel** developed a series of **Gifts**, simple wooden resources to help children understand 'the concepts of shape, dimension, size, and . . . relationships' (Staff, 1998, cited in Ellington).

- **Occupations**, such as clay, paint and natural resources, were provided for children to freely explore solid 3D shapes and flat 2D shapes in a meaningful context, rooted in and linked to the child's everyday life.

- Similarly, **Montessori's** didactic 'multi-sensorial learning resources educate children's sensory perception and facilitate the exploration of their world' (Papatheodorou, 2009: 6). Focussing on specific senses or planes of development, these could be independently accessed once the child received instruction.

- **Susan Isaccs'** (1885–1948) nursery environment was an extension of home rather than something distinct and 'none of the equipment was chosen haphazardly' but was 'intended to stimulate the child's powers of inquiry and curiosity, and thus they would learn' (Smith, 1985: 64, cited in Mickelburgh 2010).

RELEVANCE

Froebel believed the exploration of solid objects supports children's move from 'concrete to abstract thinking' (Bruce & Dyke, 2017: 27), an approach also shared by Montessori's didactic materials. Froebel's **Gifts** could not be transformed, simply rearranged and viewed from different perspectives, helping the child understand the properties and affordances of 'concrete' objects and their relationship to the surrounding world. Just as the **Gift's** solidity made them 'tangible and perceptually stable' (Kiese-Himmel, 2008: 321), the laws of solids and liquids ensure consistency as children use all their senses in their exploration and decoding of materials.

The child-initiated activities or **Occupations** gave opportunities for linking exploration of solid objects to the everyday world, helping children, 'externalize the concepts . . . within their creative minds' (Staff, 1998, cited in Ellington). Unlike the **Gifts**, these could be modified and transformed, like messy play materials, as well as introducing opportunities for cognitive disequilibrium (see page 32). So the more opportunities children encounter, the firmer their grasp of their world, a pre-requisite to feeling safe and secure.

Messy play resources have the potential to provide sensory stimulation and introduce scientific concepts, as we will explore in Chapter 7. The use of real rather than plastic tools is as relevant to children's mastery and control of material encounters as it is to Montessori's Practical Life Activities. Consider the contribution of real china teapots and cups to a tea-making activity (on page 141) and it is plain to see how impoverished this experience would be if toy cups were provided instead. Not only does this realism introduce a wealth of physical challenges and convey the adult's trust, but it forges links with home, as advocated by Isaccs and Bronfenbrenner. Steiner recognised the appeal of baskets and containers for arranging resources and stimulating children's imagination, and we will return to this topic and their affordance in Chapter 5.

Giving children responsibility

- Children in both **Steiner's** and **Isaccs'** nurseries were expected to share in daily chores and take responsibility for the nursery environment.

- **Montessori** practice developed children's skills, self-discipline, independence and ownership.

RELEVANCE

With clearing up identified as one of the biggest obstacles for messy play (Gascoyne, 2018a), it may be worth considering whether practitioners can foster children's responsibility, independence and mastery through everyday actions such as children pouring their own drinks, using real cups and tidying up after activities, as this 'apprenticeship' role will support material encounters.

> **Reflection**
>
> Honestly reflect upon any actions that you take that children could do for themselves. What changes are needed to give children the necessary time, permission and skills?

Attentive noticing

The adult's role is key in supporting children's active sensory explorations:

- **Froebel** labelled his approach to education 'self-activity' – allowing the child to be led by their interests and free to explore, with the 'teacher' as a guide rather than lecturer. This requires careful noticing and a sensitive approach so that 'practitioners offer children what they need now' (Early Education, 2018) and skilfully support or divert them without causing shame, an approach in keeping with **ARC**.

- Positioned as role-models for children to imitate, the adult's role was observing children, rather than 'hurrying to intervene' (Early Education, 2018), a philosophy which resonates with pioneering Play Therapist **Virginia Axline's** principles (1964).

- **Montessori** warned against trying to teach or dominate a child, urging practitioners to focus on providing 'the child's natural development with the best environment in which to unfold freely' (Gettman, 1987: 21).

- Similarly, Isaccs believed children should be given space and sustained time to play while adults observed children's play.

RELEVANCE

The parallels with messy play are clear as adults are key in creating enabling environments; observing to better understand children; and modelling and supporting **autonomy** by not rushing or shaming children, all potential minefields for messy play. Limiting interruptions enables children to become absorbed in their play and reduces unnecessary tidying up stresses.

Adults as curators of the emotional environment

John Dewey (1859–1952) positioned adults as co-learners:

- Suggesting a cooperative learning environment with flexible planning to follow children's learning, and like Vygotsky and Axline, a role for adults in supporting children's insights.

- Adults were encouraged to become 'permanent students of education' (Wirth, 1966: 54, cited in Mickleburgh, 2010). This dovetails with the practical activities provided throughout this book to increase reflective practice and the inquiry-based approach to learning advocated in Chapter 7.

- Dewey saw 'the skill of a good practitioner in balancing adult direction with . . . children's freedom to explore' (Mickleburgh, 2010), a challenge which we will investigate further using Deci and Ryan's Self-Determination Theory (SDT; 2000) on pages 37 and 133.

Virginia Axline (1911–1988) established a set of eight principles (summarised below and explored in detail in Chapter 8) which form a cornerstone of non-directive Play Therapy (1964). Axline's principles have also been used in mainstream settings where practitioners want to give children greater **autonomy**. The Toy Free Kindergarten, piloted in Germany in 1992 and replicated in settings around the world (Schubert & Strick, 1996), uses these principles.

RELEVANCE

While *warm and friendly relationships* (1) would certainly be expected in mainstream practice, when considered through the lens of messy play, principles like *accepting the child as is* (2) even if caked in mud; establishing *a feeling of permission* (3) to freely explore; *reflecting back to give children insight* about how the gloop or Gelli feels (4); giving the child *responsibility to make choices* (5) about what they mix together and if and how they use resources; with *the child leading* (6) may feel too scary a proposition for many adults. *Not hurrying children* (7) when we know how much there is to clear up and how little time there is to do so would test even the most patient and enlightened adult, but sometimes we also risk hurrying children's precious 'aha' moments of discovery too (Gopnik, 2000). Consistent boundaries are essential for developing children's wellbeing and supporting material engagements, but consideration of what *limitations* are needed (8) will avoid us simply exerting more control over children's messy play, an area which we return to in Chapters 7 and 8.

Reflection

Consider each of the eight principles (listed above) in relation to your existing practice. Notice which of the principles need caveats to tick them off. Think about each of the 'ifs', 'buts', and 'maybes' in terms of whose need they fulfil. Are there any actions that you should take individually or as a team to bring practice closer to these?

Lev Vygotsky's (1896–1934) most renowned contributions to the early childhood landscape include:

- The **Zone of Proximal Development** (ZPD), essentially the difference between what a child can do unaided and what they can do with **scaffolding**, and

- The importance of social pretend play for the development of higher mental functions (since termed **Executive Functions)**, pre-requisites for self-regulation.

RELEVANCE

Extreme reactions to messy play are common. For an adult or child with a loathing of wet sticky resources, any interaction with gloop is in danger of pushing them into the panic zone of learning (Ritson, 2016). Contrast this with Vygotsky's ZPD and the importance of adult attunement is apparent. With close and respectful relationships and attentive noticing comes an understanding of the child, their developmental needs, interests and sensory aversions as well as confidence in the child's abilities. Of course, peers, an enabling environment and well-judged resources which 'speak to' a child can all provide scaffolding, extending learning (Bodrova & Leong, 2017: 66). For a child with a sensory aversion to wet sticky resources (described in Chapter 1 as tactile defensive), the adult may support their interactions with a tool, then play with a favourite toy in the resource, before finally touching with hands or feet. Each of these baby-steps will represent a major achievement to this child, only made possible by the positive emotional environment.

Children's thinking and learning

Understanding how children think and learn is essential for navigating the challenging role of deciding if and how to support children's messy play encounters.

Curiosity

'The inquisitive nature of children' was central to **Dewey's** concept of how children learn (Mickelburgh, 2010). Likening children's curiosity about the world to scientists, Dewey suggested:

- That each experience was a springboard to the next, drawing from all the child's senses and their interconnections.

- A transactional relationship between the child and natural environment (Jeffs & Ord, 2018: 44), an underlying principle for Pacini-Ketchabaw et al (2017) too.

- Closing 'the artificial gap between life [and] school' (Dewey in Cohen and Garner, 1967: 136, in Mickelburgh, 2010) so that learning occurs within a meaningful context, a recurring theme which resonates with Bronfenbrenner.

RELEVANCE

Although access to objects and resources which are 'concrete' is vital for learning, Dewey saw a need for the adult to 'determine the environment of the child, and thus by indirection to direct' (Dewey, 1968: 31, cited in Cohen & Garner, 1967: 213). Urging practitioners not to be 'spectators' in children's play (Dewey, 1966: 71), we will return to this in Chapter 6 when a sliding scale of adult involvement will be introduced.

Cognitive disequilibrium

Piaget offered two concepts for understanding children's learning:

- *Assimilation* occurs when new knowledge fits within the parameters of a child's existing knowledge, either reinforcing or extending thinking.

- Where knowledge does not fit, it creates a state of cognitive disequilibrium, forcing the child to change their thinking to *accommodate* this new knowledge.

RELEVANCE

As many messy play resources share similar special qualities and ways of 'behaving', plentiful encounters with these support children's understanding of the world around them and their assimilation of knowledge about solids, liquids and properties. Messy play resources provide rich fodder for exploring causal relationships and predicting and reaffirming these patterns of 'behaviour'. They also offer opportunities for disequilibrium, such as when solid gloop behaves like a liquid, which challenge children's existing thinking, requiring them to accommodate new learning.

Neuroscience, sensory experience and learning

We now turn our attention to unpicking what's happening in a child's body and brain when they experience sensory materials. The value of sensory-rich environments for healthy development is apparent from our tour of theorists, but it's only in the last decade that our knowledge of how they support children's cognitive development has grown exponentially, thanks largely to the contribution of neuroscience. Although understanding is still evolving, research confirms that language acquisition changes the structure of the brain, how information is categorised within it and how we see and experience the world (Kuhl, 2011), creating a distinction between:

Sensory Beings 'whose experience of the world, and meaning within it, is primarily sensory', and 'in the now' (Grace, 2018: 8), and

Linguistic Beings for whom the acquisition of language has severed these sensory roots.

According to Grace, there are four stages[5] of sensory interaction marking a transition from a sensory to a linguistic being, as shown in Table 2.1.

Table 2.1 Four stages of sensory interaction (Grace, 2018)

SENSORY BEINGS	1	2	3	4	LINGUISTIC BEINGS
	Getting Wired	Search & Discover	Explore & Connect	Specialising	

Parallels can be seen with Piaget, Jennings and Montessori's developmental stages, as will become apparent when we focus on each of these:

1 Getting wired

- Typically associated with babies and toddlers, this is a complex process of connecting the sensory systems with the brain. The brain processes information from the sense receptors located all over and inside our body, 'turning experience into knowledge' (Grace, 2018: 24).

- With repeated experience, wiring between the brain and the senses is established and neural pathways form. Learning occurs when these previous acquisitions are connected by use or meaning (Gettman, 1987: 11).

- Initially, the brain processes everything that the senses perceive as it doesn't know which bits are important.

This is a physically exhausting process as this example demonstrates:

> For an infant to see a mixture of dried sand and rice they need their eyes, visual cortex and optic nerve, which relay information from the eyes to the brain, to function effectively. The brain doesn't just receive this information and process it, but also sends instructions to the eyes about how to receive that information, e.g. which muscles need to be adjusted, how big the pupils need to be, etc. To elevate vision from wobbly video camera footage, which would make focussing difficult, the brain needs to combine this with information from the proprioceptive and vestibular senses to understand and factor in, whether it is the sand or the child that is moving. Only then can they accurately scoop, pour, sort or explore the materials.

RELEVANCE

For those of us who have moved beyond this phase, and no matter how playful we are that includes all early years practitioners I'm afraid, we may have lost touch with the wonder, excitement and all-encompassing absorption of sensory experiences. Grace eloquently reminds us what the children in our care may be experiencing when engaging with messy play, using the analogy of laying on your back looking up at a star-filled sky.

> There is no sense of boredom, no sense of there being something better out there that you would rather see or hear/taste/touch/smell/sense in any way . . . being in the 'getting wired group is pure experience and expression, mixed with awe and amazement'.
>
> (Grace, 2018: 26)

Each experience is enjoyed wholly in that moment, without guilt, loss or regret. As Higashida's inspirational account of what it's like to be autistic reminds us, 'sometimes I pity you for not being able to see the beauty of the world in the same way we do. Really, our vision of the world can be incredible' (2014: 91).

We've all witnessed a child's inability to resist splashing in an inviting muddy puddle, or thrusting their hands into mud, cake batter or dough, much to an adult's annoyance or bemusement. But for children in this stage this is essential, as 'the more experiences [we] find that register with their sensory systems, the more stars [we] place in that inky black sky' (Grace, 2018: 27). The aim is not to hurry children on to the next learning milestone (echoing Axline's seventh principle) but rather to widen children's sensory repertoire by offering more of the same sorts of sensory experiences. As Crowe (1983: 39) explains:

> children's senses cry out to be used *first* to provide the experiences that they will later need . . . to connect [to words]. Children must feel the world, listen to it, see it, taste it, smell it, 'know' it . . . That takes time and . . . silent investigation.

> ### Reflection
>
> The *Getting Wired* stage highlights four key points for sharing with parents and other practitioners:
>
> - Sensory experiences bring sheer **joy and wonder**.
> - Children need **plentiful and varied opportunities** for **unhurried** exploration.
> - Children are **genetically programmed** to explore, so jumping in a puddle is not an act of wilful disobedience.
> - Messy play is a vital tool for supporting children's **cognitive, language and physical development**.
>
> Consider how best to convince others of the benefits of material engagements.

2 Search and discover

- Children are driven to seek out as many sensory experiences as they can, both novel and familiar.
- Unless viewed through the lens of 'star hunters in that dark night sky' (Grace, 2018: 28), this can appear random, repetitive or lacking in focus.
- An enabling physical and emotional environment gives children opportunities and permission to explore and amass billions of knowledge points.
- To assist knowledge retrieval later, children need a broad spread of 'random points of knowledge' (Grace, 2018: 29) rather than focussing on just one part of the 'sky', a view which resonates with children as generalist learners, to which we return in Chapter 7.

RELEVANCE

Long since passed this stage, it can be difficult to understand and value the importance of these seemingly disparate sensory experiences. In training sessions, I often talk of the need for us to view objects, environments and practices with child-like eyes to appreciate their significance. Similarly, Grace urges us to 'walk in [children's] shoes, see with their eyes, sense with their senses, [so] we discover the delightful newness of the[ir] world' (2018: 28), an approach which will strongly enhance our appreciation of children's messy play encounters.

As parents and practitioners, we act as meaning-makers providing children with plentiful opportunities to experience wide-ranging sensory experiences as well as time to return to these to galvanise thinking. The randomised way in which this happens means that pieces of information will be more readily connected than a linear learning process. So, a single word like 'mud' yields a host of eclectic words, images, feelings and memories rather than one thread of thinking. This connectivity comes to the fore in the *explore and connect* stage.

3 Explore and connect

- As children experience the world through their senses, they notice similarities and differences, colours, shapes, properties or the way that objects and materials 'behave'.

- Threads of thinking emerge as the individual points of knowledge, or stars, become joined-up like a constellation.

- Children actively test their ideas and extend their thinking about materials as they acquire knowledge through containing and transforming schemas (Athey, 2007).

- Given wide-ranging and repeated sensory experiences, the brain begins to organise this information, making connections which bring 'new meaning . . . from what was previously a sea of random points of knowledge' (Grace, 2018: 29) and assimilating or accommodating learning.

RELEVANCE

During this stage we can expect to see young children testing and developing their thinking. If the child's knowledge funds, from their Micro, Meso, Exo and Macrosystems (Bronfenbrenner) are the result of rich, varied and random experiences, then they will start to make the links between these. For example, an encounter with blue Gelli will link with separate knowledge points about other liquids and solids and other things which are blue. Much as an internet search can yield a host of results, 'the randomness of early exploration is wonderfully fruitful later' (Grace, 2018: 30).

Reflection

Di Stead (2015) uses jelly to helpfully encapsulate children's learning. But in a book about material engagements, it would be remiss not to try this!

Follow the packet instructions to make a jelly in a round bowl. When set, turn onto a plate and stand in a washing-up bowl/container. Carefully pour some hot (kettle) water over the jelly. Watch as rivulets start to form. 'Children make sense of the world based on their experience' (2015: 7), and the rivulets in the jelly represent these early theories and ideas. If you pour more water, it will tend to run down the existing rivulets rather than taking a new path. Similarly, young children and (adults) tend to try to fit new evidence into their existing ideas rather than rejecting this earlier thinking. It takes exposure to lots of situations (water in our experiment) to challenge this thinking so

> that water eventually takes new paths. It is the combination of returning to ideas to test thinking (i.e., continuing to pour the water), as well as experiences interlinking (i.e. pouring the water over the same part of the jelly), that helps thinking evolve.
>
> At some point the water will be on the cusp of overflowing. Notice momentarily how you feel. Once it starts to over flow, be mindful of whether you experience a sense of delight, release, wonder, intrigue or discomfort? (Although contained within another container, this can still provide a sense of overflowing.)
>
> Now that you have a container of wonderfully sticky jelly take the time to experience its soft squidgy feel, colour and scent, before offering it to children to explore. Notice the range of sensations, what you like or dislike about it and any memories that come to mind.

4 Specialising

The final stage, necessary for functioning in a multi-sensory world, involves:

- Analysing what knowledge is being used and pruning those bits that are not so the brain only focuses on sensory feedback which is most relevant to the individual.

- Understanding sensory feedback in terms of if and how it fits with existing knowledge, rather than as separate, discrete experiences in the now.

RELEVANCE

Without filters to manage sensory feedback, children experience overload and the world is an exhausting cacophony of sensory bombardment. As we'll discover in the next chapter, the calming and absorbing qualities of messy play resources can bring welcome relief as well as fine-tuning a child's understanding.

A foundation for children's explorations

In Chapter 1 I briefly introduced Deci and Ryan's **Self-Determination Theory** (SDT; 2000) as a framework for considering children's and adult's psychological needs:

Autonomy – Structure is essential for a child to feel safe to be curious and explore.

Relatedness – A sense of belonging is relevant to messy play on several levels:

- **Relatedness or attachment to caregivers** – Positive relationships provide support and 'exert a positive influence on how we perceive and relate to events' (Morris, 2015: 18).
- **Relatedness to resources and environments** – For children to 'feel' rather than 'know' they need to connect to the natural environment and elements.

– **Relatedness to self** – Bodily awareness is a pre-requisite for developing self-awareness and a positive disposition to exploration. Essential for understanding and decoding sensory information, it supports agency and mastery, 'function[ing] as a bridge for children' between their inner and outer world (Baldwin, 1906 cited in Russell, 1996: 172).

Competence – For children to feel they can make a difference, they need a balance between the familiar and novel (see pages 106 and 156). Routines and attachment free the brain to concentrate 'attention and energy on the novel' (Morris, 2015: 91), a key driver for children's learning.

RELEVANCE

While many messy play resources like sand, dried rice and water behave predictably when explored in a cause-and-effect way, part of the fascination and appeal of materials like gloop, Gelli and moon sand is their potential for disequilibrium too. With safety and structure provided physically by a trusted adult, or from visual cues like aprons, containers and appropriate cleaning tools, the child can immerse themselves in their playful explorations of novel and possibly scary messy play experiences. A medley of logistical considerations like the number of children, messiness of resource, location and time available will be key to deciding the degree of structure deemed necessary. But as importantly, the adult's emotional context (whether feeling stressed or adequately supported, personally and professionally) will determine their resulting relaxed laissez-faire approach or tighter rein.

'Young children are endlessly interested in and biologically programmed to explore the stuff of the earth, how materials behave and what they do' (White, 2014: 48). These explorations furnish the child with 'experiences with the senses focussing on similarities and differences between themselves and objects' and it is 'through an awareness of differences [that] they can begin to view themselves with new appreciation' (Oaklander, 1978: 284) a key step in raising self-esteem.

Children with a poorly developed body sense need opportunities to discover the boundaries between themselves, tools and the sensory materials with which they are engaging. Equipped with an understanding of a child's interests, schemas and funds of knowledge (Moll et al, 1992), an attuned practitioner can provide a stimulating environment offering a balance between the familiar and novel, the ZPD of resource provision, if you will.

The most important aspect of a safe and predictable environment is the caregiver and their reaction to messy explorations provides an indicator of a child's acceptance or otherwise, (Axline's second principle). 'Having an environment that is predictable and over which one has some control' is fundamental to wellbeing (Morris, 2015: 92), presenting a particular challenge to material engagements, as both the adult's and child's sense of **Autonomy**, **Relatedness** and **Competence** need to be maintained, and often these can appear to be diametrically opposed! Picture a sliding scale with an adult's **autonomy** at one end and a child's at the other (a concept which we return to in Chapter 6). Our objective is giving children appropriate opportunities for developing **autonomy** and **competence**, without eroding adult confidence and wellbeing. Key to this is increasing our understanding of material encounters, the focus of Chapter 3.

IN THIS CHAPTER WE HAVE COVERED:

- The importance of attachment and an enabling emotional environment.
- The value of sensory-rich environments which spark curiosity, active sensory exploration and movement.
- Adults' role in shaping the emotional and physical environments.
- How children learn and the theoretical foundations of messy play.

Notes

1 Various parent and practitioner verbal and written comments on messy play (unpublished). For example, 'I'm twitchy about doing painting and the real messy play stuff at home and prefer them to do it at nursery or at one of my classes.'.
2 Several social media threads from parents and practitioners strongly support the view that messy play should take place in settings not at home. Some settings even impose limits, e.g. 'mess is limited to 10 minutes, 2 children at a time' (June, 2007). Some practitioners recognise the value of messy play at work but wouldn't contemplate offering it at home!
3 Only the earliest stages are referred to.
4 Gettman (1987: 17).
5 Development from one stage to another is not necessarily a linear progression as some individuals will remain in, or return to, these phases, due to accidents, autistic spectrum disorders or illness.

3 Investigating and quantifying messy play

In Chapter 2 we explored the historical, theoretical and scientific roots of messy play. Our attention now turns to challenging the idea that messy play encounters are a homogeneous landscape, providing an important quantitative dimension to an otherwise qualitative experience. Research evidence will highlight the special qualities of messy play, and the different types of resources and typical stages in messy play will be introduced. Tools for quantifying the spread of mess and links to emotions will provide a useful framework for considering children's material encounters with fresh insight.

Categorising types of messy play resources

As a fan of messy play (in both mainstream and therapeutic environments), sometimes a lack of quantitative measures can make it difficult to spot potential patterns, frustratingly clouding individual experiences. Drawing from the world of Play Therapy, this chapter introduces a series of lenses for viewing and quantifying children's material engagements. Given the subjectivity and extremes of reaction which surround messy play, this will add an important dimension to our understanding, furthering our appreciation of the importance of **Autonomy**, **Relatedness** and **Competence (ARC)** (Deci & Ryan, 2000) to children's and adults' experiences of messy play.

With an open mind and a playful approach, most materials can be used for sensory-rich encounters. A quick search in the kitchen would yield plentiful messy play resources, be it dried porridge oats, squidgy sultanas, crunchy cereal, silky custard powder, creamy yoghurt, slimy tinned tomatoes, baked beans or rice pudding, floral tea, pungent coffee, herbs and spices not to mention a plethora of ingredients for baking, including trusty favourite cornflour – the key ingredient for gloop! Venture outdoors and you can probably add pea shingle, seedpods, leaves, flowers, sticks and mud to the mix. But just because these foodstuffs and resources are suitable for messy play does not mean they are uniform in the way they feel, perform, respond to touch or appeal. Gburczyk (2012) suggests a useful classification of messy play resources in terms of their wet or dry qualities. Although simplistic, this classification has a lot to commend it as it addresses some key physical and perceptual barriers to these divisive resources.

Table 3.1 Types of messy play resources

Classification of messy play resources	Examples of resources
Dry textures	Dried lentils, rice, split peas, porridge oats, couscous, salt, etc. Leaves, seedpods, wood shavings, compost and natural treasures. Sand, shredded paper, fabric scraps, maize packing peanuts, powder paint and objects.
In-between textures, i.e., resources that are not dry but don't stick to the skin	Playdough/Play-Doh, clay, kinetic sand, artificial snow and water beads (sometimes called 'Orbies'). Cooked spaghetti and tapioca. Messy Pots, ice, soap and water.
Messy textures	Shaving foam, gloop/oobleck, Gelli, slime and finger paints. Tinned tomatoes/beans/rice pudding, dough and yoghurt. Mud, wet sand and clay.

Reflection

Look at the list of resources in Table 3.1 and notice any which arouse feelings of worry, stress, shame, guilt or loathing in you or a child that you work with.

Try to pinpoint what it is about this resource that sparks negative feelings, then spend a few minutes coming up with ideas for reducing these negatives.

RELEVANCE

Problems accessing resources

For a child or adult with sensory processing issues, touching some resources can be so distressing that the prospect of messy play fills them with dread. Whether sticky wet substances, dry powdery resources or any combination of textures is the problem, this continuum from wet to dry qualities reminds us of the physical challenge facing tactile-defensive adults and children. With an awareness of this obstacle to inclusion, steps can be taken to ensure that certain textures are (initially) avoided, or spoons, tongs and gloves provided to create an interface with the 'offending' material. Far from being the preserve of special educational needs, the ever-increasing number of children with sensory processing difficulties makes a review of the setting's resources essential.

An aversion to mess among children is also increasingly commonplace as a learnt (rather than physiologically rooted) behaviour. Here also an awareness of the wealth of textural messy play possibilities available may be key to children's inclusion, as wetter, stickier, messier resources tend to elicit more negative reactions. As practitioners and parents, we also need to be aware of our own sensory preferences and aversions to ensure that these don't limit what we offer children. Like the practitioner who loathed messy play and realised that by not offering this, children were missing out on opportunities for positive sensory experiences. As important is how we convey our personal likes and dislikes in our interactions and responses to children's mess. With parents firmly positioning early years settings as the preferred location for messy play (see note 6), practitioners have an incredible opportunity to furnish children with non-judgemental experiences to engage with and explore materials, and model how best to respond sensitively and appropriately to children's concerns.

Reflection

Think back to the child with a muddy hand or sand in their shoes in Chapter 1. Consider what underlying message these children received and how you would respond to these children's seaside encounters to sensitively foster joy, curiosity and wonder.

Managing a fear of mess

Gburczyk's simplistic classification can also help us perceptually. Sometimes the worst is expected when we envisage messy play and this subconscious focus on extremes can inadvertently push people far beyond their comfort zone, into the unhelpfully disabling panic zone (Ritson, 2016: 47). Whether the practitioner, valiantly overcoming their phobia so they can offer messy play experiences, or the child unsure of whether to please the practitioner and give in to their natural urge to explore and get messy, knowing they'll face the wrath when they get home, the panic zone of learning is an undesirable place to be.

By recognising that there is a lot more to messy play than wet and sticky gloop, shaving foam, mud or Gelli, practitioners can better respond to children's differing sensory needs. Starting with safer dry resources and gloves or tools for accessing these, children (and adults) can experience and master the stretch zone of learning (Ritson, 2016: 47), creating a solid foundation for future exploration, and the first step in rewiring negative associations. The knowledge that only some messy play resources are wet and sticky enables practitioners, for whom messy play doesn't come naturally, to start with less-threatening textures first, gradually building up to more challenging wet and stickier resources, when their confidence allows.

If messy play is lumped together in a 'one-size-fits-all' category, then one negative experience can taint a whole spectrum of resource opportunities, even though the nightmare might only have been cooked couscous or tinned plum tomatoes! This simple classification also helps us understand the potential for material engagements, as dry resources such as lentils, wood shavings and leaves will have very different affordances, or ways of being used, (Gibson, 1979), to wet and sticky clay and in-between textured playdough, an area which we will explore further in Chapter 4.

Patterns in messy play

We have seen how personal and qualitative an experience messy engagement can be. Perceptions of mess vary with an individual's own attitudes, experience, skills and confidence, not to mention changing moods and circumstances. To try to understand the unique role of messy play in the early years it's helpful to focus on the special qualities of resources. Gascoyne (2016) identified six attributes of therapeutic messy play, which are also highly relevant (in a simplified form) to mainstream provision.

1 Sensory and experiential

As we discovered in Chapter 2, a child's experience of the world is multi-sensory and active. Sensory receptors located in our sense organs (the skin and sense-specific cells) receive energy from the environment and relay this to the Central Nervous System, resulting in a response or action. The more times a child's sense receptors and nerves are stimulated by encountering sensory-rich materials, the easier they become activated as the stimulus threshold decreases. This reminds us of the importance of giving children plentiful sensory and motor opportunities, as 'previous experience and emotions . . . can profoundly modify stimulus thresholds' (Pagliano, 1999: 27).

Sometimes engagement takes the form of children's 'little toes creeping to the edge of a puddle' inching forward with delicate movements . . . which is very different to jumping in with your wellies on' (Brodie & Godfrey, 2018). In other instances, a mound of sand invites large arcing arm movements, fast and frenzied or calm and slow; or a child mesmerised by the tiny soap bubbles on their palm, or sand trickling between their fingers or toes. Using their senses, babies and young children discover about themselves and the world around them and begin to differentiate themselves from this (Crowe, 1983). As such, open-ended resources like those listed in Table 3.1 give children the opportunity to be curious, 'explore and to discover things for [them]self' (Arnold, 2003: 113).

Where motor and sensory experiences are restricted due to a disability; the child's emotional and physical needs not being met; an unstimulating environment; child-rearing equipment or approaches restricting mobility; or limited opportunities to explore, the child's motor and sensory development will be negatively affected. Thinking about every activity from a multi-sensory perspective encourages us to consider if and how our actions or inactions might unwittingly detract from an experience. Such as when practitioners talk to each other while a child plays with sand or soapy water, effectively cancelling out some children's ability to concentrate on the sensory experience at hand.

> **Reflection**
>
> We can gain an insight into what this might feel like through this activity. Divide into threes – one practitioner takes the role as the child exploring a sensory resource such as a container of dried sand, shaving foam, gloop or clay; the other two practitioners take-it-in-turns talking to and prompting the child or talking to each other. Reflect on how each of you felt and the impact, if any, on the quality of the sensory experience.

2 Restoring and calming

'Nature for the child is sheer sensory experience' (Cobb, 1977: 28) so perhaps this provides a clue as to the root of messy play's appeal. Certainly, calming restorative benefits have been associated with water (Oaklander, 1978), sand (Gascoyne, 2016) and clay (Axline, 1964; Case, 1990; Rabiger,1990; Sagar, 1990; Dalley, 2008). A wealth of research points to the emotional and restorative qualities of the outdoor environment and how play outdoors or with open-ended sensorial resources may act as a buffer against the stresses and problems of modern life (Schubert & Strick, 1996; Wells, 2000; Wells & Evans, 2003; Tomkins & Tunnicliffe, 2007; Sigman, 2011). While evidence for this is convincing, the absence of children's words to explain what this feels like makes Crowe's insight fascinating. Sparked by a hands-on activity, a mother describes her childhood, as the oldest of five children, 'all of whom were seriously maltreated physically and emotionally.' She recalls:

> a bitterly cold day and I was shut out of the house as usual in a cotton frock and knickers and without shoes but I didn't feel the cold, I was playing in a deep cart-rut puddle and I was totally absorbed in what I was doing. I could feel the soft mud squelching up between my toes and round my ankles ... I forgot everything except that it was wonderful. I just sat and drifted and didn't want to come back.
>
> (Crowe, 1983: 6)

As memories like these suggest, children experience the natural environment (the most natural form of messy play) 'in a deep and direct manner, not as a background for events' (Sebba, 1991). With this level of absorption come opportunities for physical and emotional repair and growth.

Kaplin and Kaplin (1989: 782) identify four qualities of sensory environments: Fascination; Being Away; Extent; and Compatibility, all of which have important attention restoration benefits for the brain and implications for messy play. As Table 3.2 shows, these therapeutic qualities can be found in a range of messy play resources, including several early years staples. With such self-regulating benefits potentially to be gained from material engagements it is essential these are not undermined by the wider environment (as we will explore further in Chapter 6).

Table 3.2 Attention restoration qualities and messy play

	Explanation	*Play example*
Fascination	Environments which fascinate allow the neural inhibitory mechanism to rest.	Child noticing the surprising feel and solid/liquid movement when they draw their finger through gloop. Child fascinated by the transformation of water into fluffy Gelli.
Being away	The experience of taking a mini-holiday from daily concerns.	Child noticing tiny soap bubbles on their hand and watching these pop. Child dreamily scooping sand with their hands.
Extent	An experience which allows immersion.	Child's immersion of their whole arms in a bucket of soapy water. Practitioner's immersion (up to their arm pits) in a feely bag of interesting objects!
Compatibility	The match between the environment and one's inclinations.	Child exploring what sinks and floats in Gelli. Child exploring what happens when they sprinkle powder paint onto shaving foam and mix it with a spoon.

Source: Adapted by Gascoyne (2018b) from Kaplin and Kaplin (1989: 782)

3 Transformation, autonomy and mastery orientation

Messy play gives children ample opportunities to develop **autonomy**, mastery orientation and creativity by deciding what to add to a resource to change its texture, consistency, colour and usefulness. The open-ended affordance of messy play materials makes them ideally suited to transformation, the importance of which should not be underestimated as children may feel 'powerless to control other aspects of their life' (Good-Year Brown, 2010: 105, cited in Hastings, 2013: 105). Transformation may occur on several levels:

- **Structure** – Starting as sensory play this evolves into a 'more ordered and controlled projective activity' (Jennings, 2014: 85).
- **Form** – Hastings (2012) and Gascoyne (2016) describe a transformation in the colour and texture of messy creations, as we will explore later in this chapter.

- **Use** – Transformation is also evident in children's creation of 'harnessed mess' – making something positive from mess (Dalley,1984: 25) or self-cleaning, themes which we will return to in Chapter 5.

- **Agency** – Changes in ownership, for example an adult-initiated buried treasure activity, develops into a child-led game of hide-and-seek.

- **Emotions** – Changes in energy and emotion to which we return at the end of this chapter.

4 Communication and self-expression

If 'toys are children's words and play is their language' (Landreth, 2012: 313) then it is no surprise that children choose to use messy play resources to express their feelings. With materials infinitely flexible, Bender (1937) and Woltmann (1943) recognise their value for self-expression, as within an enabling environment they 'can be torn apart, restructured, destroyed, and recreated over and over without causing guilt or worry' (cited in James, 1997: 81). It is this affordance which makes them ideally suited to the 'release of pent-up feelings' (Moustakas,1953,1959b, cited in James, 1997: 81). Materials such as paint, clay, playdough, sand and water are invaluable as 'they do not require spoken language, and yield to the child's inner creative urges' (West, 1992: 65). Reminiscent of Vygotsky's notion of 'self-talk' and its role in supporting young children's thinking, if the sensorial qualities of materials mirror the child's emotional world or match their interests, this can actively support thinking. Rather than a one-way process, materials become agents in their own right, suggesting different ways of being used and tools for children to think with (Kind, 2018, unpublished Skype interview).

5 Containment and attachment

Messy play and containment, or a lack of containment, go hand in hand and are apparent on several levels, a theme we return to in Chapter 5:

The 'containing' adult – The adult has a key role to play in providing safety by containing and shaping the emotional environment within which messy play flourishes or withers. In a stay-and-play session in Southern India, children and adults encountered playdough for the first time on a sheet of polythene:

> I circulated a ball of playdough, which I had made at home so they could feel it. The parents were as excited as their children. I made them sit facing each other around a large polythene sheet. Then I distributed the besan flour to each child and asked them to touch and feel it. Later, I gave them water and asked them to mix it with their hands into dough. While they were busy kneading the dough, I introduced the food colours as a surprise element. Most of them were seeing the food colour for

> the first time. I gave them the powder and when they mixed it with their flour and water, the colours became evident. They became more excited and interested in the activity. Even the most silent in the group was actively participating. A girl who initially didn't want to make her hands dirty was the one who asking me for more and more flour and colour. Once they had kneaded the flour, I added a few drops of oil to their dough to make it a bit softer. I had given them orange and yellow as these are commonly available in our market, but they were demanding green, blue etc. so I advised the parents to [crumble] water colour 'cakes' to get a variety of colours.
>
> This activity lasted for about 30 minutes and at the end I could see a lot of Dough Vadas (a traditional [doughnut-shaped] snack in Kerala), Dough Laddos (a round sweet Indian snack), and some Dough Snakes.... Some just wanted to retain their mixture in a semi-solid texture or thick paste.
>
> (Anjali Rajan, 2018)

In this potentially very messy session, containment was provided virtually by the limits set and structure introduced by the recipe instructions and established aim of replicating the dough. Physically, too, the adult's presence, arrangement of seated adults behind children and provision of ingredients also acted as a 'container' for children's mess.

A containing natural environment – A natural extension of Malaguzzi's idea of the environment as the third teacher is children forming meaningful connections with Mother Nature, the ultimate attachment figure. Puddles, stones, mud and sticks make a perfect arena for messy play, but 21st-century childhood has seen a growing disconnect with the natural environment. Containment in the natural environment may be provided by the extent of a puddle, the focus of one Reception Class teacher's creative tool for introducing a wealth of measuring and scientific inquiry (Anon. In Dixon, 2005: 58–60) or discovery of a pot of ice. With clearing up stresses minimised outdoors, this also reduces the need for containment.

A continuum of containment – Drawing upon a myriad of messy play engagements (both therapeutic and mainstream) suggests to me a pattern in children's containment of mess. Children typically move from uncontained to contained mess, probably a reflection of the child's age as younger children may not have the fine motor control to initially contain their messy play; or developmental stage, with a child at Jennings' embodiment stage (1990) deliberately immersing themselves with resulting spillages and mess. This is a necessary precursor to a child experiencing **competence** from working within the confines of a container. The addition of a discrete 'container' such as a piece of card or larger tray beneath a pot can be all that is needed at this stage to enable the child to succeed. Conversely, for children new to messy play they may first move from contained to uncontained play, tentatively testing the adult's boundaries and permission to get messy, before letting go.

Messy Pots – For most children, the process of making mess rather than any end product is the important part. However, sometimes children may choose to contain some of their mess, because they're not yet ready to deal with it or to discover if and how it changes over time. Saunder's Messy Pots (cited in Rice, 2013: 15) give children **autonomy** to decide which of their messy creations to keep.

6 Fun and enriching

Play is the lifeblood of children, bringing with it positive health benefits from the release of endorphins and opportunities for problem-solving, creativity and self-expression. Motivated by satisfaction rather than extrinsic rewards, fun features highly in adults' views of messy play (Gascoyne, 2016; and Gascoyne, 2018i).

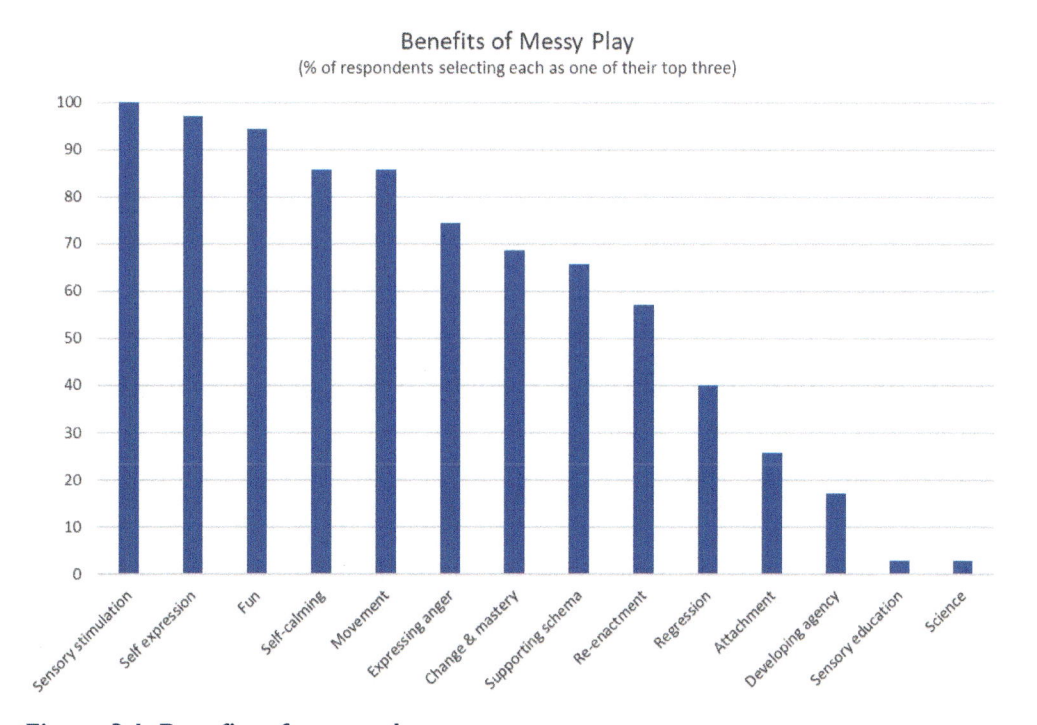

Figure 3.1 Benefits of messy play

Hastings developed a Mood Scale (2013: 52) to provide an indication of a child's mood before and after messy play sessions. With 0 representing extremely sad, 5 happy and 10 extremely angry, this is better suited to the extremes of a therapeutic context, but it does raise the issue of just how powerful messy play engagements can be and reminds us that not all messy play is boisterous and fun.

The Leuven Wellbeing and Involvement Scales (Laevers, 1994) provide a useful indicator of what high levels of engagement (level 5 on the scale) look like. Conversely, levels 1 to 3 can be a useful barometer for identifying areas which, contrary to our hopes and expectations, are not currently working for children. In its modified POMS (Process Oriented Monitoring System) format (Laevers & Declercq, 1997), these are excellent tools for evaluating children's engagement, providing a useful indicator of fun and Csikszentmihayli's 'state of flow' (2008). Described as the essence of being 'a fish in water', and resonating with the mud-caked children described in Chapter 1, according to Laevers, a child's satisfaction that comes with:

> involvement stems from one source: the exploratory drive, the need to get a better grip on reality, the intrinsic interest in how things and people are, the urge to experience and figure out. [This] only occurs in the small area in which the activity matches the capabilities of the person, that is in the 'zone of proximal development'.
>
> (Laevers, 2005: 5)

Quantifying messy play

Having introduced the special qualities and different types of messy play resources, we now explore a range of quantitative measures.

Spatial patterns

Messiness Scale

The Messiness Scale developed by Hastings is a useful tool for spatially measuring the messiness of play, whereby 0 equals 'no messy play', 4 'small areas for contained mess' and 10 'whole room used for messy play' (2013: 48). When applied to fifteen Play Therapy sessions, differences were apparent 'between the actual spatial spread of mess and the therapist's anxiety and perception of chaos' (Gascoyne, 2015: 14). A key factor in this appeared to be when within the sessions the mess had been created. When the mess increased gradually the therapist scored the mess lower than it was. However, where there was a rapid acceleration of mess at the end of the session, this impacted upon the adult's sense of chaos versus control and subsequent higher scoring of mess.

SIGNIFICANCE

This can help us review mess to see whether any changes are needed:

- To simplify the environment and increase or decrease lines of flow (e.g. increasing flow to the sink for clearing up).

- Reduce the amount of resources or size of containers provided, e.g. switching from large squeezy paint bottles, where paint is quickly used up, to small containers of powder paint which take time to be mixed.

- Increase protective covers and aprons or provide more containers for limiting the spread of mess.

- Change the location.

This can also raise adults' self-awareness:

- If a practitioner feels stressed by the amount of mess, quantifying this can give them a greater sense of control.

- It helps put mess into context, especially if it reveals that the mess is less than they thought.

- Realisation that the actual spread of mess is less than on prior occasions can buoy confidence as they have successfully managed it before.

- Comparing with other practitioners' mess thresholds brings self-awareness and team-working.

- Recognising that other factors are contributing to the stress can help practitioners own these feelings and avoid deflecting or instilling a sense of guilt or shame on children.

Temporal patterns

It's also useful to consider mess temporally, in relation to a child's age, within sessions, throughout the day and across weeks, to see if any patterns emerge.

Child's age – As already discussed, the child's chronological and developmental age will likely impact upon the degree of containment and embodiment, and how the resources are used. Examples include infants mouthing and exploring with hands and feet to understand what the material is, or older children discovering what materials can do and become as they experiment and role-play.

Over time – Drawing from Play Therapist's experiences in a 12-or-more-week interaction, the messiest stage in a child's process typically occurred between week 4 and 8 (Gascoyne, 2015). This may coincide with the establishment of the adult/child relationship as part of the psychological need for **relatedness** (Deci & Ryan, 2000). It may also reflect the growing confidence of the adult in their own abilities (**competence**) and trust in the child's ability to contain the mess (**competence** and **relatedness**), leading to their offer of more messy resources over time. Exceptions to this have been identified, such as the peaking of paint and dry sand in sessions 1–3, possibility due to their familiarity (Gascoyne, 2015); and children who immediately engage in extremely messy play which may reflect the child's age, embodiment stage or significant trauma (Hastings, 2013; Gascoyne, 2016).

The 'Introduction to Messy Play' session in Southern India (described on page 47 and explored further in Chapter 6) raises a relevant point. For their first encounter, children created playdough on a large polythene sheet, without bowls. The children's lack of familiarity with messy resources and cultural context potentially helped limit mess but it would be interesting to see whether, with repeated exposure and greater familiarity, any temporal patterns (or need for greater containment) emerge as children's reaction to messy play evolves and the balance of power, **competence** and **relatedness** changes.

Within the day – As anyone that works with young children knows, it's worth considering when messy play opportunities are offered within the day, as this may significantly affect children's experience and energy levels.

> In one nursery a collection of interesting objects were buried within a deep trug of sand, with some spoons, scoops and magnets arranged on a floor mat. As the 2-year-olds woke from their afternoon nap, they gravitated to the trug and quietly started scooping and pouring the sand. I shall never forget the calming meditative feel in this room (not something typically associated with 2-year-olds' messy play), as they purposefully engaged with the resources, and gradually awoke.

At a different time of day this same resource could have generated much more energised play with very different outcomes.

Reflection

Consider when in the day or week messy play is typically offered, and if and how this might impact upon children's range of experiences, enjoyment and energy levels. Factor in practitioners' best and worst parts of the day or week too and plan opportunities accordingly.

Within sessions – Where children's mess tends to occur at the end of sessions, a conscious awareness of the clarity and maintenance of boundaries may be necessary. This could include putting in place a series of simple steps to support children's choices and minimise stressful pinch points, or making organisational changes such as:

- Restricting the use of new resources in the last 10 minutes.
- Ensuring longer uninterrupted periods of time are available to reduce children's need to rush.
- Providing storage so that children can return to unfinished work.
- Reflecting to the child that they still have more to do and that they will be able to continue.

Reflection

As we shall explore further in Chapter 8, children's **autonomy** stems from having clear limits but a permissive flexible approach.

Consider how bounded a practitioner you are and whether this sometimes unhelpfully constrains children's development of **autonomy** and **competence** because of too many or too few limits.

SIGNIFICANCE

- If older children immediately engage in extremely messy play this may indicate their need for embodied messy play opportunities, introduced in Chapter 2.

- Minimising unnecessary interruptions within the day increases focus and decreases unnecessary clearing up.

- This brings awareness of the need for appropriate boundaries, not so tight and inflexible as to stifle play but providing the necessary limits to develop a child's (and adult's) **autonomy** and **competence**. Consistency is essential, but flexibility will also be needed to respond to different material engagements – as one practitioner's deliberations over appropriate clothing for puddle play reveals in Chapter 8.

- It may be appropriate to avoid certain times within the day or week for wet and sticky messy play, such as when children and adults are tired, and offer drier materials when calming relaxation is needed.

Emotional and material patterns

At an early years training session that I was leading, I was struck by several insights into the potential mirroring and emotional qualities of resources.

> Keen for adults to experience the joys of sensorial play first-hand, to appreciate its captivating qualities and intrinsic appeal, I provided sand, water, gloop, Play-Doh, plasticine and clay to explore in silence. After experimenting with each resource, we discussed their sensory appeal. Several commented on Play-Doh's unmistakable smell, which instantly transported them back to children, others on the satisfying sound of water. Several shared their dislike of the sticky feel of plasticine, others were disappointed by the difficulty they experienced in manipulating clay when compared to Play-Doh, describing it as 'too hard work'.

Reflection

Try this for yourself and then discuss which experiences were most enjoyable or calming and which senses were stimulated. Consider whether your choice of materials may artificially restrict children's ability to:

- express emotions like anger?
- discover more about themselves and the world?
- use them in a range of ways to think with?

We will now briefly consider the implications of the texture, resistive qualities, predictability, colour and scent of resources.

i) Texture, wetness and resistance

The above practitioners disliked the challenge of manipulating clay, but for a child needing to express anger, a lump of clay or plasticine needs more physical effort and will release more energy and frustration, than easily malleable Play-Doh. Within mainstream environments we may not wish to dwell on how we can support a child to express anger, yet West (1992) reminds us of the importance of children being able to manipulate resources to vent anger. Apart from the parallels with a child's earliest sensory exploration – exploring the contents of their nappy – manipulating clay is a very physical experience which can't be rushed. The process of gradual transformation and re-engaging with the senses, builds resilience and focus, contrasting markedly with the immediacy of 21st-century life. Hasting's work with 'looked after children' (LACYP) revealed a strong preference for sticky wet materials which were typically investigated as 'scientist[s] or chef[s]' (2013: 103). Similarly:

> the surprising resistive qualities of Gelli frustrated and physically challenged a child as he tried to submerge objects. The apparent lack of rules (about what would sink and float) and chaos mirrored perfectly his situation and needs.
>
> (Gascoyne, 2015: 17)

ii) Predictability

The unpredictability of the Gelli was key to the above child's play. Sand by comparison was far too stable and predictable. Similarly, playdough would have probably been too easy and mouldable to mirror a sense of chaos. Just because a child does not gravitate to a resource on one occasion is not an indicator of its unsuitability per se. On another occasion, dry sand was perfectly suited to a child's need to create a sandstorm by moving their arms in a large circling motion, gradually calming and relaxing them, as the 'storm' subsided.

iii) Colour and appearance

Far from being random, the colour and appearance of children's messy creations (in a therapeutic context) also suggest potential patterns in the darkness/lightness, transparency/opacity, and dullness/sparkliness of mess (Case, 1990; Sagar,1990; Jung, 1959; Hastings, 2013; Gascoyne, 2015).

- **Appeal of dark colours** – Described by Kaplin and Kaplin (1989) as 'Compatibility', some of the appeal of dark-coloured resources may stem from their greater ability to mirror a child's negative feelings than pastel colours. They may also convey a sense of naughtiness stemming from their similarities to bodily products (Case, 1990; Dalley, 2008). Interestingly, practitioners in one training session declined to explore the chocolate playdough provided, because they were put off by its uncanny resemblance to poo!

- **Creation of dark colours** – Many children choose to mix dark colours, a finding noted by Hastings (2013); Case (1990); Sagar (1990) and Gascoyne (2016). A common theme in children's interactions with paint (and other resources) is 'the familiar stage of needing to use all of everything' (Sheehan, 2015: 16).

> The children start with mixing all the colours of the paint together wondering how much they can use and what happens if all the colours are mixed. The resulting brown liquid is a fascination. Does it work like paint? What does it feel like? What does it taste like? What happens if you add other substances to this liquid?
>
> (Aldridge, 2008: 2)

How often have you found yourself hoping that a child's painting will cease before being 'ruined' by brown? (An idea that we return to in Chapter 8.) When reframed as alchemy, 'a seemingly magical process of transformation, creation, or combination' (Oxford Dictionaries, 2017, cited in Powell, 2017: 4), it becomes easier for adults to accept and treat this stage of learning and **autonomy** with the significance that it deserves.

- **Creating 'cleaner' mess** – Many children's messy creations, from potions to meals, are often characterised by a transformation in colour. Jung suggested three stages common to many alchemical processes (Jung, 1959). The 'nigredo' or blackening state, linked to chaos; the 'albedo' or whitening stage; and the 'rubedo' stage, representative of 'vitality [and] symbolised by the colour red' (Powell, 2017: 4). These physical colour changes, apparent in therapy (and potentially in children's play generally), were believed to signify underlying changes in the child's subconscious. Sagar noticed a pattern in children's therapeutic messy play to create 'new cleaner kinds of mixture' (1990: 110). Similarly, Hastings (2013) and Gascoyne (2016) documented a trend towards the lightening and brightening of children's experimentations. As children transform their brown or black creations into white or sparkly forms, they experience a sense of **competence** and **autonomy**.

Reflection

Review the colour (and texture) of existing resources offered and permission, or otherwise, for children to mix resources to create darker colours to ensure that children can access materials that are compatible with their feelings and needs.

- **An emotional barometer and communication tool** – Over an 8- and 9-month period respectively, a striking transformation in colour and texture from lumpy forms and shades of brown, to pure white then colourful sparkly creations was apparent in two children's mess (Gascoyne, 2015, 2016). When compared with Strengths and Difficulties Questionnaire (SDQ) data (Goodman et al, 2000), measuring children's emotional and behavioural state, a parallel improvement in scores indicated that as children played with their mess they developed strategies to control their inner mess too. Like a visual barometer of a child's emotions, Gascoyne (2016) questions whether the colours that children purposefully create in their messy explorations represent another communication tool in the 'hundred languages' (Malaguzzi, 1998: 3). Before reaching for a DIY colour chart to analyse children's mess it's worth emphasising that this is an unproven theory, worthy of further exploration in case it provides further proof of the value of children's messy play explorations.

iv) Changing moods

Hastings (2013) found a positive correlation between messy play use in Play Therapy sessions and children's increasingly calm mood, underlying the myth of messy play just being fun. Associated with the oldest limbic part of the brain responsible for memory formation, there are strong links between smells, memories and moods. With many messy play resources featuring distinctive or strong scents, an awareness of the child's and our own reactions to smells is key.

When we compare which materials children use (in Play Therapy) to express widely differing emotions like anger and self-calming (Figure 3.2), it starkly reveals the impact of practitioners' choices, and the difference that the addition of water to sand; provision of clay rather than playdough; or choice of scent can make to enabling children's exploration of a range of emotions. Within mainstream environments too, children may capitalise upon sand's calming qualities, clay's anger-releasing effect, Gelli's surprising qualities or water's calming yet equally exciting properties, to amplify their interests and needs. Parallels can be seen with Kaplin and Kaplin's notion of 'compatibility' and 'extent' (1989), as some children spend entire play episodes exploring and experimenting with a single resource, while other resources lack appeal.

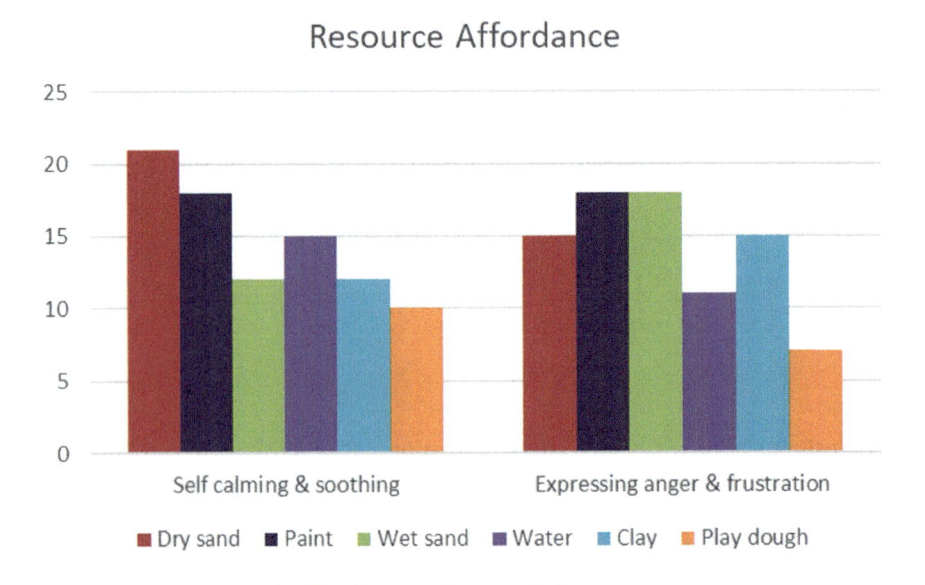

Figure 3.2 The emotional affordance of materials

SIGNIFICANCE

The relevance to children's experience of **ARC** is evident:

- We need to be aware of the different qualities and therefore affordance of materials to ensure we offer a good range of opportunities to experience **relatedness**, as well as learning from increased resilience, focus, problem-solving, scientific inquiry, language and creativity.

- The addition of scent should be a conscious choice, with a legitimate reason for picking or avoiding smells. (**relatedness**)

- The resistive qualities of clay or plasticine will release more energy and frustration, than easily malleable alternatives. (**relatedness** and **autonomy**)

- Children need to be able to access or create darker materials which may be more compatible with a child's negative emotions than pretty pastels and enable them to change these by lightening, adding colour or sparkle. (**autonomy** and **competence**)

- Resistive or repetitive qualities of resources will invite different emotional, problem-solving and scientific responses. (**relatedness**)

- Acceptance of the child (Axline, 1964) is signalled by permission to play and accepting their mess – even the brown stuff! (**relatedness**)

- Attentive noticing increases our understanding of why children aren't using resources, e.g. is it because it is not fit for their purpose; considered babyish or gender specific; out of sync with their emotions; too challenging for them to touch; or ruled out as they're scared of being shamed by making a mess? Each of these will have very different implications for practitioners. (**ARC**)

- If mess is 'magicked away' children lose opportunities to explore transformations and the associated benefits to problem-solving, personal, social and emotional development and scientific thinking. (**ARC**)

Patterns in use

While the permutations of material engagements are potentially limitless, it is possible to identify a series of stages in children's messy play which can typically be expected. Developed by Gascoyne (2016) following an analysis of Play Therapy clients as well as a trawl of secondary data, as is apparent from Figure 3.3, evidence of each of these stages is also apparent in mainstream environments (Gascoyne, 2018a).

Stages in Messy Play Use
(% of respondents who have witnessed each stage)

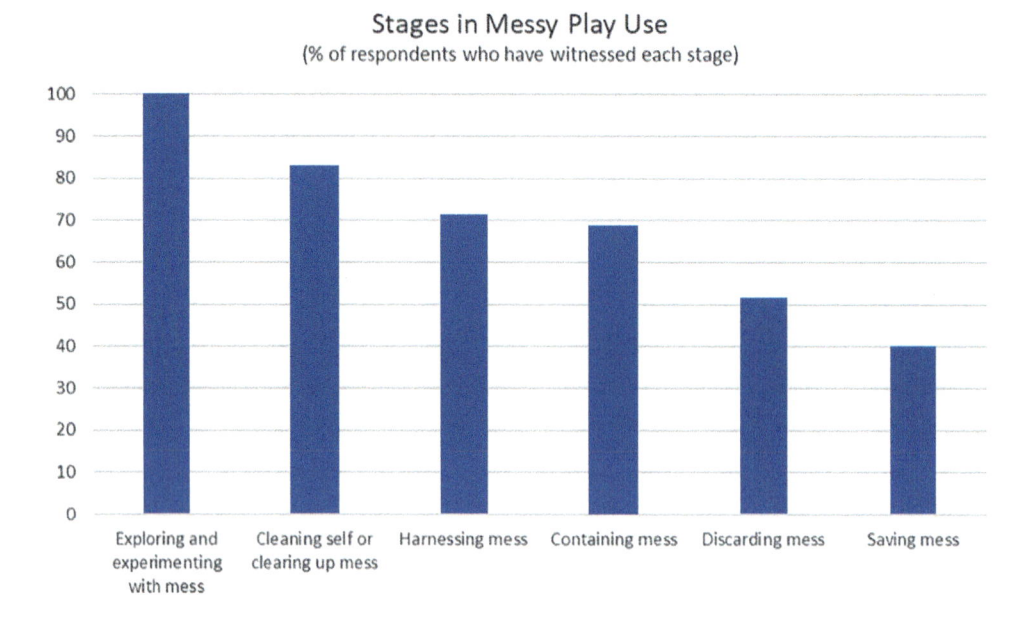

Figure 3.3 Stages in messy play use

Typical stages in messy play

We end this chapter with a focus on the following 'stages' in the lifecycle of messy play interactions:

- **Exploring and experimenting**
- **Containing**
- **Harnessing**
- **Saving**
- **Clearing up**
- **Discarding**

Rather than 'painting with a broad brush', these non-linear and potentially cyclical stages are provided as a guiding framework for better understanding and planning children's material engagements:

Exploring and experimenting – Sensory experiences like infants playing with food in their highchairs or pre-schoolers exploring water are vital for cognitive development and for supporting children's understanding of the world and their interactions with it (Perry et al, 2013). Characterised by a range of active sensory exploration and investigations, this process evolves as a child's **ARC** develops.

Containing – Once children have had opportunities to play with their mess in an unbounded way they may begin to contain it in containers, if provided. Children's messy play engagements and feelings of **autonomy** and **competence** are inextricably linked to the type and degree of containment of materials, an area which will be amplified in Chapter 5 where we unpick the implications for resourcing appropriate containers for messy play.

Harnessing – Sometimes a positive bi-product emerges, such as the creation of a magically sticky paint, made from glue and paint, or a eureka moment, when points of knowledge connect. Described by Dalley (1984) as harnessed mess, transforming resources brings satisfaction and **ARC**. The child may then move to another round of exploration, by seeing what happens if other resources are added, and so on.

Saving – Sometimes children chose to save their mess, such as storing the magic paint for later use or to see if it changes. Not always present in children's play, as adults rather than children are generally concerned with end-products, the provision of a range of containers enables children to develop their **autonomy** and **competence** in deciding if and what to keep.

Clearing up – The cleaning of themselves may happen immediately, or even during a messy encounter (such as the 6-year-old boy who frequently wiped his hands with paper towel during his investigation of Gelli) and can be a wonderfully calming act of self-care. Clearing up the mess may be similarly therapeutic and important for a child's sense of agency, or if space permits, may be left to see what happens, much like a scientific experiment. Again, the lifecycle may start again if the clearing up process highlights something unexpected, such as what happens when a running tap disperses dried paint.

Discarding – If children can choose when to move to the final stage of discarding mess this can be a carefully considered, almost cleansing, step-by-step process or, if the resulting creation and mess holds no value to them, a swift act. Often overlooked and falling to adults to take care of, this is an important stage in a child's emotional and learning process and in developing a sense of **ARC**.

> ### Reflection
>
> Consider whether children can experience all the above stages in the lifecycle of messy interactions. Is the magical removal of all traces of mess a good thing? What advantages might there be for children being able to take control of this cleansing process; deciding what to discard and what to keep; returning to and exploring change; and ultimately experiencing a sense of agency and closure?

Relevance to mainstream practice

These stages have interesting ramifications for practitioners because if children do not have opportunities to return to their mess, contain and harness it, clear up or discard it themselves because mess is 'magicked away' by adults, they are unable to experience the fulfilling lifecycle of messy engagements. This denies children opportunities for developing **ARC** as well as: self-regulation and self-esteem; tool use and physical development; and a wealth of scientific and creative learning. They may also experience different material engagements as discreet and unconnected activities and processes rather than being able to link these experiences, to elucidate the underlying science (Gascoyne, 2012; Tunnicliffe, 2016). For example, a child's understanding of the properties of liquids, solids and reversibility (a difficult concept for children to grasp), and sense of mastery orientation in being the agent of change, will be significantly enhanced if he or she experiences the full cycle of engaging with gloop, from powder through to liquid, back to a solid and so on, rather than the gloop being cleared away after one play.

> ### Reflection
>
> Consider for the children you work with where in Table 3.3 their existing material engagements fall, and if and how you can introduce changes to enable children to access the full lifecycle of messy play interactions.

Table 3.3 Stages of messy play interactions

Stage of mess	Benefits	Examples	Messy play themes[1]
Exploring and Experimenting	■ Sensory stimulation and awareness. ■ Understanding what a material is like and linking with existing knowledge. ■ Understanding themselves. ■ Developing skills, control and bodily awareness. ■ Scientific investigation and developing thinking.	■ Exploring soapy bubbles. ■ Comparing the marks left from 'painting' with water.	**Sensory exploration** **Scientific and mathematical investigations** **Creativity**
Containing	■ Increases usability of resource. ■ Limits mess, potentially avoiding fear, stress and shame. ■ Sparks uses, e.g. a cauldron suggests role-play. ■ Helps frame mess focus like good picture frame.	■ Making spice and mud pies. ■ Creating lavender perfume and 'wine'!	**Role-play** **Scientific and mathematical investigations**
Harnessing	■ Develops creativity. ■ Increases **competence**, **autonomy** and self-esteem.	■ Floating a toy boat on a flooded floor.	**Role-play** **Creativity** **Scientific investigation**
Saving	■ Provides **autonomy**. ■ Values child's choices and needs, e.g. wanting to add to and transform mess later.	■ Choosing a ziplock bag for wet mess and paper plate for a dry concoction (revealing thought process and the importance of the container being 'fit for purpose').	**Scientific and mathematical investigations** **Role-play**
Clearing up	■ Develops self-care and increases wellbeing, **autonomy** and **competence**. ■ Increases **relatedness** and environmental responsibility.	■ Infants gravitating to a container of soapy water to clean paint-covered hands.	**Sensory exploration** **Calming and therapeutic** **Role-play**
Discarding	■ Increases **autonomy**, **competence** and decision-making. ■ Increases **relatedness** and environmental responsibility.	■ Carefully sorting mess, retaining only those with the 'right' texture.	**Sensory exploration** **Calming and therapeutic**

Several of these stages are apparent in this 6 year old's use of messy play in Play Therapy:

> From an unsettled home, initially 'Billy's' use of messy play seemed to be communicating his life's 'mess' and lack of secure boundaries. He mixed, churned and poured paint, rice and water using his hands and arms (**Exploring**). Billy started with a small litter tray and the mess would seep over the sides of the container, so I provided a bigger tray and table cloths, but the mess always seemed to 'escape'. I had to remind him of the rules of the room while recognising what he was showing me (**Containing**).
>
> Billy would make a thick dark mixture in the tray and then sprinkle glitter[2] into it, seemingly lightening the 'mess' (**Experimenting**). Ultimately the glitter would disappear into the tray, which felt very pertinent to what was happening in his life.
>
> Sometimes Billy took his shoes and socks off to get in the messy mixture. There was lightness and laughter with the slipping and sliding (**Exploring** and Jennings's embodiment, 1990). He would abruptly get out and wash his legs, feet and hands in the water with a baby sponge, as if the mess was suddenly too much, and he needed to be cleansed and cared for (**Clearing up**).
>
> As the sessions continued, Billy started to use the messy play to calm himself. It was like he was connecting with the sensory nature of it, relaxing and helping himself regulate (**Exploring**).
>
> (Lynne Latham, 2018)

Another child highlights a similar transition through these stages:

> 'Bobbie' carefully mixed-up lots of different 'ingredients', looked at it, played with it revelling in how it felt (**Exploring**) then put it into a plastic box with a lid and named it (**Containing**). Each week Bobbie would check it (**Saving**) and over the summer the smell became so bad that he made the decision to throw it away (**Discarding**). It felt very symbolic as during that time things at home started to improve.
>
> (Lynne Latham, 2018)

As we will discover in the next chapter, an awareness of these different stages in messy play can prepare us for what to expect, as well as ensuring that children get opportunities to benefit from the lifecycle of material engagements. Our attention now turns to the affordance of different materials, and how this influences their use.

> **IN THIS CHAPTER WE HAVE:**
>
> - Covered a variety of different tools for quantifying children's messy encounters.
> - Unpicked their significance for the adult's role in planning enriching messy play opportunities.

Notes

1 We return to these themes in Chapter 4.
2 Glitter is no longer recommended due to environmental damage. A similar effect could be achieved with yellow powder paint.

4 Patterns in messy play use

> Far from being a uniform 'one-size-fits-all' area of provision, this chapter challenges the myth of the simplicity of messy play, introducing the idea of different materials behaving, appealing and working in widely differing ways. This chapter takes us on a journey towards the development of a messy play continuum, from wet and sticky consistencies, to in-between and dry textures, each with their own unique characteristics, qualities, appeal and potential uses. We explore how children's typical interactions challenge the idea that material encounters are a one-dimensional experience and highlight a spectrum of messy play possibilities.

We explored in Chapter 3 how children's material engagements can be considered in terms of their special attributes, physical qualities and stages. A range of quantitative lenses were introduced for viewing spatial, temporal and emotional patterns, as well as transformations in colour, form and containment. Now we will focus on the emergence of key messy play themes before unpicking the specifics of different materials and their implications for use.

Messy play themes

As well as the various stages of play identified in Chapter 3, several themes (and activities within these) emerged from children's mainstream messy encounters (Gascoyne, 2018a; Gascoyne, 2018b), many of which will no doubt resonate with readers.

Although communication and literacy are not, of course, listed separately, since these would rarely be a child's chosen play theme, that doesn't mean that benefits aren't apparent, as children's sensory engagement instils the essence of words, scientific discoveries give children something worth talking about, and children's tool use and mark-making support writing. Similarly, with children freely able to engage in a whole-bodied way, physical development strength and skills will be nurtured in everything the child does. As is apparent from Table 3.3 (page 61) these common messy play themes, which will be apparent in the vignettes provided throughout the book, also dovetail with the different stages of messy play. What warrants further consideration is whether the themes are:

1. Sparked by the affordance of the **materials**, e.g. bottles inspiring perfume-making or a cauldron, potions;

2. A product of the **child** and their 'stage' in their relationship to their mess and therefore readiness to experience, contain, save or discard it; or seeds of inquiry or knowledge funds? Or

3. The result of **adults'** provision, context and expectations?

We unpick the relationship between these in Chapter 8 when we explore the plethora of decisions involved in shaping material engagements. Our attention now turns to the affordance of messy play materials, (1), before we bring into focus the plethora of materials that create the messy play landscape and shape children's and adults' choices (2, 3).

Material affordances

Without a doubt for most children messy play has a special appeal. Perhaps this is because of its highly sensory qualities; potential for creativity and fun (being different to everyday play or

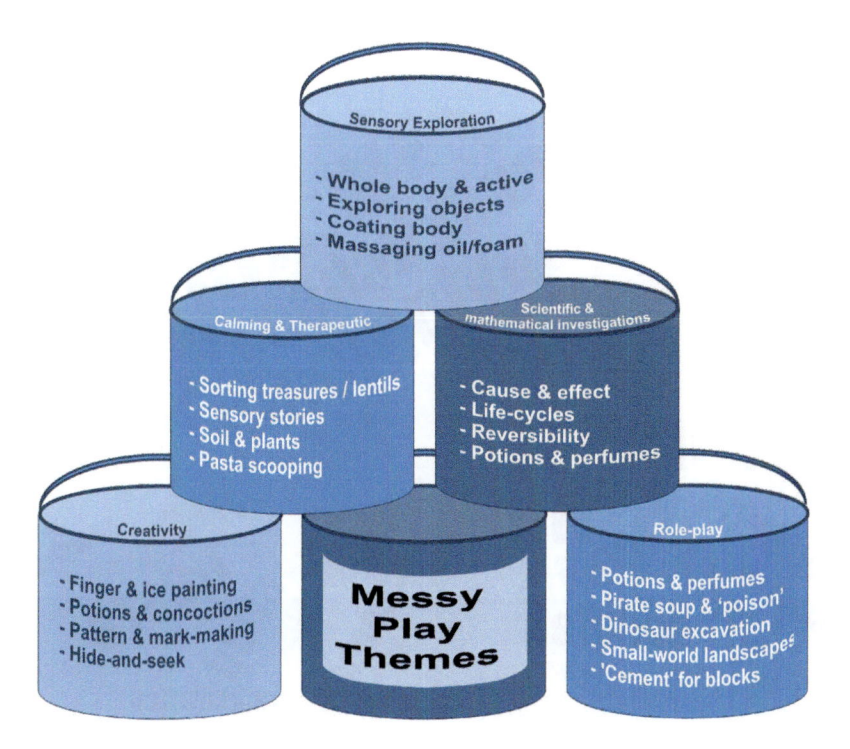

Figure 4.1 Key messy play themes

school); or the fact that making mess may feel rebellious and therefore exciting? According to Gibson, what is perceived when looking at objects (or materials) is not their dimensions or properties but their affordances: 'what they can provide or offer' (1979). This open-endedness of materials, so that the same resource has the potential to be used in a multitude of ways, is particularly apt for messy play.

Take gloop, common to many early years settings, it is an intriguing 'cognitively discombobulating' (Duffy, 2007) substance, because it behaves in unexpected ways. In some play episodes children play calmly with it, quietly absorbed in its feel; for others its surprising solid/liquid qualities cause wonder and surprise; some will experiment like a scientist; still others will be wowed by its transformational qualities and empowered by their ability to change it over and over again; some will enjoy the challenge of creating a ball; or like a child that I worked with therapeutically, the focus may be on pouring it from one container to the other, mirroring their life of constant movement between separated parents.

We discovered in Chapter 3 the importance of children having a range of materials for messy play investigations, and as is apparent from the list below and in Figure 4.2, many of these are readily available in early childhood settings and homes, without recourse to specialist provision:

Natural materials – e.g. mud, clay, sand, water, leaves, soil, flowers, seedpods.

Foodstuffs

- **Wet** – e.g. yoghurt, rice pudding, tinned tomatoes, baked beans, whipped cream.
- **Dried** – e.g. rice, lentils, couscous, herbs, spices.

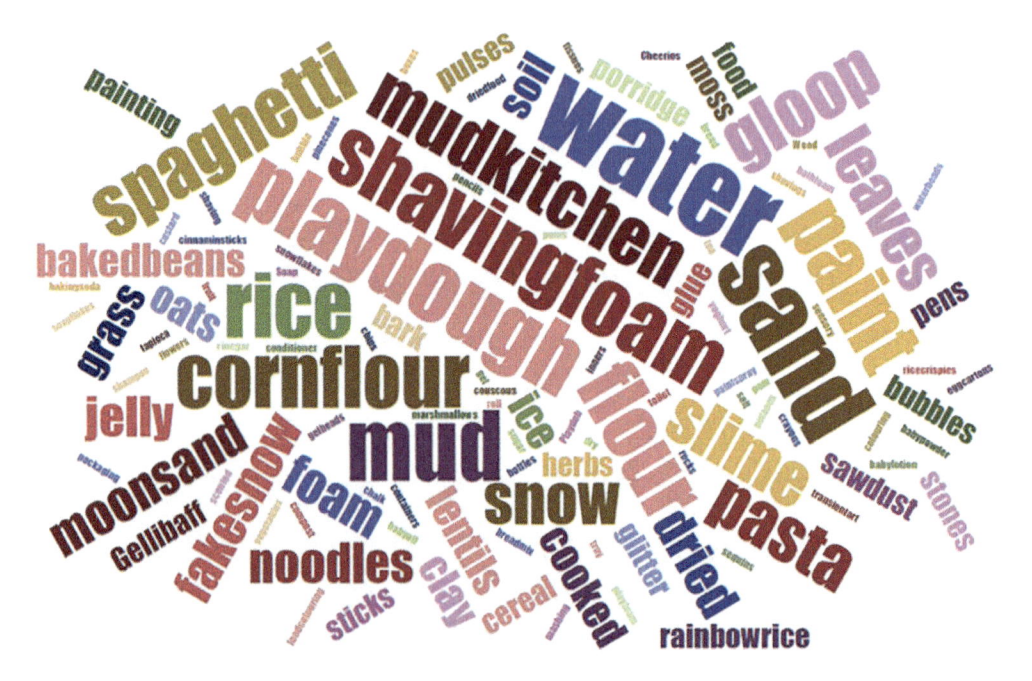

Figure 4.2 An array of messy play materials[1]

Early years staples – e.g. paint, playdough, gloop, shaving foam, glue, paper.

Recycled materials – e.g. wood shavings, shredded paper, maize packing 'peanuts'.

Specialist materials – e.g. Gelli Baff/Gelli Play, kinetic/moon sand, slime, water beads (orbies).

'The kinds of play materials ... we offer provides the framework within which children communicate' (McMahon, 2012: 76), develop and express themselves. This is particularly true of messy play materials given the myriad of choices (for adults) and wide-ranging affordance (for children), which will shape a child's play and learning process.

Resource affordance and use

When we compare how the same resources are used by children in a therapeutic context (Figure 4.3) we gain further insight into their varied affordances and compatibility, or otherwise, with children's use.

Hutt et al (1989) identified an assumption among early years practitioners that dry sand contributes to children's imagination and sharing skills. However, unless offered with other resources, which increase its play value, dry sand generates a very limited repertoire of hand movements (and therefore categorisation in the brain). While its repetitive nature may calm and support wellbeing, other benefits were not apparent, highlighting the importance of practitioners' attentive noticing to ensure informed decisions are made about what resources to offer and why. Observation of several early years staples revealed that children 'are often thwarted in attempts to make their own associations between materials' such as paint being used on the easel not in the water tray and sand cakes not allowed in the home corner (Hutt et al, 1989: 98). We will return to this in Chapter 8 when we consider the importance of Laevers' Wellbeing and Involvement Scales to check and fine-tune resource provision.

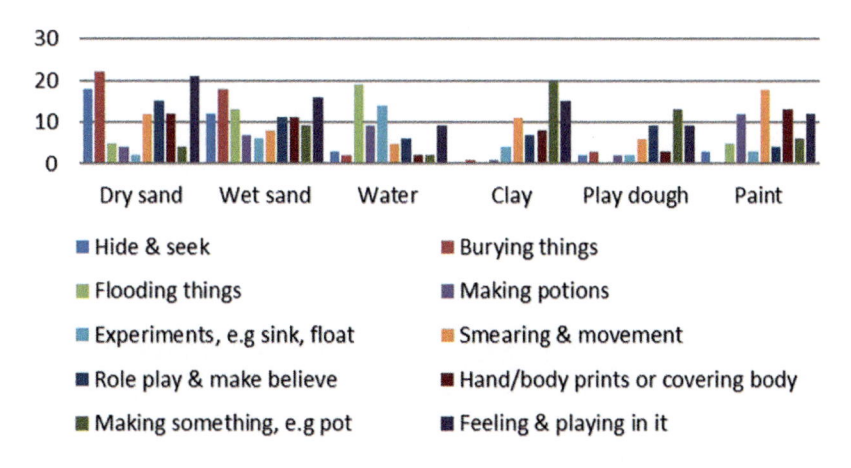

Figure 4.3 How messy play materials are used

> **Reflection**
>
> Consider as a team what types of messy play materials you offer. Do these include wet and sticky, dry and in-between textures? Do children have opportunities to change, store and return to their creations? Are children able to take control of clearing up? Are value judgements passed on the mess created, such as pastels being preferable to pooey-browns? How does children's play compare to Figure 4.3?

The importance of scale

Offering materials on a range of scales will have a bearing upon the child's perception of affordance, containment and use. Imagine offering children dried rice in a mini dolls house-proportioned copper saucepan, a large cauldron, 'sand' tray or almost completely uncontained on a sheet of tarpaulin. Each of these contexts and scales will invite different energies, affordance and play. Giving children opportunities to engage at a range of scales, be it water in a bucket, jug, puddle or clean dustbin; or water beads in a rubber glove, bucket or tray, also provides continuity through connecting knowledge points.

An example of the benefits of continuity on deep-level thinking was evident in one setting:

> Asked if I could think of a use for some sturdy cardboard tubing I arranged these in a small box, added a cable reel as a table, guttering and basket of conkers and pinecones to create a focus for a material encounter. Within minutes this became a hub of activity with children discovering what happens when objects are fed into the tube, how far do they roll, what happens when the incline is changed? A hole in the guttering became a positive feature as the children played peek-a-boo with dropped objects when they appeared at the hole. Sometimes this doubled-up as an observation point for locating a blockage. Working as a team to get objects through the tube within the quickest time, the 'posted' resources careened across the floor in a fun and energised activity.
>
> What united this and the myriad of other inventive engagements that these materials generated was the high levels of involvement and wellbeing observed – level 5 and 4 on Laevers' scale.
>
> Moving to another room in the same setting, I noticed a 4-year-old girl sat quietly at a table exploring dried rice using several containers arranged on a tray. With echoes of Montessori practice, she transferred the dried rice from one container to another, captivated perhaps by its calming sensual feel. Watching this child fill a tiny jam jar with the dried rice, pat it level (as I have seen so many children do with sand) then continue to add more rice, sprinkling this with her fingers, I was surprised by her addition of

Patterns in messy play use 69

> two pieces of dried penne pasta, which I had not previously noticed. Pressing these into the jar of rice so that the tubes protruded from the top, one-at-a-time she added rice grains to the pasta tubes, a challenging act requiring considerable manual dexterity. This ingenious approach to increasing the capacity of the jar by filling the protruding pasta tubes, provided a clue perhaps, to her self-set challenge of seeing how much rice she could fit in!

What this and play with the cardboard tubes share is the same potential for children to test and develop their knowledge acquired through transporting, enclosing and trajectory schemas. By offering opportunities to return to and explore the same principles but at very different scales, this provided an age-appropriate way of connecting threads of thinking, as well as enabling each child to differentiate the activity according to their ability and needs. The children in these examples experienced learning inspired by the thoughtful (or accidental in the case of those pasta tubes) provision of resources and permission, space and time to explore self-set challenges.

Reflection

Next time you're planning a provision take a few minutes to reflect upon:

- Whether it should be offered at that scale or if an alternative scale might be more fruitful?
- Whether a variety of scales is preferable?
- Are there opportunities for introducing continuity?

Consider what might happen if materials are offered on a different scale, be it large flowing rolls of paper, or tiny pots of powder paint?

A continuum of resources

In Chapter 3 a categorisation of materials, based on their texture and composition, was introduced. Its benefits for practitioners, in managing mess and for children, in accessing wide-ranging opportunities, were outlined. Using this as a framework for considering which resources to offer and why, we will now focus on a range of low-cost materials, exploring their characteristics, benefits, challenges and ideas to try. Drawing from the spectrum of types of messy play resources listed on pages 66 and 67, examples of natural materials (mud and clay); dry and wet foodstuffs (pulses and yoghurt); early years staples (sand, water, paint, paper, playdough and shaving foam); and speciality materials (Gelli and water beads) are provided, giving a taste of the breadth of messy play materials available. We start our journey through the landscape of messy materials, with the driest textures:

Dry textures

If you, or children, are remotely concerned about the prospect of messy play and resulting mess, this is the place to start!

Paper

CHARACTERISTICS

This undervalued messy play resource is remarkably varied and relatively cheaply available, especially if you're able to re-purpose packaging. Its properties and appeal vary markedly with size, colour, texture and density. Sensorially it's also surprisingly noisy – just try holding a piece of scrunched-up tissue paper near your ear!

BENEFITS

- **Dry** – Limits mess.
- **Availability** – Widely available, non-specialist resource.
- **Affordance** – Wide-ranging affordance depending upon the type, scale, weight and colour of paper, e.g. newsprint, tissue, shredded, corrugated, sugar paper; and how it is offered, whether on its own, whole, in small pieces, on a roll, with water or glue, outdoors or near a fan.
- **Versatility** – Ability to challenge 'functional fixedness' (i.e. that a resource can only be used in a certain way, limiting creative thinking; Brown & Kane, 1989, cited in Goswami, 2004: 287), proving there is more to paper than A4 sheets!
- **Emotional mirror** – Varies with resource, e.g. shredded paper can be calming or exciting, a huge canvas or roll liberating or scary; papier mache or 'clean mud' (made from a roll of toilet paper, soap and water or its food-safe alternative, from cornflour, coconut oil and water, www.powerfulmothering.com/how-to-make-clean-mud-recipe-taste-safe/), sensory or challenging.

SENSORY QUALITIES AND VOCABULARY

Rustle, bright, white, coloured, flat, fold, smooth, cool, floating, movement, torn, shredded, absorbent, spread, pattern, marks.

CHALLENGES

- Paper and dust spread.
- Paper cuts are surprisingly painful.
- Overcoming concerns about waste, e.g. ripping-up pristine sheets of tissue paper.

TRY . . .

- Introduce a 'walking water rainbow' experiment where capillary action mixes different-coloured water (Citro, 2015) and then provide different types of paper (e.g. kitchen towel, toilet paper, greaseproof paper, tissue paper and plain paper for children's investigations).

- Introduce surprise by painting paper with vinegar and leaving to dry for children to discover fizzy painting with a mixture of paint and bicarbonate of soda.

- Hang up a huge sheet or roll of paper to explore paint and movement.

- Bury some objects, treasures or figures in shredded paper to be discovered.

- Provide containers of different materials, including shredded paper, for children to walk through and explore, possibly with a story like *We're Going on a Bear Hunt* (Rosen, 1989).

- Leave paper in the sun with objects on for children to discover and create their own prints.

- Invite children to paint without brushes or paint, e.g. using objects and natural colours instead.

- Provide sieves, tea strainers, flour (check allergies) and paper or crocheted doilies for exploring patterns.

- Create dens for 'hibernating' in paper.

- Tear up tissue paper to create an inviting mound and experience its new affordance.

Reflection

Consider what types of paper you currently offer and whether these inadvertently introduce functional fixedness, which hinders creative thinking.

Consider whether play opportunities are sometimes restricted because of concerns over wastage. Are these legitimate concerns or unhelpfully limiting?

Dried pulses, grains, pasta, oats, sultanas, spices and herbs

CHARACTERISTICS

These store cupboard staples tend to be widely and relatively cheaply available. Their colours, textures, smells and sounds add a richly sensory dimension to messy play.

BENEFITS

- **Dry mess** – Mess may be restricted and relatively contained.

- **Safe** – Depending upon the child's age, allergies, chosen resource and whether cooked or not, many of these are 'taste' safe for children to explore and mouth with close adult supervision. Avoid raw kidney beans as these can be toxic if not properly cooked. Care needs to be taken with uncooked resources which could represent choking hazards.

- **Learning** – Familiar resources, like oats and rice, may build upon children's knowledge funds and forge links to prior learning about solids (Perry et al, 2013), e.g. how cooked and raw porridge or rice compare. Unfamiliar pulses like split yellow peas and lentils may extend learning about the environment and food we eat.

- **Minimise waste** – These are a great way of using up 'best before' essentials. Mess may be compostable.

- **Environmentally friendly** – With the use of glitter and sequins damaging to the environment, dried continental or orange lentils, split yellow peas and lavender provide natural alternatives.

- **Imagination** – Inspire domestic role-play, especially if complemented with some miniature pots and teacups.

SENSORY QUALITIES AND VOCABULARY

Trickle, pour, same, different, flat, smooth, round, orange, shiny, dusty, soft, hard, pointy, warm.

CHALLENGES

Overcoming criticism of wasting food:

- Playing with food has been identified as an essential part of infant's learning about properties and themselves (Perry et al, 2013).

- Alli Sonnier provides excellent advice on this topic (see the next Reflection).

- One survey respondent shared an unexpected positive of messy play with food – 'Being able to play with [noodles] encouraged a very fussy eater to try them and he loved them' (Gascoyne, 2018a).

TRY . . .

- Shake in a sealed bag with food colouring to cheaply and quickly transform into visually exciting provocations.

- Add a sensory dimension to stories like *Goldilocks and the Three Bears*.

- Fill empty chocolate box trays with different dried grains, pulses or herbs and provide a range of tongs, chopsticks, utensils and other containers for exploration and sorting.

- Create trays of different pulses and grains for children to explore and walk through. Link to sensory stories or story books with resources providing textures, sounds or smells.

- Mix into dried sand or soil to add visual and textural interest and support scientific thinking of volume, capacity, big, small and same and different if offered with sieves or tea strainers.

- Create environments for safe and sensory small-world play.

Reflection

Read Alli Sonnier's advice (2012) and then consider your approach to the use of food for messy play. Does this change your view of what should be offered to increase children's opportunities or minimise waste?

Sand

CHARACTERISTICS

Dry sand is a predictable repetitive resource and it is these qualities which make it very calming and emotionally soothing. When wet however, sand is very different, offering opportunities for developing a sense of agency and control from varying the consistency, projecting the child's mark, building and exploring cause-and-effect.

BENEFITS

- **Transformation** – Exploring change and developing a sense of control, e.g. by changing consistency with the addition of water, beads, buttons; or if adding to dry sand, dried rice, lentils and couscous.

- **Flexibility** – Sand is good for transporting, enclosing, pouring and filling but its flexibility significantly increases when offered with utensils and containers.

- **Learning** – Supports wellbeing and physical development when used on its own or with tools. Supports problem-solving and knowledge of the world when combined with other equipment such as funnels, spoons, sieves and a selection of different-sized containers. Invites creativity and mark-making, inspires imagination and provides a rich foundation for language.

- **Early years staple** – As a familiar and accepted part of everyday practice it doesn't need to be explained or instructions provided.

SENSORY QUALITIES AND VOCABULARY

Cold, hot, smooth, soft, powdery, squeaky, flowing, golden, calming when dry. Mouldable, resistant, sticky, gritty, squidgy, clumpy, solid, cold, warm when wet.

CHALLENGES

- Some people don't like the feel of sand beneath their fingernails so provide utensils as tools.
- If thrown, the grit in sand can scratch children's eyes.
- Spillages of sand on some surfaces can be a slip hazard.
- Children's play with sand can lack value.

TRY...

- Provide a selection of different-sized wooden and metal spoons and brushes or magnets and brushes for an archaeological dig.
- Offer with a variety of containers, some metal and wooden, but also some recycled pots.
- Provide utensils and containers for pouring, filling, transporting and role-play.
- Provide in small containers, such as takeaway plastic trays for individual work.

- Provide water (a jug, tap or bucket) for mixing to the desired consistency.
- Provide washing-up liquid or cornflour for mixing, if wished.
- Provide plastic bottles for experimenting with solids, liquids and sounds.

> ## Reflection
>
> Notice …
>
> - How you initially feel about touching the dry sand? Does this vary with its dryness/wetness/consistency?
> - Did you use the utensils provided?
> - Did you explore in silence?
> - Would you have liked to have explored the sand with different parts of your body?
> - How could the experience have been improved? E.g. in individual containers, outdoors, with the provision of other resources?

In-between textures

Once adults and children feel comfortable with dry textures, these in-between textures are a great stepping-stone as they don't stick to the skin.

Playdough (or Play-Doh)

CHARACTERISTICS

Unlike shop-bought Play-Doh, homemade playdough is a sensorially varied malleable resource, limited only by individuals' creativity.

BENEFITS

- **Early years staple** – As a familiar and accepted part of everyday practice it doesn't need to be explained or instructions provided.
- **Sensory appeal** – Unmistakable smell of shop-bought Play-Doh. Scents and textures of homemade playdough.
- **Variety** – Limitless recipes to change the colour, texture, smell or even taste.
- **Cost** – Cheaply made with no specialist resources.
- **Learning** – Making playdough is a wonderfully sensory messy play activity, or if measuring quantities, a science experiment. Children can explore colour mixing, if allowed.

SENSORY QUALITIES AND VOCABULARY

Smooth, soft, squidgy, squishy, scented, stretchy, squashy, print, flat, roll, ball, shape, mould.

CHALLENGES

- Limited play value other than as a malleable or for pretend meals, especially if using Play-Doh.
- Colours can constrain play if children feel they need to be used appropriately.
- Adults' reluctance to mix different colours, particularly if dough has been made at home at practitioner's cost.
- Some children are resistant to touching playdough if already used.
- Easily mouldable so limited resistive qualities for fine motor strength and venting emotions.
- Tendency to become gender biased if offered with pink baking equipment.

TRY . . .

- Add sand, lavender, beads, polystyrene balls, googly eyes or porridge oats for textural and visual interest.
- Use herbs, spices, food flavouring, flower petals, herbal tea leaves for scent.
- Make edible versions with sweets, custard powder or instant pudding mixture. (Search online for recipes.)
- Put some powder paint into the centre of playdough balls for a surprise. Add more than one colour for colour mixing.

> ## Reflection
>
> - Consider whether children are given adequate opportunities to freely explore and transform playdough without judgement.
> - Discuss how the team feels when different-coloured paints or playdough are mixed together.
> - Consider how decisions are made about which colours and scents to offer and whose preferences they reflect, e.g. not brown playdough?

Water beads

CHARACTERISTICS

Affectionately known by children as orbies, this is an incredibly appealing messy play resource. I recommend getting the ones that include a selection of opaque and transparent beads as they are visually more interesting and have greater play and learning potential.

BENEFITS

- **Wow factor** – An exciting resource that is likely to appeal to adults and hook reluctant messy players.

- **Safe** – Child safe for three years plus **provided you buy the ones packaged for child use. Avoid floristry versions**.

- **Cost** – Good value.

- **Mirrors energy** – Very calming, but if trying to move them into containers can cause excitement as extremely bouncy.

- **Transformation** – Great for exploring change (and the difficult concept of reversibility) as the orbies will grow, shrink and even dry out depending upon the water level.

- **Versatility** – You can vary qualities and appearance by offering in different-sized/depth containers.

- **Responsibility** – They foster **relatedness** if a child takes responsibility for keeping them topped up with water.

- **Age appeal** – Unlike playdough, which may be considered babyish, orbies are cool enough to appeal to older children.

SENSORY QUALITIES AND VOCABULARY

Shiny, cold, bouncy, iridescent, round, smooth, slimy, squidgy, squishy, slippery, opaque, transparent, colourful, ball.

CHALLENGES

- Containing spillages and beads going everywhere if dropped!
- Keeping topped up with water.
- Some children may not like their slippery feel.
- Avoiding contamination with substances that would make them 'go off'.

TRY...

- Put in different depth containers to see how it changes their appearance and appeal, e.g. one-layer deep on a yoghurt/margarine pot lid, or deep enough to submerge the whole hand in a deeper container.
- Fill a latex-free glove and then carefully tip out the excess water and tie the top. This has a wow factor and feels wonderful. Great for tactile-defensive children.
- Explore on a light table or overhead projector.
- Freeze and explore change.
- Mix with Gelli for creepy concoctions.
- Provide pots for colour-sorting with utensils. Be warned: their bounciness makes this very challenging!

Reflection

- Take some time to notice the different sensory qualities of this resource and how it makes you feel.
- Compare the different sensations from plunging your hand in a deep container of water beads compared with the dazzling reflections of light when just a single layer.
- Be aware of how changing their presentation affects your experience and consider if and how you can apply this to other resources too.

Water

CHARACTERISTICS

Water is incredibly versatile as it can be relaxing and calming or playful and exciting. It mirrors and amplifies a child's emotions, and some water experiences such as sporadic fountains and water pistols incite playfulness as an agent of play.

BENEFITS

- **Early years staple** – A familiar and accepted part of everyday practice, it doesn't need instructions and complements a child's knowledge funds.

- **Mirror to emotions** – Can be quiet and calming or exciting, lively and fun.

- **Versatile** – Great for exploring, experiments, sensory stimulation, potion-making, role-play, science and developing a range of fine and gross motor skills.

SENSORY QUALITIES AND VOCABULARY

Wet, cool, warm, splash, splosh, bubbly, soapy, slop, spill, leak, plop, drop, soaked, drip, fill, trickle, dribble.

CHALLENGES

Health and safety – All water play should be supervised.

Risk of slipping from spillages.

Limitations – Familiarity might make it difficult to look afresh and creatively.

Play could be repetitious depending upon what resources are used with the water.

TRY . . .

Offer opportunities for children to engage with water at several scales and in different forms:

- A running tap provides a sense of agency and introduces children to the phenomenon of natural chaos (see the next Reflection).

- A jug provides opportunities for developing physical motor strength and skills as well as agency and mastery over materials. The ability to pour in a directed way supports accuracy and skill, and the weight of the jug encourages careful usage.

- A deep container, such as a bucket or recycled soup pot, offers opportunities to experience suction pressure and a sense of immersion.

- A transparent tray gives a view of sinking, floating and refraction.

- Guttering, tubes and a water wheel introduce movement.

- Warm body-temperature water de-sensitises and is less painful than extremes.

- Contrast reactions, e.g. does powder paint or Gelli act differently in warm or cold water? What difference does stirring make?

- Set up a laboratory with bottles, scoops, ladles, a pestle and mortar and large mixing bowl for perfume-making.

- Provide resources for water-related role-play such as car, baby or clothes washing.

- Provide alternative ways of exploring water, e.g. sponges for squeezing and pressing, a rubber glove filled with water, or laminated pouch/sandwich bag filled with water, oil and food colouring.

Reflection

Notice . . .

- What happens to a pot of puddle water when it is left to separate, resources are added to it, or a puddle or ice evaporates in the sun? Imagine that you are seeing this for the first time. Really take the time to notice and appreciate, as if a curious child.

- Place a small piece of tin foil under the slow drip of a tap so that you hear the regular beat of the drip. Turn the tap a little further and the rhythm will change to an irregular pattern as you hear 'alternate long and short beats'. Turn still further and you will experience deterministic chaos, which is also evident in a falling leaf (Percival, 1992: 12). Consider other everyday science opportunities to explore.

Wet and sticky textures

Our final stage in a focus on resource consistencies is wet and sticky resources. These are likely to be the most challenging and messiest for children and adults so not the ideal starting point for a messy play journey!

Shaving foam

CHARACTERISTICS

This creamy frothy material is a longstanding messy play staple. Its clean smell and appearance potentially makes it more acceptable for adults and children.

BENEFITS

- **Early years staple** – A familiar and accepted part of everyday practice, it doesn't need to be explained or instructions provided.

- **Sensory** – Its smell and visual appearance may appeal, and sensitive options are available.

- **Cause-and-effect** – If allowed, squirting the aerosol can increase a child's **competence** and **autonomy**.

SENSORY QUALITIES AND VOCABULARY

Velvety, smooth, creamy, white, scented, frothy, jet, plume, aim, splatter, squirt.

CHALLENGES

- Some children (and adults) may have skin sensitivities to this or find the smell nauseous.
- Due to cost, adults rather than children tend to be in control.

TRY . . .

- Squirt on a safety mirror or glass for sensory exploration and pattern-making.
- Add powder paint for colour mixing, patterns and mark-making.
- Add balls for a sensory and visual contrast.
- Add to sand to create a lovely smooth texture.
- Provide small-world vehicles and people for role-play.
- Use to enhance an arctic provocation.
- Use to explore change by comparing frozen, dried-out and fresh foam.
- Provide for role-play with mirrors and other barbers' props.
- Freeze to create 'artificial snow'.

> One primary-aged child took the role of Spiderman, squirting his web (shaving foam from an aerosol) over a target. His feelings of **ARC** were evident as he mastered one-handed squirting.

A playful practitioner addressed children's concerns about getting messy head-on in this session in Southern India:

> I sprayed the shaving foam onto their clothes and hands. At first, they were surprised because I made their clothes dirty. Then I re-assured them that I had their parents' permission. When their hands were almost foam-filled, I asked them to clap, so it 'rained' foam. They loved this, and some enjoyed spreading their foam-covered hands on the polythene sheet in circular motions.
>
> (Anjali Rajan, 2018)

Paint

CHARACTERISTICS

We tend to think of ready-mixed or wet paint, hence its inclusion at the wetter end of the continuum, but as we explore in Chapter 5, powder paint has even more play and learning potential. Food-safe and natural paint substitutes are also good options.

BENEFITS

- **Early years staple** – As a familiar and accepted part of everyday practice it doesn't need to be explained or instructions provided.

- **Flexible** – Paint can be used flexibly if permitted, especially if we offer alternatives to ready-mixed paint.

- **Cost** – Powder paints, water and mud are low/no cost.

SENSORY QUALITIES AND VOCABULARY

Velvety, smooth, oozing, squelchy, silky, thick, watery, congealed, powder, run, spread, prints, patterns, brush, colours, tint, tone, hue, shade, mix, splatter.

CHALLENGES

- Adults tend to be more bothered by the need for a range of colours (see powder paint vignette on page 100).

- Adults can be resistant to children mixing to create the colour brown.

- An over-emphasis upon primary and secondary colours can be at the expense of exploring the spectrum of tints, tones and hues available, and supporting children's 'language' of colours.

- Consider whether fit for purpose, i.e. watercolours not poster paints, if exploring blending.

- Ready-mixed paints can prove expensive if children have free use or adults may feel tense about wastage.

TRY . . .

- Add powder paint to a puddle of water, block of ice, snow or squirted shaving foam to watch colour(s) dissolve, spread and mix.

- Put dollops of paint in a sandwich bag for squishy mess-free exploration.

- Squirt paint onto paper and then cover with clingfilm (see page 139) for disequilibrium (at clean hands and feet), colour mixing and mark-making with objects and toys.

- Add watercolour paint (or food colouring) to a cup of milk, then dip a cotton bud in washing-up liquid to spread the paint with.

- Add sand or rock salt to create textured paint.

Patterns in messy play use **85**

- Make your own paint colours from natural plant, vegetable and flower dyes or using tomato ketchup or adding food colouring to yoghurt or whipped cream.
- Experiment with different consistencies and shades of mud-painting.
- Inspire paint exploration by reading *Cave Baby* (Donaldson, 2010).
- Create a paint slide or explore body prints.

Reflection

Consider the **Challenges** identified and whether changes are needed to the resources offered, limits set, or permission given for children to explore.

Homemade natural yoghurt

CHARACTERISTICS

A wonderful sensory-rich resource, whose texture and consistency can be varied, if homemade, by how long the yoghurt is left to set.

BENEFITS

- **Safety** – Healthy and safe to eat (check allergies).

- **Affordable** – Cheap and easy to make.

- **Learning** – Unlike quick and impressive volcano (vinegar and bicarbonate of soda) experiments, this scientific reaction takes time and therefore is great for supporting 'self-regulation, attention, resilience, self-control . . . curiosity, self-esteem and [a child's] ability to defer gratification' (Pascal et al, 2018: 36).

- **Cleanliness** – Reinforces self-care as cleanliness is essential when growing live yoghurt cultures.

- **Mastery** – The finished result delivers satisfaction, magic and mastery orientation.

SENSORY QUALITIES AND VOCABULARY

Soft, velvety, creamy, smooth, grainy, gloopy, runny, set, solid, liquid, white, milky, bubbles, glossy, healthy, slimy, gloopy, sloppy, thick, wobbly.

CHALLENGES

- If children have a milk allergy, use a vegan recipe, soya milk and a soya yoghurt starter.

- Adult involvement is essential as the milk needs to be heated.

TRY . . .

Making your own yoghurt is so easy and a real-life science experiment on how materials change. You will find simple instructions on www.playtoz.co.uk.

- Laboratory coats and goggles will add to the experience and reinforce the serious science behind children's creation, as we shall explore further in Chapter 7.

Use for a range of material encounters:

- Add a few dollops to a large child-safe mirror. Babies and young children will enjoy exploring, spreading and smearing the yoghurt, as well as tasting it. Unless a child is tactile defensive, there is no need to provide any utensils. Children will feel the cold slimy yoghurt with their whole bodies, as they sit, crawl and walk over the mirror discovering cause-and-effect; spread and smear; and eventually make marks and patterns.

- Add a few drops of food colouring to some firmly set yoghurt in a tray for exploring colour mixing with hands or brushes (Lil Bebe Academy, 2018). Large brushes will help develop children's gross and fine motor skills and strength.

- Offer spices and herbs for mixing with yoghurt for multi-sensory appeal, mixing and science.
- Create a yoghurt slide on an old shower curtain for some sensory fun outdoors. Provide a bucket of water or hose for easy cleaning.

Gelli Baff or Gelli Play

CHARACTERISTICS

This is an amazing jelly-like substance, which varies greatly in appearance, qualities, play and learning value, depending upon the amount of warm water that it is mixed with. Available in primary colours, it looks fluffy, light with opaque jelly-like flakes when concentrated. When diluted it has a rich dark glossy appearance.

BENEFITS

- **Versatility** – Provides calming sensory feedback or can be used to vent frustration.
- **Wow factor** – Transformation and resistive qualities engender surprise and cognitive disequilibrium.
- **Learning** – Introduces problem-solving and the science of cause-and-effect, sinking, floating, reactions, change, cycles, reversibility, and effect of temperature on reaction time.
- **Transformation** – Develops **autonomy** and control as children add water or objects, mix or freeze it. Its resistive properties vary with consistency, so some objects sink while others float.
- **Cost** – If you use the powder sparingly, store Gelli in a lidded-container/refuse bag, avoid contamination and don't rush to the Step 2 dissolving powder; it lasts for ages.

SENSORY QUALITIES AND VOCABULARY

Fluffy, jelly, sticky, wet, sloppy, velvety, shiny, resistant, crystalised, liquid, stir, mix, add, powder, change, cold, glossy, runny, thick, lumpy, opaque, warm.

CHALLENGE

- Not everyone likes touching Gelli.
- Some resources will cause the Gelli to 'go off' so:
  - Explain that adding things like sand, shaving foam, lentils, dried rice, glue, shredded paper etc to the Gelli will mean it has to be thrown away.
  - If desired, help children put some Gelli into a smaller container for mixing and experimenting with.

TIP

- Slime versions have significantly less exploratory play potential, so beware when buying.
- Only a tiny amount of powder is needed. Store the dissolving packet and remainder somewhere dry.

- If it's not thickening don't be tempted (as I have) to add more powder. It can take up to 20 minutes to fully thicken and the water needs to be warm **and** the Gelli mixed (or agitated) to make the reaction work. If it is too thin, try stirring in some very hot water (adult only).
- Some people dislike the feel of Gelli when 'fluffy' but can tolerate it when diluted. Help children desensitise by gradually increasing its thickness.
- If using the dissolving powder, do so with children to explore change and science as well as developing mastery orientation and **autonomy**.

TRY . . .

- Provide a range of spoons and utensils for tactile-defensive children to use.
- Explore colour mixing with different-coloured Gellis.

- Offer plastic mini army figures/insects/dinosaurs, wooden blocks, buttons, stones, shells, gems, orbies, sequins, rubber 'eyeballs'; provide in a cauldron (see image); and arrange a selection of spoons and containers for mixing, pouring and role-play.

> ### Reflection
>
> Notice how you initially felt about touching the Gelli. Did this vary with its consistency or different states?

Clay

CHARACTERISTICS

Clay comes in many colours and forms, each with their own qualities and characteristics. Although clay is a wonderfully natural resource, it tends to be less familiar to children than Play-Doh and plasticine.

BENEFITS

- **Sensory** – Provides wide-ranging sensory feedback as it offers the extremes of cold/warm, hard/soft, dry/squelchy, and all manner of stages in between.
- **Emotions** – Good for releasing and expressing emotions through pummelling, bashing, pressing or calmly moulding. Brown clay's resemblance to poo can increase its appeal.
- **Transformation** – Children can explore cause-and-effect and gradually shape and mould it to explore change, save creations and develop a sense of control.

SENSORY QUALITIES AND VOCABULARY

Soft, hard, squidgy, slimy, cold, warm, squelchy, smooth, velvety, patterns, thump, roll, ball, flat, earthy, lumpy, powder, pummel, knead, force, crack, crumble, squish.

CHALLENGES

- Challenges fine and gross motor skills as harder to work and takes longer to achieve results.
- There may be resistance to its mess or colour.
- Safe storage is needed to avoid it drying out.
- Keep wet to avoid hazards from clay dust. Dampen dust before sweeping up (Weinstein, 2016).

TRY . . .

- Provide a bucket of water for children to change consistency.
- Offer outdoors on wood offcuts or modelling boards for saving and transporting.
- Provide stones, shells, twigs, buttons etc to be incorporated if wished.

> **Reflection**
>
> - Notice how you feel about touching it? Does this change as it warms up and softens; water is added; and it begins to yield?
> - How do your fingers, hands and wrists feel as they get a workout from pummelling and bashing the clay?
> - Try using your feet instead. Notice the sensation, hardness and then feeling of warm clay oozing between your toes.
> - Notice the earthy smell and any memories that spring to mind.
> - How do your hands feel afterwards? At first slightly sticky, then drying to a flaky crust that cracks and powders when moved.

Gloop or oobleck

CHARACTERISTICS

Defined by Oxford Dictionaries.com as a 'sloppy or sticky semi-fluid matter, typically something unpleasant', gloop is made by mixing cornflour (or cornstarch) and water together. It is a cheap and potentially very messy resource, commonly used in early years settings.

BENEFITS

- **Sensory** – Provides captivating, calming sensory feedback.
- **Surprise** – Its solid/liquid qualities provide surprise and cognitive disequilibrium.
- **Transformation** – Good for exploring change and developing **autonomy** as children change its consistency, add water/powder and leave it to dry.
- **Science** – Introduces problem-solving, understanding properties, cycles and reversibility as the powder transforms from solid to liquid and back again.

SENSORY QUALITIES AND VOCABULARY

Soft, velvety, runny, hard, shiny, dull, flaky, caked, smooth, liquid, solid, powder, change, dry, cracked, drip, shape, force, plop, white.

CHALLENGES

Spillages can be tricky to wipe up as the stain re-appears when dry.

TRY . . .

- Explore after reading *Bartholomew and the Oobleck* (Dr Seus,1949).

- Add Glow Water (made from non-toxic highlighters and water) and use in a room with black light.
- Add ice cubes for added sensory interest.
- Spray water into a tray of cornflour.
- Explore colour mixing with gloop.

Reflection

- Notice how you initially feel about touching the powder, liquid or dried gloop. Is it more/less appealing in its different states?
- How does it change when you squeeze it; let it ooze between your fingers; draw a finger through it; put it in a plastic container and shake it; roll it into a ball; or let your fingers sink into it?

Mud, soil and compost

CHARACTERISTICS

The colour, earthy smell and dirt-factor of mud, soil and compost can make them irresistible to children, if they are given permission to explore and change their consistency with the addition of water.

BENEFITS

- **Cost** – Cheaply or freely available.

- **Availability** – Familiar and generally accessible at home and in the setting, thereby supporting the child's knowledge funds.

- **Sensory** – Interesting texture, smell and consistency.

- **Transformation** – Ability to transform consistency with water or washing-up liquid; its smell with tomato ketchup, herbs or spices; its texture with pea shingle and seedpods.

- **Science** – Can add water to explore separation into parts, experiment with consistency and explore puddles.

- **Role-play** – Wonderful for mud pies and potions.

SENSORY QUALITIES AND VOCABULARY

Crumbly, messy, sticky, wet, dry, earthy, dirty, mud, caked, cracked, parched, puddle, squelchy, splash.

CHALLENGES

- Need to take precautions to ensure that the soil is safe for use.

- Appropriate clothing and footwear, if needed (see page 193).

- Deciding limits and boundaries.

- Potential adult and child resistance to getting hands messy (see mud pie-making on page 143).

TRY ...

- Create a makeshift worktop from a shelf, bench, pallet or log for a mud kitchen, together with a selection of pots, pans, bun trays and utensils.

- Vary the water supply available, i.e. a jug, tap, bucket or hose will illicit very different consistencies and affordances.

- Make lengths of guttering and pipes available together with mounds and slopes for exploring flow.

Reflection

Even fans of messy play may struggle with the feel and appearance of soil or mud-caked hands. Cast your mind back to the definitions of mess in Chapter 1 and it is probably these types of materials that adults find most challenging. Try experimenting first-hand to familiarise and desensitise yourself.

The spectrum of resources

As we have discovered in this chapter, the term messy play engulfs a myriad of materials from dry to wet and sticky. Each of the low- or no-cost resources described offers individual affordances which will shape how the materials can be accessed and used, whether for science investigations, sensory calming, creativity or role-play. A knowledge of these, together with how complementary resources and careful planning can extend children's fruitful engagement, is essential for practitioners. Our attention now turns to these in Chapter 5 as we consider preparing the environment and individuals for enriching messy play with a view to minimising anxieties about mess.

> **IN THIS CHAPTER WE HAVE:**
>
> ■ Explored the special qualities, benefits and challenges of a range of low- and no-cost messy resources on the messy play continuum.
> ■ Introduced a spectrum of messy play possibilities.

Note

1 Resources identified by participants in a seminar at Childcare Expo (Gascoyne, 2018b).

5 Planning enabling messy play environments

> In the last chapter we explored the varying affordances of different materials. Our attention now turns to the types of resources to offer with these, to enrich children's messy play and learning. Using the stages of play introduced in Chapter 3 as a framework, we will consider the process of identifying resources and planning enabling environments, through to the clearing up stage. A set of core essentials will be provided for safely maximising affordance and managing mess, with a focus throughout on the lynchpins of **Autonomy, Relatedness and Competence, ARC** (Deci & Ryan, 2000).

Preparing for messy play in all its guises

We're told 'Fail to prepare and prepare to fail' and it's easy to see its relevance to the potential minefield of messy play! One of the biggest barriers to material engagements is the resulting mess[1] (Gascoyne, 2018a), and with confessions such as 'loathe it' and 'makes me gag' (Childcare Expo seminar; Gascoyne 2018b) simple and effective measures are needed to minimise these anxieties. Enjoyment of messy play experiences can depend upon appropriate safeguards for limiting stress. As we will discover in this chapter, as well as preparing the immediate environment and resource in question, be it sand, gloop, soil or slime, it's also worth considering if and how the child, parents and practitioners' expectations need preparing, as these are also key for successful material engagements.

Planning and preparation

Investing considerable time in preparing resources is sadly not a guarantee of success, as this practitioner discovered.

> A carefully crafted city of cereal bricks was flattened within minutes by the pounding fists of the young children. Once a desert of crumbs, adults had a choice about if and how to proceed. Whether to remove the flattened city to minimise mess; add some scoops and containers for children to use with the dry crumbs; or if they dared, provide water to enable children to form their own structures from the sticky paste, a truly messy resource with cement-like qualities, as most parents (myself included) can testify!

Reflection revealed a myriad of factors that contributed to this frustrating outcome:

- Having given up her own time and money to create the provocation, she was naturally personally and financially invested in her creation. (**adult relatedness to resource**)

- As it was 'her' vision and creation, the children (and colleagues) didn't have shared-ownership from its planning or creation. Ironically, as these children pounded the structure their **relatedness** and ownership increased.

- The children were not developmentally ready to make the link between these cereal towers and skyscrapers. (**relatedness**)

- No adults modelled appropriate use of the cereal, perhaps due to their lack of confidence, understanding, or sensory aversions. (**ARC**)

- Most likely the children had no interest in using the resources for role-play as they were still at Jenning's sensory embodiment, or projection stage (2011), exploring trajectory schemas and the irresistible science of cause-and-effect, such as what happens if I apply a force to this structure? However, with time and permission to interact in a whole-bodied sensory way they might have begun to mould the paste into sculptures, then challenged themselves to create taller and more substantial constructions, not dissimilar in shape and form to the practitioner's 'city'. (**relatedness**)

Reflection

This practitioner invested considerable time in planning the provocation, but this did not extend to preparing staff and children for its use. Consider instances where this has happened to you or colleagues and what you've discovered as a result?

Managing preparation time

When we are too attached to resources, objectives and outcomes, it's doubly difficult to ditch the plan in favour of planning in the moment. In fact, there's an argument for reducing time spent preparing provocations and investing this in preparing the wider physical and emotional environment instead, so that we can shape the quality of children's material encounters and respond more flexibly to children's interests and needs. The above provocation (described on page 68) sparked a wealth of posting, problem-solving and schemas but took just minutes to assemble, thanks to the fortuitous gift of some cardboard tubes.

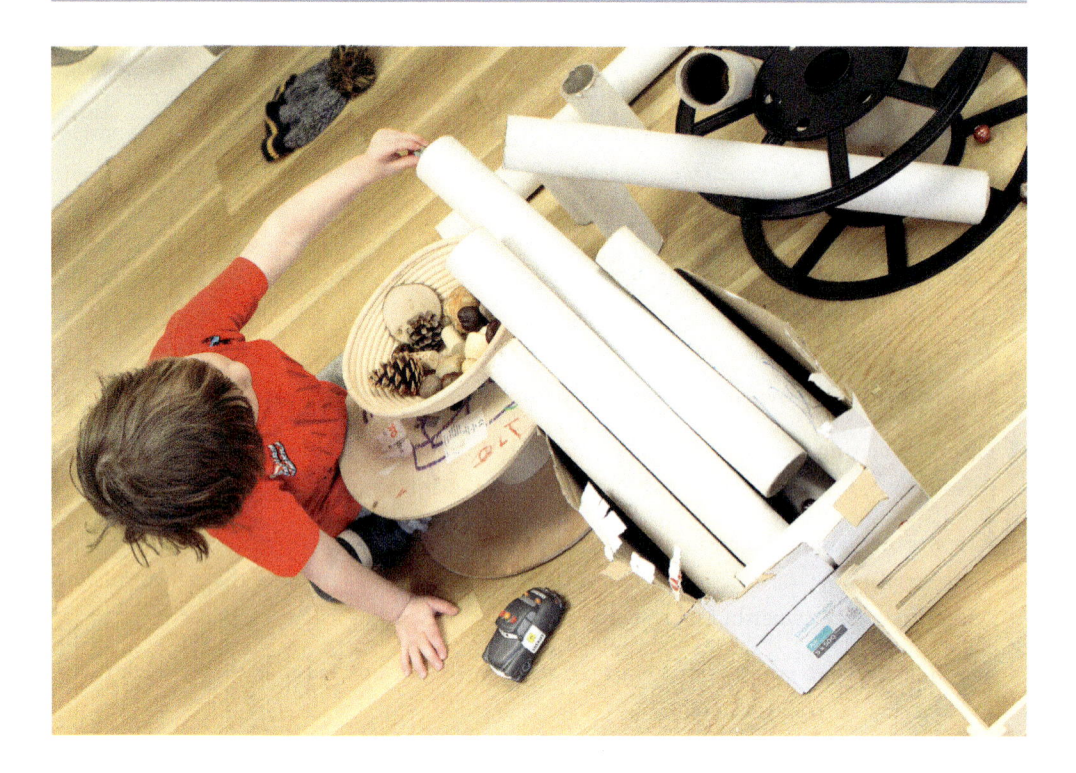

Choosing resources

When deciding which messy play resources to offer with the materials explored in Chapter 4 and how these should be arranged, several factors will impact upon the quality of children's resulting material encounters:

- Context
- Legibility and affordance
- Choice
- Continuity
- Safety
- Time and space available

We will now consider each of these in turn:

1) CONTEXT

Busy environments and backgrounds compete with children's attention, making it difficult to focus. Visual busyness often stems from too many resources or a plethora of colour and displays; however, a neglected environment can be just as challenging, as it's hard to discern areas of focus and flow. As well as detracting from meaningful material engagements, this can negatively affect adults' wellbeing, undermining their **relatedness** to the environment and **competence** and **autonomy**. If the environment already feels chaotic then the prospect of adding to this with messy play becomes considerably less appealing.

With children increasingly unlikely to experience silence at home and its potential as a mindfulness tool (Kaplin & Kaplin,1989; Veilleux, 2017), auditory disturbance can be equally damaging for focussed engagement.

> While observing play in a nursery I noticed a 3 year old deeply engrossed in soapy water. Pressing her hands flat on the base of the tray, feeling the water, she noticed the tiny bubbles. Selecting a bubble, she inched her forefinger into the suds to pop it. She slowly lathered her hands with the bubbles which had clung to them, before drawing these to her nose to smell, all the time her face etched with focus and concentration. With arms raised and water now trickling down her sleeve she used the towel protruding from under the tray to dab this dry. In the background *Old Macdonald* was playing loudly.

Although deeply engaged in her self-set explorations, I can't help wondering whether this might have been sustained even longer without music?

The context for an activity is also key for children's acquisition of new information, with a disconnect between the two introducing inaccuracies in children's thinking. A recurring theme throughout this book, the context of an activity also contributes to legibility.

II) LEGIBILITY AND AFFORDANCE

Norman (1988) considered legibility (the extent to which it is apparent what things do and how they can be used) to be an important factor in maximising the affordance of objects. Material engagements will be influenced by the legibility of resources and environments and the child's prior experience and knowledge. So, if children have had ample opportunities to engage with open-ended resources, they may be 'unconcerned with the intended use of any object they play with, [and] make everything their own' (Szekely, 2015: 17). However, where children are more familiar with prescriptive toys, then they may benefit from cues, such as creating 'hubs' for focus (like the tubes and objects), with space for flow in between, which increase the legibility of the environment and indicate the adult's expectations.

The careful choice and positioning of tools and equipment can provide important visual cues. For example, a variety of containers or utensils next to a sandtray hints at their suitability for a wealth of pouring and filling activities. As importantly, it also indicates the adult's permission for the sand and utensils to be used in this way and that it is ultimately the child's choice whether to do so. In one setting a hose left outdoors indicated permission for this to be used as an exciting mud-slide! Here are some simple ideas for increasing legibility and affordance:

- Arrange magnets, spoons or containers next to a tray of sand, water or Gelli.
- Use silhouette templates on shelves and walls to support tidying up.
- Consider the complementarity of resources, such as utensils and containers, conkers and tubes. Or provide Montessori-style, on a tray for individual use, such as dried rice, containers, tweezers or spoons.
- Bury a cobblestone (dinosaur's egg perhaps?) or treasure in sand with utensils for digging or magnets for metal-detecting.
- Provide questions or prompts next to a water tray for self-directed investigation, such as heavy, light, sinks, floats, metal, wood.

The intention of these simple cues is not to dictate and therefore stifle children's creativity or **autonomy**, but rather to indicate acceptance of their investigations; noticing of their interests (such as transporting schemas); and if needed, an ice-breaker into interacting with the resource – a sad reflection of some children's lack of familiarity with open-ended objects. Best of all, none of these actions requires a significant investment nor radical change of approach to existing practices.

III) CHOICE

Open-ended experiences are the antithesis of creativity-limiting worksheets and templates. However, for many a blank page can be as paralysing as the thick black lines of a photocopied sheet. When faced with a huge blank canvas few creative adults would, I suspect, feel able to immediately commit paint to canvas, as the fear and expectation of getting it right can suffocate creative urges. The same can be true of an unused lump of clay, although the ability to rework it gives us the confidence to try, as we can start afresh if it goes horribly wrong! This is an area in which messy play resources can be particularly liberating as it is enough simply to notice and enjoy feeling gloop, shaving foam or dried lentils with outstretched fingers or toes; move paint or shaving foam around a surface, watch patterns emerge, disappear and re-emerge, without feeling the need or expectation to create an end product.

Morris (2015: 49) offers a middle ground when it comes to resourcing, with 'structured freedom', a balance between having enough but not too much choice. A careful decision-making process which Quackers Playgroup Lead Practitioner, Menna Godfrey, shares in relation to paint.

> I had attended some CPD led by Dr Kathy Ring. She challenged us to consider the type of paint we used and how this supported children's understanding of materials, suggesting that by providing ready-mixed paint we were limiting children's learning and that the provision of powder paint and water would increase these possibilities. ... Kathy didn't think many young children were particularly concerned about colour, but rather had a fascination with exploring what certain media could be used for. I reflected on the way children used coloured paint in the setting and realised that most of the time children were more interested in the things that they could do with paint than the colour. E.g. children used paint to make marks on paper, to cover surfaces, to paint themselves, hands, feet, legs and faces and then to use themselves as a printing tool. When they asked for more than one colour it was rarely to use that colour to represent anything but rather to increase the volume of paint ... all paint became brown as we allowed free exploration with brushes and other ways of mixing and applying paint.
>
> (Menna Godfrey, 2018)

The decision to replace ready-mixed paints with a single coloured powder paint was controversial, with practitioners voicing concerns over whether restricting choice infringed children's rights. As we shall explore in Chapters 6 and 8, this brave and difficult decision to limit choice had important ramifications for children's and staffs' sense of **ARC**.

Hutt et al (1989) describe the physical challenge of too much equipment getting in children's way, something which resonates with this child's experience:

> A 2-and-a-half-year-old plays with spoons and containers in a makeshift sand tray, clearly frustrated by the presence of a plastic digger and cement mixer from his earlier play. After digging around these obstacles, he eventually discards these from the sand. His movements instantly become freer.

If we consciously offer tools and utensils *next to*, rather than *within*, a material (as shown overleaf), we avoid cluttering and detracting from their appeal (as we shall see on page 111). We also need to be aware of the message that this potentially gives children (legibility), about this being the only 'right' way to use the sand, in case the child's desire to please the adult (**relatedness**) exceeds their own self-motivation (**autonomy**). Pedagogically, there is a big difference between making attuned resources available, based on the adult's observations, and tightly prescribing the child's play, an area we will return to in Chapter 8, where the adult's role in supporting an 8 month old's investigation with sand is explored.

Quality, not just quantity is also important. Picture this hypothetical situation in a nursery. A trainee practitioner notices a child's interest in transporting materials and decides that some spoons will support this child's schema and enable another child, who is tactile defensive, to engage with sand. Three identical spoons are arranged next to the tray for the children to use, but these remain barely touched. Disappointment sets in as the practitioner doubts their ability to read children's cues and her sense of **Autonomy**, **Relatedness** and **Competence** are diminished.

How different might the children's reaction (and adult repercussions) have been if an enticing assortment of spoons had been provided instead? A huge wooden one, another dotted with intriguing holes and a third featuring one large hole in its centre? A tiny hand-carved spoon in a richly scented wood, a large metal spoon – shiny and cold to the touch, a strange metal spoon with a wiggly handle and another, perforated with hundreds of holes. Each of these spoons, picked for their quality, distinctiveness and play value, would afford children a different experience of essentially the same resource and potentially highlight different areas for further investigation and learning. Given an eclectic selection of spoons or utensils and a mix of dried rice, lentils and sand, children may have discovered about volume, capacity, thermic qualities and size as the smallest grains fall through the perforations while the rice grains are captured.

Of course, selecting individual spoons, each with its own distinct characteristics, will take longer and cost more, but crucially their affordance as play and learning tools will be magnified as children encounter first-hand the essence of big, small, same, different, hot and cold.

Reflection

Try this for yourself and then observe children's play to understand the true meaning of affordance when resources are looked at laterally rather than literally.

IV) CONTINUITY

Another important factor in supporting the legibility of resources and processes is providing continuity of experiences. Particularly relevant to scientific engagements, but important for mastery orientation in all areas of learning, continuity in provision enables children to test and develop their thinking, enabling comparison and deeper learning. With multiple opportunities to explore acid/alkali reactions, volume and capacity, solids and liquids in a variety of situations, or simply wet and dry porridge oats, children's knowledge funds and connectivity of thinking, are greatly enhanced.

V) SAFETY

Safety is paramount so it's worth investing in quality equipment that will withstand repeated use. If sourcing metal tea strainers or mini sieves, avoid cheap versions with a narrow rim, as the wire mesh can quickly work its way loose, exposing sharp edges. Similarly, cheap whisks should be avoided as the metal prongs are potentially hazardous. With common sense the following simple steps can help ensure safe yet enriching material engagements:

- Follow the instructions and age restrictions of manufactured resources.
- Avoid chemicals like Borax – if making your own slime.
- Position resources outdoors or take steps to contain to minimise slipping.
- Ensure adequate supervision, if mouthing is likely or water play.
- Check children's allergies.

VI) TIME, BOUNDARIES AND SPACE

In Chapter 3 we discovered the importance of picking the best times for satisfying material engagements. It's also crucial to allow enough time for each of the stages of messy play outlined in Chapter 3, to minimise the stresses of the clearing up stage. Planning for opportunities for children to revisit their messy play interactions will minimise unnecessary tidying up stresses. Deciding whether to locate play outside or inside may affect practitioners' and children's enjoyment, as the limits which need to be set and clearing up time and stresses will vary, as will become apparent in Chapter 6.

Messy play stages and implications for preparation

Although children's material engagements are infinitely varied, as we discovered in Chapters 3 and 4, if allowed, several stages of messy play can be identified, helping to prepare us for what to expect:

1. Exploring and experimenting
2. Containing
3. Harnessing
4. Clearing up
5. Saving
6. Discarding

We now return to these as a useful framework for structuring preparation.

I Exploring and experimenting

We begin with a focus on protective equipment and the plethora of decisions to be made about utensils and tools to ensure fruitful exploration.

i) Protective equipment

With appropriate equipment such as aprons or old clothes; table or floor covers; a readily available water supply or bucket of soapy water; dustpans, brushes and brooms; or an outdoors location, the stresses of messy play can be limited so that its positives can be enjoyed. Preventatives such as these need to be understood in terms of their impact upon both the child and adult's experience since it is the latter who shapes the emotional landscape. Careful consideration is needed, like Menna Godfrey's reflection on dressing for mud, (on page 193) in case choices unwittingly detract from the child's experience.

> In one Forest School session, a group of 4-year-olds attempted to balance on slippery wet ropes and crawl along fallen tree trunks wearing cumbersome waterproofs and wellies. These kept them dry but were ill-suited to balancing and climbing. Other children stood waist-high in a muddy puddle, insulated against the oozing-wet feel of the mud. Although their uniforms were protected, I can't help wondering whether their sensory experiences would have been richer if able to feel the cold wet mud?

ii) Utensils and tools

In Chapter 4 we discovered the importance of not restricting materials to just dry or wet and sticky, so their different qualities and affordances can be appreciated. Similarly, tools shouldn't be pigeon-holed as one-size-fits-all. Utensils and tools are essential for material engagements as they support investigation and enable some children's involvement. When selecting utensils to facilitate and extend children's material engagements, it's important to follow Montessori's lead and choose wisely. Here are some factors to consider:

A) VARIETY

Spoons and scoops An eclectic mix of wooden, metal and natural spoons in a range of sizes is essential. A richly carved spoon, giant-sized coconut shell spoon and metal sweet shop scoop will each offer something different for interactions with a mixture of dried rice and sand.

Other utensils There's a lot more to utensils than spoons. Included in my repertoire of utensils for children's material explorations are melon and meat ballers, tongs, chopsticks, tea infusers, spatulas, butter pats, whisks, a teaball and turkey baster. Metal jam-making funnels offer different tactile and auditory sensory appeal than plastic and may be a novelty to children. Think about opportunities for introducing cognitive disequilibrium, such as utensils and containers with holes, as children rarely notice these.

One 3 year old repeatedly filled a mini-terracotta pot with dried rice before he noticed that much of the material had spread across the carpeted floor.

Brushes are great for using with sand and a range of dry resources. As the same 3 year old discovered, each has a very different way of working when trying to clear up a spillage of dried rice!

[He] picks up the pastry brush, which he uses to brush the floor. The rice pings in all directions and is discarded. He tries stroking [a nailbrush] across the carpet and a smile spreads across his face as the short bristles move the rice.

(Gascoyne, 2012: 120)

Reflection

Compare your existing provision of utensils and brushes to those shown above and on page 102. For each item consider:

- How they could be used with different materials?
- If and how they will add value to existing provision?
- How children will react to them?
- What, if anything they will contribute to investigations?

Specific tools and specialist equipment   While creative approaches to object affordance are essential, we shouldn't dumb down the role of specialist tools and the importance of these being appropriately sized for child use. Furnishing children with real tools, a pre-requisite of Montessorian practice, enables them to master the skills and bodily control to engage in meaningful material investigations. This could be scientific tools such as pipettes and tweezers, or arts-based resources like good-quality brushes.

B) SCALE

Scale can magically elevate a mundane spoon into something quite special which will have children clambering to use it. As well as having to use their whole body and gross motor skills to mix with a large spoon, they will need strength, skill and balance to control its movements, particularly if the challenge is to spoon a mixture into small containers or sacks. An over-sized spoon can transform a cauldron of mud into giant's gruel, while miniature spoons which ignite interest and spark role-play require precision and a focus on detail.

C) NOVELTY

Szekely (2015: 16) suggests that 'any object can be an art supply and freely integrated into play, no matter what the object's original purpose' and this is no less true of messy play. Although a carefully developed collection of utensils is a pre-requisite for some material engagements, this doesn't mean that we shouldn't take a creative approach to tools. Imagine children's reaction and the impact of offering celery sticks as stirrers in the mud kitchen?! Here's an opportunity to let your imagination go wild and signal to children the value of creativity. It's also an excellent approach for reducing functional fixedness (Brown & Kane, 1989). As well as empowering children to look at objects as naturally divergent thinkers, it shifts from resources which only have one right way of being used and therefore can erode confidence and mastery. Instead of a conventional spoon, try sticks, celery, cinnamon sticks or even candy canes – available cheaply at Christmas and bargain prices afterwards!

An element of surprise and challenge also comes from re-purposing sensory equipment like dinosaur or shark puppets, tentacles and snake fingers as tools. Building on children's interests, these are great for attracting attention and providing challenge in manoeuvring them, as well as supporting those who are tactile defensive and would struggle to touch materials.

D) CULTURALLY REPRESENTATIVE

If we want children to feel at home in the setting and tap into their knowledge funds, it's important for them to be able to access a range of culturally appropriate, authentic utensils and containers. Available cheaply in discount stores as well as in local and specialist shops, consider including Balti dishes, lassi cups, Thalis of inviting metal bowls on a tray, tiffin tins and elegantly shaped spoons, spice scoops and spatulas from India; beautifully decorated Moroccan tagines; a delicately painted Chinese tea set and chopsticks; or inviting coconut-hewn spoons and bowls of South East Asia. Whether references to a child's cultural heritage (and Bronfenbrenner's systems) or exciting provocations, culturally varied utensils and containers add interest and shape the affordance of messy play materials.

E) COMPLEMENT AND CONTRAST

Of course, a collection of utensils really comes into their own when offered with containers, as we shall see in the **Containing** stage. Children can happily spend hours filling and pouring and with the range of messy play textures available, from wet to dry, the challenge is choosing which combination of resources, tools and containers to use. Appropriately sized tools for child-size hands give opportunities for fulfilling play and mastery orientation as children successfully achieve their self-set objective. But that does not mean avoiding age-appropriate opportunities for problem-solving, challenge and humour too, such as needing to fill a tiny cauldron or container with an over-sized spoon, or vice versa. Provocations like these introduce challenge and give an insight into a child's resilience and problem-solving. Through children's material engagements we are afforded a glimpse of their threads of thinking:

> A 3 year old chose to use a large spoon to extract dried rice from a partially opened drawer. A range of smaller spoons were available, and the drawer could easily be pulled out, so one can only assume that his skilful manipulation of the tool was a self-set goal.

Another child persevered with balancing a large heavy stone egg on a tiny wooden salt spoon, a challenge which he eventually mastered. Open-ended resources and adult acceptance enable children to self-differentiate challenge, such as filling an over-sized or miniature container with an ill-suited tool. It's only by attentive noticing of children's widely differing interactions with materials that their interests and underlying thinking becomes visible. We will now explore the broad spectrum of containers.

2 Containing

As we discovered in Chapter 3, containers serve a range of purposes, from shaping the child's process to containing their mess, giving practitioners a sense of control and minimising tidying. It would be wrong to suggest that there is a simple adult/child divide, such that the containment of experiences is always an imposition upon the child's freedom. Some children and adults may need an element of containment before they can engage with a resource, otherwise this might feel as overwhelming as that blank canvas. For others the need for containment may wax and wane, varying with the resource and location; knowledge funds and emotional state; relationship with the practitioner; or any number of other factors. Just as the affordance of individual materials suggests and shapes their use, so too the scale, style, number and type of containers offered can either fit with or provoke a child's thinking and interests. When deciding which types of containers and how many to provide for children's material investigations, it's worth considering the following key attributes.

i) Material properties

Choose pots, bowls, bottles and boxes made from wood, metal, rubber and cardboard as well as ubiquitous plastic. Their unique qualities and affordance will not only shape a child's sensory experience, for example the tinkling sound of a metal spoon in a glass jar; hollow resonance of wood on wood; or cold feel of metal or stone but will also influence how the resources are used. Recycled plastic containers and interesting packaging are ideal compliments to a selection of containers. A transparent container gives children a different perspective on their messy creations than a solid or opaque one. Similarly, it's worth including some containers with lids for children to store their creations, in the **Saving** stage.

ii) Variety and shape

Although egg cups, sugar bowls and bun cases are ideal, some unusual containers and a range of shapes will infinitely increase play value. A leaf-shaped dish hewn from wood, rustically carved olive wood bowl, woven basket or old-fashioned perfume bottle will enrich and inspire children's material engagements. Shape is also important so include some containers with handles and spouts for facilitating directional pouring. Think tall and thin, low-sided, wide and accessible, robust buckets with handles, delicate miniatures, cauldrons, special one-off items as well as multiples such as yoghurt pots, as all of these will influence the resulting play.

The more playful and open-minded we are when thinking about containers, the greater the potential for children to experience a 'place of possibilities' (Pacini-Ketchabaw, Kind, & Kocher, 2017) or what Bogost describes as the 'possibility space' (2016). Hodgman (2011) suggests an interesting alternative to the conventional container:

filling several bags with different materials such as sand, soil, rocks, gravel and bark provides . . . the opportunity to explore the materials using their senses. Adding some containers, scoops, spoons or shovels enables children to engage in large-scale physical activities, by filling and emptying the bags with the different materials.

This clearly evokes a building site, builder's merchant or garden centre and plays to children's need to experience a sense of weight. The flexibility and lack of solidity of the containers introduces problem-solving, gross motor strength and manipulative challenge as children need to manoeuvre tools to extract contents or fill the bags. A range of bags could also prove interesting such as hessian, rubble and fibre postage bags.

iii) Size

Deciding what size and type of containers to offer and when is by no means clear cut as I discovered when working therapeutically with a group of boisterous 4-to 5-year-olds.

> Activities quickly became chaotic, with paint or water being flicked, sprayed and smeared around the room. These children needed sensory embodiment opportunities and structure to support them in self-regulating and containing themselves. Initially I offered them each a Gratnel tray of sand and some objects. However, keeping the sand within the tray and limiting the number of objects proved difficult. After much deliberation I provided each child with a plastic takeaway container, cup of water and five stones. With such a tiny container to work in, keeping the sand contained would be a challenge, but each child carefully created a sculpture representing how they felt, and incredibly barely any sand was spilt in the process! These tiny containers, which could so easily have been dismissed as being too small, turned out to be perfect.

These children remind us of the value in challenging our pre-conceived ideas and assumptions. By offering containers of different sizes, shapes and properties, children can explore same and different, volume and capacity. An assortment of containers also opens opportunities for using them together to manage and contain their own mess:

> For one child some yoghurt pots enabled them to create concoctions, each with varying quantities of different-coloured paints, water, glue and glitter, within the safety of Play Therapy. By placing these pots within a larger tray, it made storage easier, but more importantly enabled the child to experiment with flooding and containment. As they added to the already overflowing pots they unexpectedly harnessed it (Dalley, 1984), creating an amazing multi-coloured picture within the tray.

Sometimes the addition of a larger container gives young children a chance to succeed in their investigations, by containing the spread of mess. For one 4-year-old I believe this 'managed overflowing' was instrumental in helping them cope with a bereavement, as well as affirming their self-esteem and need for personal control. Not all containers need to be rigid and watertight to limit mess. A towel under a water tray or polythene sheet beneath a mound of sand will achieve similar results, giving children (and adults) the confidence to play and explore in the knowledge that mess will be limited.

iv) Quantity

Providing the right number and variety of containers to maximise explorations is also something of an art. Too many and the area can feel cluttered and the child overwhelmed with choice and too few and the potential for exploration, investigation, transformation and containment may unnecessarily limit outcomes. Bogost (2016) uses the term satisficing to describe the optimum number of resources to avoid overload and as the chockerblock sandtray in a baby room (on page 101) shows, this may have invited very different kinds and depths of engagement had the tools been arranged next to, rather than in, the sand. With barely any sand left to beckon a child's hands, feet or bottom, the tools intended to extend play may have limited this instead. Compare this with these children's experience of sand in the image, and it is evident which offers greater appeal.

v) Legibility and function

Gone are the days when the very colour and shape of bottles gave a strong clue to their contents. While it's important not to be constrained by function, there is sometimes value in resources being used as intended. Some children struggle with knowing what to do with open-ended objects, so the provision of mini metal saucepans, teacups, large cauldrons, potion or perfume bottles can open the door to wider material engagements.

> For two young children on holiday, the discovery of some interestingly carved glass perfume bottles, a large jam-making pot and ladle was all that was needed to spark several days of productive perfume-making. They collected marigold petals and lavender to infuse in water, stirred with the huge ladle, cooperatively manoeuvred the cauldron-like pot to fill the bottles, then decorated the bottes, with their by now agreed company name – *Bottletastic* of course! Some paper was found for writing labels and then came a serious discussion about what price to charge. Surveying their products, these budding entrepreneurs (4- and 7-years-old) recognised the need for point-of-sale embellishment, adding sprigs of lavender with string (see image on page 108).

Child-led material encounters like these are essential for galvanising sensory memories and developing self-esteem, self-regulation, mastery orientation and even resilience, as sadly the resulting smell was frequently disappointing! An adult's choice of containers also communicates to the child their expectations and permission, whether it be to freely explore or not. As Anjali Rajan explained her rationale for the playdough Stay-and-Play session introduced in Chapter 3:

> I wanted to give them total freedom while exploring, which is why I opted for a plastic sheet and no containers. I was afraid that giving bowls ... would limit the scope of the activity. At home I give bowls to my son, but I felt that a larger space would bring a lot more fun.
>
> (Anjali Rajan, 2018)

vi) Shaping affordance

This practitioner recognised that uncontained play, be it with mud, water, sand, yoghurt or orbies, will have very different qualities and potential to contained play. As well as influencing how a child interacts with a resource, the containment of some resources can also change their characteristics and affordances. Take flour, when sprinkled through a sieve it spreads a thin film of dust over everything, creating fascinating negative prints if objects get in the way! Drop it from a height onto paper and it makes a surprisingly loud thud. However, when tightly sealed in a strong sandwich bag with the air removed, the qualities of the flour change, giving it surprising solidity and gloop-like characteristics. Similarly, when gloop is momentarily contained within your hand, the force of pressure changes its qualities, miraculously forming into a ball, before dripping through fingers as liquid.

vii) Learning potential

Different-sized and shaped containers, such as a pond, bucket, clean dustbin or water tray, give the potential for varied water (or resource) levels so children get to experience what it's like to immerse whole arms or legs and feel the forces from plunging hands deep into water or Gelli. With greater depth, a sink or float investigation can yield more interesting and varied results which will enrich scientific thinking. Puddle water decanted into a transparent pot will eventually settle revealing lines of sediment and water. This will invite different forms of investigation than the original puddle, water tray or chocolate-brown mud pit. Sometimes the container can elevate a simple resource, making it more inviting, special or eye-catching. A great example of this is the tiny copper pots, cauldrons and jugs that I have collected from charity shops. Miniatures such as those on pages 85 and 166 instantly elevate humble resources like orange or brown lentils, dried rice, porridge or couscous to exciting provocations, sparking creativity and role-play and prompting us to viewing them differently.

3 Harnessing

When children feel secure, this can give them the confidence to transform their mess into something positive, an incredibly rewarding experience, enriching **ARC**. For one child it was the accidental creation of a Cheesy puff (Chapter 1), for another, a lino-flooded floor was perfect for floating a toy boat. A group of 4-to-5-year-olds used a hose to create a waterfall on an earth mound (see Chapter 7). From their reaction when one child fell, it's clear that creating a mud-slide was not their intention, but this did not stop them exploiting their surprising discovery to the full! For another child a messy encounter with shaving foam resulted in a calming hand massage, where the child experienced safe touch and embodiment.

> **Reflection**
>
> Consider whether we deny children the opportunity to harness mess by:
>
> - Clearing up mess and spillages too quickly?
> - A lack of time or throwing the process away?
>
> Adult acceptance was key in all these examples, so are any changes needed to make this possible (safety permitting of course)?

Of course, increased opportunities for harnessing mess become possible when mess is saved.

4 Saving

This stage of mess is often overlooked in mainstream practice yet can contribute significantly to minimising stress. For some children it's important to be able to store some of their mess, in which case takeaway containers or robust mini jam jars are ideal. Whether their intention is to track material changes like a scientist at work; save a 'magic paint' which they've created; or safely contain their (emotional) mess for another time, making decisions over what to keep and what to discard is an important source of **autonomy** for children.

Drying area and storage

If some shelves or an area can be repurposed to enable children's work to be left as ongoing projects, this will reap dividends in children's growing capital of knowledge, as they enjoy the opportunity to return to and extend thinking. It will also minimise the need for so much tidying, to which we now turn.

5 Clearing up

Preparing for mess

Material engagements can feel chaotic, so it's important to start on the right footing. Decluttering the environment can bring order to chaos (Bettelheim, 1977) as well as crystallising our thoughts. I experienced this firsthand when a debunking of physical and mental clutter while tidying, gave my mind 'a holiday' (Kaplin & Kaplin, 1989), incubating ideas and allowing writing to flow. I also realised that rather than seeing tidying as a chore, it increased mindfulness.

Benefits of tidying

These unexpected meditative qualities led to the startling conclusion that Montessori made over 100 years ago. Clearing up after ourselves is part of developing a relationship with our environment and others, and essential for self-esteem and **ARC**. It's through clearing up that children discover the corkscrewing pattern of blue paint swirling down the plughole, 'chaotic motion' in action (Percival, 1992: 12); or colour mixing as paint trays are washed, but also an opportunity to experience mindfulness and agency. Put like this, then 'magicking' mess away denies children valuable opportunities for self-regulation and discovery.

Developing a clearing up routine

There is, however, a method to mindful tidying and it begins with having the right tools, storage spaces and adequate time. A calm yet purposeful approach is best in a process, which like Montessorian practice, sees the putting away as much part of the process as the actual doing. Children's lives are increasingly rushed and stressful, so while 'tidying up ditties' are effective, they can instil a sense of urgency or need to move onto the next thing, rather than a slower and calmer ending of a cycle of exploration.

If we can make clearing up a communal act of togetherness, rather than an individual's chore, then we also reframe what for many is an obstacle to messy play. Positioning paint next to an indoor or outdoor water supply and providing accessible aprons supports children's responsibility, implicitly signalling the adult's acceptance of experimentation, an expectation that this may result in mess and that the child is capable of clearing this up. We can support children's agency of their mess by:

- Preparing children and the environment:
    - Setting up outside or on wipeable flooring.
    - Using preventative covers and aprons.
    - Providing child-sized tidying up equipment.
    - Creating 'hubs' for focus with space for flow in between.
- Supporting children with cues:
    - Aprons and water supply near resources.
    - Using silhouettes on storage to increase children's **ARC**.
- Evaluating the quantity of resources needed to ensure satisficing rather than over-abundance.
- 'Apprenticeship' opportunities, where time is given to learn how to do things for themselves.
- Modelling positive strategies and values.
- Providing adequate storage for ongoing or wet-work.

Reflection

Discuss with colleagues your existing approach to tidying up, considering the following questions for starters:

- Who tidies up? Mainly adults or children too?
- Who tidies the messy stuff? Are children trusted and able to do so?
- Consider how this is done. Speedily, methodically, calmly, respectfully?
- Is it necessary to always tidy up? Could some of the materials or mess be left for children to return to and revisit thinking?
- Could the activity be repositioned, or the number of resources reduced, to minimise tidying?
- How do you help children take responsibility for their mess? Is there time for children's apprenticeship, so they can learn, and opportunities for them to share with others their knowledge funds from home, such as what happens when you try to clear up spilt rice!!

Positioning tidying as an essential part of activities

In Chapter 6 we will discover how clearing up the aftermath of ice eggs can be a rewarding activity, providing fun, learning and sensory opportunities. In this example too, a spontaneous activity helped foster an awareness of our impacts, an essential aspect of mindfulness.

In one busy stay-and-play session in an adventure centre I had arranged containers and utensils on the floor next to trays of sand/dried rice/gems. A range of playful investigations and role-play emerged with children exploring pattern-making, filling and pouring from different-sized containers as they tentatively explored volume, capacity and number as well as creating some wonderful meals! Fortunately, I had covered the floor with a huge sheet of material as at the end of the session sand had spread everywhere! Conscious of my need to clear up quickly a fun idea came to mind. I invited the children to stand around the blue sheet holding its edges in their hands, then started a story about the little waves in the sea rolling backwards and forwards on the beach, moving the material as we did so. As a storm grew the waves and our movements became more pronounced. The storm gradually passed, and the children noticed for the first time how their actions had moved the mixture into a neat pile in the middle. I invited them to pick containers to collect the spillage and within minutes the room was tidy. We'd enjoyed an energising yet calming story, plentiful fine and gross motor movements and the surprise and satisfaction of working together to harness the mess.

What both these examples demonstrate is the importance of a playful adult recognising the potential for satisfaction, learning and fun in everything, be it clearing up or cleaning trikes.

Self-cleansing and care

Although children's creations should of course be treated respectfully, an important distinction can be made between cleaning the self and the environment. For many children, touching wet or sticky resources can be challenging so it's important to value and plan flexibly for this to avoid limiting involvement. Understanding this helps us avoid situations where routines unhelpfully prevail over children's needs, such as denying a child the opportunity to wipe their hands until the activity is finished, or all the children are ready to go to the bathroom. By responding sensitively to a child's immediate need to wipe their hands during an activity, we can support their sustained interaction with the resource in question and develop their sense of **autonomy** (over their body and resources), **relatedness** (to the adult, environment and setting) and **competence** (which comes from self-care).

For many reluctant children, a bowl of warm soapy water and accessible paper or fluffy towel is all that is needed to provide a safety net for touching messy materials. Like a 'get out of jail card' in a game of Monopoly, this enables them to take risks, giving them the knowledge that they can clean their hands when needed. If allowed, some children can literally yo-yo between touching a sticky substance and wiping their hands clean, before repeating the cycle again. In an accepting judgement-free environment, a child can find ways of responding to their sensory needs and aversions, persisting with uncomfortable yet compelling experiences for extended periods of time.

The provision of latex-free surgical gloves and a range of spoons and utensils can act as a bridge for a tactile-defensive child (or adult), although frequently they may choose to discard both when they discover their limitations! By providing such intermediaries we are giving children a strong message that their needs are noticed and accepted. Returning to Deci and Ryan's SDT (2000), actions like these reinforce a child's perception of **relatedness** as it signals that the child belongs and fits in; their unique needs are valued; the caregiver is attuned to their needs; and as importantly, through these actions they can increase their sense of **relatedness** to the environment. **Autonomy** and **competence** increase with the child's successes and growing agency over their actions and environment.

The value of a bucket of warm soapy water should not be underestimated:

> In a Splat stay-and-play session, I noticed children gravitating to a trug of soapy water. This popular 'station' served both as a messy play resource and a cleansing opportunity in between, during and at the end of messy play encounters! For some the soapy water was a metaphorical full stop in between different materials, a bit like a palate cleanser in a meal. Like animals drawn to a watering hole, some of these toddlers paused to wash their hands or feet before moving to another messy station, while others lingered for a while, noticing the bubbles or enjoying sucking or squeezing a

soapy sponge. With no adult input needed, these young children were able to enjoy immersion and take responsibility for their own self-care.

Similarly, walking through paint, a 2-year-old boy sat next to a towel and spent time carefully drying himself, a wonderful moment of **ARC** (see page 119).

In another setting the child's sense of fascination, compatibility and taking a 'mini-holiday' (Kaplin & Kaplin, 1989) are evident:

A 3-year-old used the protruding towel from beneath a container of soapy water to dry the water dripping down her arm and sleeve. Intently focussed she tracked the progress of the water with her eyes, then purposefully dabbed her arm and sleeve.

As these examples demonstrate, for some children cleaning themselves with soapy water during and after messy play can be a powerful act of self-care. This should not be rushed or punctuated with loud talking, music or tidying up songs. A respectful environment which does not intrude upon the child's mind-wandering has the added benefit of providing another sensory experience – the pleasure of soothing clay or paint-caked hands and arms with soapy bubbles before patting dry with a towel.

Reflection

- Next time you engage in messy play, take a moment to appreciate the calming dimension of self-care as you wash the mess away. Notice how you feel about being clean.

- How does it feel immersing your hands and arms in warm water? Does the heightened sense of enclosure and depth of a bucket offer a different experience than a sink or running water?

- Avoid antibacterial gels and soap which contain triclosan, associated with liver and colon disease in mice (Gees, 2018) and hormone dysregulation (Taylor, 2008, cited in Swim, 2017: 196). A slippery bar of soap provides more sensory, fine motor control and self-regulating opportunities.

- Provide a soft towel for drying and even hand cream in dispensers for hand-massages.

Changing our view of clearing up can open up a mindful process of meditation and self-care as well as a continuation of material investigations. It also firmly places responsibility for tidying up in the hands of many rather than few, thereby hopefully minimising the associated stresses and strains of messy play. We now move to the final stage in the cycle, discarding mess.

6 Discarding

The value of tidying up resources being accessible and empowering children to take responsibility for their mess is evident from this 4 year old's encounter with soil.

> Noticing a child deliberately throwing soil indoors, the practitioner's calm and non-judgemental re-stating of the rules avoided the child experiencing a sense of shame and reinforced their **autonomy** and responsibility. The child showed high levels of engagement and wellbeing while clearing up the soil, a process which lasted significantly longer than the act of throwing! Problem-solving was evident as he developed the best strategy for brushing up the soil and after an unsuccessful attempt, he worked out the complex sequence of actions needed to manoeuvre the contents of the dustpan into the bin without spilling them. Watching this child, it was evident that the very process of clearing up had developed into a satisfying activity, increasing his sense of **autonomy** and **competence**, which could so easily have been undermined, and developing **relatedness**, as he frequently watched others' reaction and even extended his clearing up to include another child's mess!

Far from being a chore, for this child clearing up his own mess introduced enriching opportunities for absorption and discovery and a wealth of executive functions. By taking responsibility, he developed **autonomy** and **competence**, cementing his **relatedness** to both adult and environment. Our focus now turns to the delicate balance between adult and child-led material encounters and giving children responsibility for messy play.

IN THIS CHAPTER WE HAVE:

- Considered the importance of preparing the optimum environment for material encounters.
- Explored how, with attentive noticing and an awareness of these six potential stages of mess, we can better support children's material engagements.
- Introduced ideas for minimising unnecessary stresses.

Note

1 In a survey of 35 practitioners, clearing up time and the attitudes of others were identified as the biggest barriers to messy play (Gascoyne, 2018a).

6 Creating enabling environments for messy play

> In this chapter a Messy Play Framework is suggested. On the Microlevel it helps meet children's and adults' need to experience **Autonomy, Relatedness** and **Competence** (**ARC**) in material engagements (Deci & Ryan, 2000). On the Macrolevel it serves as a tool for planning a balance between adult/child-led activities. Messy play cameos will be explored at different points on this sliding scale, unpicking the plethora of decisions involved and importance of planning for continuity.

Creating enabling environments

In Chapter 5 we explored some tools and approaches for minimising the stresses associated with messy play, including the importance of preparing not just the resources but also children, adults and the wider environment. We now turn our attention to the challenge of creating enabling environments for material engagements. Chances are you've already started mentally ticking off enabling aspects of your physical environment, but the emotional environment is equally important in determining the quality of children's messy play explorations. Shaped by our actions/inactions, words, body language and choices (over the resources, environments and time that we make available), the emotional environment can signal to children our complete acceptance of their mess or disappointment and shame. With so much potential for messy play interactions to be charged with anxiety, guilt and fear, and each person's reaction to mess shaped by their own personal circumstances and history, a positive enabling emotional environment is arguably the most important determinant of quality messy play.

A framework for planning messy encounters

Deciding whether to offer children opportunities for material engagements is not a simple yes/no matter. In part, as we've seen, because the special qualities and therefore affordances of messy resources vary widely, but also because every provision involves multiple conscious and subconscious decisions, each of which will shape and inform the resulting interaction. Howard and McInnes' work play continuum (2013: 45) conveys how a series of factors, including an activity's location, child's degree of choice and the presence or otherwise of an adult, subtly influences whether something feels like work or play. Similarly, the resource consistency, location, degree of containment, adult involvement and planning will shape the quality of material encounters and resulting mess!

Figure 6.1 provides a framework for planning children's material engagements and a tool, particularly for adults with messy play views like these:

- 'Great for children, not for adults to clear up'
- 'Love it, but what a mess we make'
- 'My colleagues will hate me!'
- 'Not a fan'
- 'Eeek …'
- 'Oh God! Chaos!'
- 'Makes me gag!!'
- 'Hate it!'

(Childcare Expo seminar; Gascoyne 2018b)

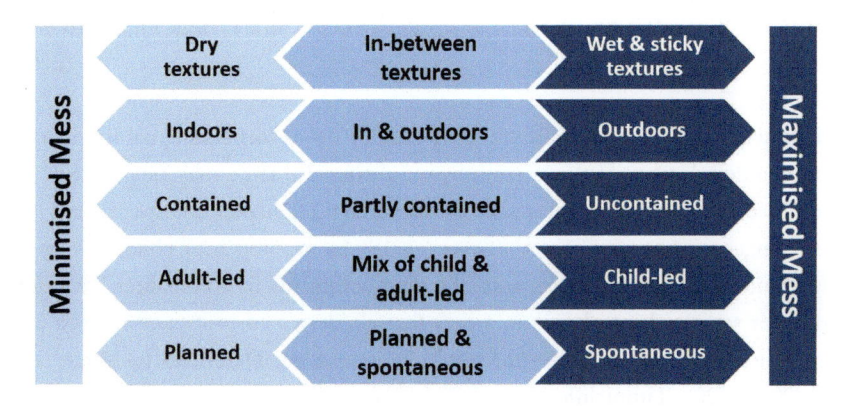

Minimised Mess			Maximised Mess
	Dry textures	In-between textures	Wet & sticky textures
	Indoors	In & outdoors	Outdoors
	Contained	Partly contained	Uncontained
	Adult-led	Mix of child & adult-led	Child-led
	Planned	Planned & spontaneous	Spontaneous

Figure 6.1 A framework for planning messy play encounters

Although simplistic, as some adults may be comfortable with more mess than children and the indoor/outdoor mess interplay is complex,[1] this sliding scale of material engagements can be applied at both the Micro and Macrolevels:

At the **Microlevel** (Figure 6.1) it facilitates the planning of material encounters to suit the individual child and adult.

At the **Macrolevel** (Figure 6.3) it supports practitioners' planning of an all-important balance between adult/child-led activities.

For example, using this framework we can immediately see that a *planned* activity with shredded paper (*dry texture*), *outdoors* in a builder's tray (*contained*) where the children find objects hidden by the adult (*adult-led*), is likely to be a more comfortable starting point than a gloop slide indoors on a sheet of polythene! As practitioners' confidence grows with each successful material engagement, they might gradually introduce changes to one of these factors at a time. Such as trying the same shredded paper activity but indoors; or removing the tray and positioning on a tarpaulin instead; or swapping the paper for gloop but keeping all the other factors constant. With each incremental change, children's **autonomy**, **relatedness** to the resource and adults, and **competence** will increase (Deci & Ryan, 2000), as will their experience of continuity (as we saw in Chapter 5), a key factor in developing threads of thinking.

By using the framework as a planning tool on the Microlevel, it is possible for practitioners to gradually build their own **relatedness** (to messy engagements) without compromising on their **competence** and **autonomy**. A win-win as children will benefit from a calmer and more accepting emotional environment for their growing **competence**, **autonomy** and **relatedness** to both the materials and adult, so that ultimately children will be trusted to choose how to use the shredded paper, whether outdoors or in!

Setting objectives

Beckerleg stresses the

> need to have an idea as to where we want to go, what do we want [messy play] to achieve, what are we going to use and how long are we going to continue. It's no good just thinking "Oh, I've got a tin of baked beans in the cupboard, I think I'll use those."
>
> (2009: 36)

Of course, when supporting children's specific sensory needs this is essential if we are to avoid causing unintended distress, but in a mainstream setting the same may not be true. Although preparation is of course important (as we discovered in Chapter 5), spontaneity is equally relevant for engaging 'sensory beings' (Grace, 2018) by tapping into children's interests and knowledge funds. It is through moments like discovering ice in a container left outdoors, or paint and water separated into layers in a pot, that children's curiosity and interest are piqued and lifelong memories and strategies for thinking are forged. Described by Waite as 'squirrel moments' (2010: 120), Tunnicliffe recognises the value of capitalising on just such moments of spontaneity as a core ingredient in developing scientific thinking.

As we shall explore in Chapter 7, 'Children don't divide themselves into curriculum areas, that is something we do' (Goddard, 2018a: 33), so setting narrow curricular-based objectives may limit the potentialities of children's encounters with messy materials and diminish learning. With the setting of objectives also comes the tendency to adopt linear approaches to move children's development on (Grace, 2018), instead of considering what else we can provide to give children similar or related experiences now. Rather than using this framework as a tickbox, it should be viewed as a series of iterative cycles, with each material encounter furnishing children with a range of experiences, scales and deepening inquiry.

A balanced approach

While adult-initiated interventions like creating papier mache birds (Featherstone, 2016) would certainly satisfy Beckerleg's call for clear objectives and planning, as **autonomy** resides with the adult, they also limit the potential and ownership of children's material engagements. Part of my motivation to write this book was to highlight an alternative to the types of messy play engagements characterised by an adult-directed, product-focussed approach. At best a tool for delivering learning objectives in a more child-friendly way and at worst a superficial gloss on what would otherwise be considered 'work', interventions like these are aptly described by Bogost as 'chocolate broccoli' (2016: 59). Don't get me wrong I love broccoli (and chocolate!), so much so that my son recently asked me if it was my favourite ingredient as I put broccoli in everything! But we all know the importance of a balanced diet and this is no less true of children's messy play encounters.

Personally, I'd love to see more genuinely open-ended material engagements like this Canadian-based project (Paccini-Ketchabaw et al., 2017).

> Three or four mornings a week, children had the opportunity to engage in open-ended self-set investigations with a range of commonly found materials, such as paper, clay, charcoal and fabric. Sometimes a mix of ages, other times single ages, some of the children attended these sessions over a period of 3-4 years. The focus was not on understanding the children's intent or learning but rather joining children as co-investigators. The order in which materials were explored was not planned. They were all available at the centre so the focus stemmed from what children or adults were drawn to and 'began to pay attention to'. Some of the encounters lasted for significant periods of time, for example the centre 'stayed with newspaper in different forms for 3 years'.
>
> (Kind, 2018, unpublished Skype interview)

By treating materials 'as active and participatory . . . they become productive moments' (Pacini-Ketchabaw et al, 2017: 2). This sustained focus and curriculum-free space offered children opportunities to think *with* materials, repositioning materials as agents in children's play and 'transform[ing] early childhood education, provoking educators to notice how materials and young children live entangled lives . . . how they change each other through their mutual encounters' (Pacini-Ketchabaw et al, 2017: 2). Continuity with familiar resources enables children to tap into and build their knowledge funds as well as being open to the potentialities of materials. By supporting children's deep and meaningful exploration of materials, these children may turn into the engineers, scientists and inventors of the future, whose creativity and problem-solving might literally save the planet!

A framework for understanding messy play provocations

For some these types of encounters with materials may feel a step too far, seemingly lacking any direction or focus, not to mention the discomfort of adults not knowing where exploration is leading. But if we remind ourselves of the framework in Figure 6.1 (page 123) we see that limits were provided as engagements took place in particular spaces and times (*location and containment by space, focus and adult*); the resources were provided by adults, which in itself contained children's encounters (*adult-provided*); and throughout investigations a series of implicit themes, such as movement and time were apparent, as if the resource qualities provided the focus (*jointly planned*). Practitioners did experience the discomfort of suspending judgement and resisting the urge to influence outcomes, something which also resonates with Godfrey's experience of powder paint shared in Chapter 8. This could not be further removed from activities whose

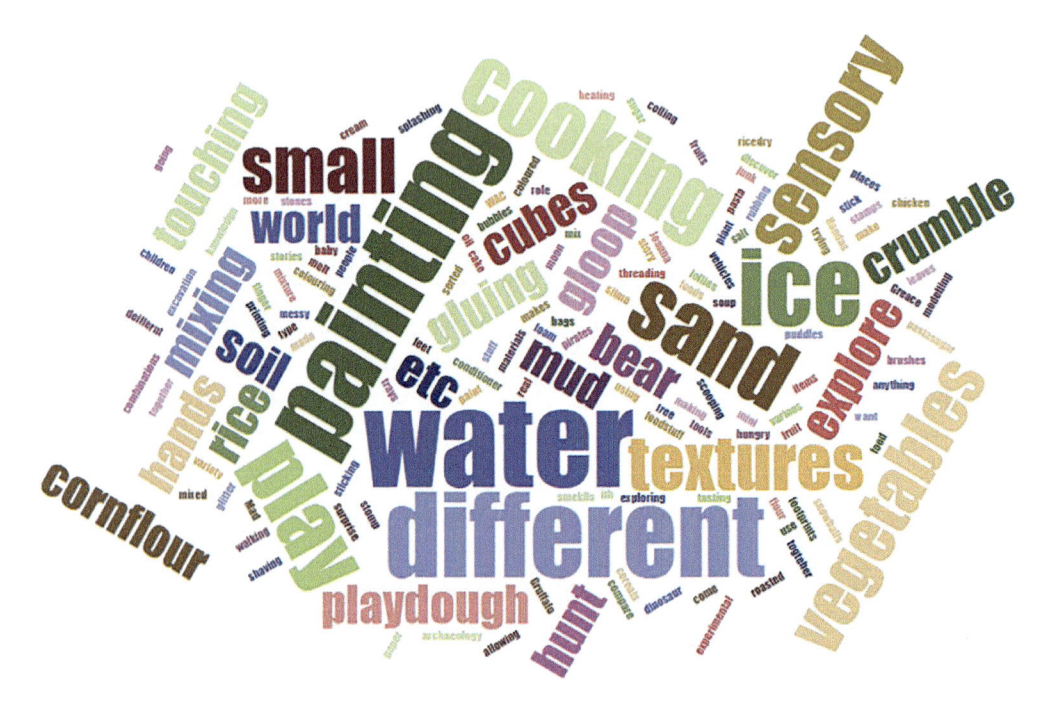

Figure 6.2 Messy play experiences are limited only by the imagination[2]

clear adult-directed, product-orientated focus position messy resources as a thin veneer for making phonics, fine motor skills or numbers fun.

As we will explore further in Chapter 8, truly open-ended free play is a rare commodity, as every decision that adults make about what to offer, how, when and where subtly influences the resulting play. With many of these decisions subconscious, there is a danger that children's **Autonomy**, **Relatedness** and **Competence** with materials becomes limited, especially given the potential for extremes in messy play interactions, be it adult or child-led, contained or uncontained, relaxed or exciting, amazing or terrifying.

A sliding scale of messy play provision

Rather than advocating a 'one-size-fits-all' approach to material engagements, a sliding scale of provision is proposed. By making apparent the different layers of decisions involved at the Microlevel in offering material provocations, this framework highlights each decision, demystifying the process.

Similarly, at the Macrolevel, picture a sliding scale of provision, from enticingly realistic, sensory provocations evocative of a jungle, seaside, Arctic or lunar scene for children to 'turn up and play with', through to truly open-ended free play (often with no adult presence or awareness), like the barefoot girl in wintry mud (page 45). As Figure 6.3 shows, between these two extremes lie a myriad of approaches, each varying in messiness, containment, location, spontaneity and the degree of adult control.[3]

With practitioners tasked with supporting children's opportunities to experience **autonomy** and plan for a balance between adult and child-led engagements it would be wrong to think that one end of this sliding scale is good and the other bad. However, it is important to understand the intentions behind our choices and the degree of freedom children have – whether this be autonomously responding to, changing and re-purposing those adult-provided resources and

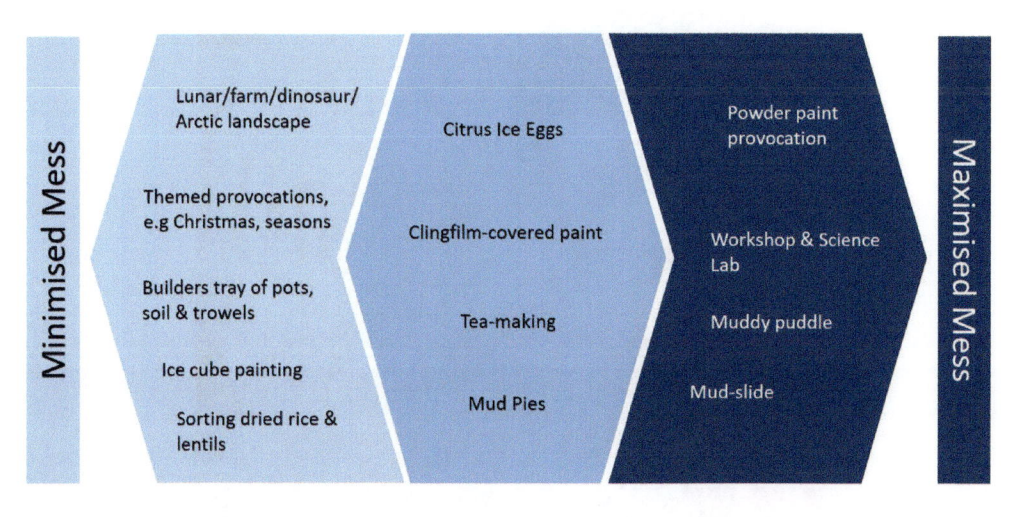

Figure 6.3 A sliding scale of messy play interactions

environments situated at the left extreme of the scale, or children being free to follow their own inspiration on the right.

Using the sliding scale

A starting point might be deciding where on the scale you would like to position a messy play opportunity. This will determine several of the other practical factors covered in this chapter, as well as the likely outcomes! Alternatively, if messy encounters don't come naturally to you or a child, you can start at the Microlevel, with decisions about which textures to offer, should these be located in or outdoors, contained or uncontained, spontaneous or planned and adult or child-led?

The range of different possibilities and affordances of material engagements is usefully illustrated by the following approaches to playdough making. Even though all five of these examples shared two factors in common – playdough and an indoor location – as will become apparent, the range of approaches, quality of experience and outcomes varied significantly.

Creating enabling messy play environments **129**

Setting 1 – A nursery practitioner sat with a small group of children sensitively supporting them to share in adding and mixing ingredients to create playdough. With practitioner support, the children took it in turns to help create the sloppy goo. The children exercised some choice over what they contributed to, by asking if they could 'sift', 'stir' or 'add', but this took place within the constraints of creating a joint resource. (Level 2–4 Involvement, Leuven)

Wet and sticky	Indoors	Contained	Planned	Adult-led

Setting 2 – In another nursery I observed children playing with playdough that had been made with practitioners earlier that morning. A range of resources had been provided, including pink silicon bun cases, rolling pins, wooden chopping boards, plastic straws, pink plastic cookie cutters, and multi-coloured shape and number cutters. On shelving to the side, further resources were available including a baking tray and plastic mixing bowl. During my visit, predominantly girls played with the playdough, rolling, shaping and cutting it or portioning and pressing it into the silicon bun cases. No conversation between children was observed and levels of involvement ranged from 2 to 3 (Leuven), albeit potentially lowered by my presence.

Even though there was no adult presence (apart from me observing play) and the children were free to focus on their individually set objectives, the types of play apparent were generally uniform, as if the rolling pins, muffin holders and cutters provided 'dictated' their use (resonating with Dewey).

In-between texture	Indoors	Contained	Planned	Adult-provided but child-led

Setting 3 – In the stay-and-play session in Southern India (described on page 47), the children were seen 'pressing, shaping, squeezing, and kneading' the dough into popular Keralan sweet shapes and 'excitement was very evident. A few of them were silent making shapes out of the dough. While most of the kids were following my instructions ... a boy, who was 6 years old was doing it his way. He was enjoying sitting with the children, mixing the flour, adding colours to it, making paste out of it.

He was not making any shapes despite my repeated instructions … he was the one who had the most mess on his clothes and hands. He was not at all worried.' (Level 5 Involvement, Leuven.)

(Anjali Rajan, 2018)

| In-between wet and sticky | Indoors | Loosely contained | Planned | Mix of adult and child-led |

Setting 4 – Four children, including one with special educational needs (aged 46 to 51-months) gathered at a table upon which were arranged playdough ingredients, food colouring, a selection of conkers, twigs, pine cones, cinnamon sticks, etc and laminated recipe pictures.

An adult was there to extend children's thinking where appropriate. The children measured the ingredients into the bowls they had chosen (creating the need to share resources but allowing ownership). Some chose to follow the visual recipe sheet to make playdough [but gradually] began to explore more. They added lots of water

> to the mixtures and discussed what they would need to make the contents a thicker consistency. (Showing the children working together and problem-solving.) The sensory resources created opportunities for lots of differing smells to be explored individually and then the children made 'potions' and explored how the smells changed when mixed together.
>
> Children explored putting different natural resources into the creations, such as stones and sticks. The consistency ... did not matter, they all explored the resources and watched some of them sink into the mixture (giving them more to discuss together as they played). The activity was planned for 20 minutes; however, the practitioner moved away after 45 minutes and the children asked if they could still play! The children were engaged at level 5 and 4 involvement and wellbeing respectively (Leuven).
>
> (Fiona Smith, 2018)

Wet and sticky	Indoors	Loosely contained	Planned and spontaneous	Adult-initiated but child-led

Setting 5 – Now let's return to children's exploration of playdough in Setting 2. When initially shown the playdough area I had asked to see the resources that children had used earlier in the session to make the playdough. I put a container of salt, two half-empty containers of flour and a huge bottle of oil with only a drizzle remaining, on the table to photograph as an aide-memoire. Moving on to look at something else I forgot to put these resources away, so was intrigued when I returned to the playdough station:

> Two boys had joined the girls at the playdough table. One (aged 4-years-9-months) chose to play with the 'new' resources for some time, pouring, transferring and mixing the resulting 'pancake' mixture' and grappling with how to pour the drizzle of oil from the huge bottle into the small metal pots. Levels of involvement (5) and wellbeing (4) for all the children were high (Leuven) and there were several instances of children commenting on their creations to each other, laughing and sharing resources. A wider range of play behaviours and movements were evident including mixing, pouring, scientific experimentation, creativity, communication, sharing, concentration and mastery orientation.

In-between wet and sticky	Indoors	Semi-contained	Spontaneous	Child-led

Although each of these examples involved making and playing with playdough indoors, the adults' influence (physically or through the selection of materials); degree of open-endedness; and **autonomy**, **relatedness** and **competence** experienced by the children differed widely, as did the range of textures of playdough created! It is interesting to note that the greatest levels of child **autonomy** and **competence** occurred when the adult was either not present (Setting 5); the child ignored the adult's instructions (Setting 3); or the adult was flexible (Setting 4).

Reflection

Consider what influences your choice and arrangement of resources.

- If and how they are used, by whom, when, where and for how long?
- Levels of involvement and wellbeing and whether gender biased?
- How open-ended are the resources, play and learning opportunities?
- What's your role in supporting play and learning?

- Is there potential for children to 'think with' materials?
- If and how do you introduce opportunities for reflecting with children?

Could you increase children's opportunities for **ARC** without compromising yours?

The framework in action

The following eight vignettes provide a flavour of what provocations at different stages of this sliding scale might look like at the Macrolevel. For each stage:

- provision is described and summarised using the framework as a visual tool;
- the essentials of **Autonomy (A)**, **Relatedness (R)**, and **Competence (C)** for the child and adult are relayed (Deci & Ryan, 2000); and
- ideas for extending provision are offered, reflecting the importance of continuity which comes from children having opportunities to return to their investigations to cement understanding and find more connections in the now.

Although activities outdoors have been classified as messier, this reflects their freer feel to the child (and adult) as it is recognised that the stresses of mess indoors may actually be more challenging!

Minimal mess – Maximum adult control

We begin our journey with examples from the 'minimal mess' end of the scale, featuring contained, adult-initiated, planned provision. Although children's use of these provocations is not actually delimited, it is limited by the resources.

Examples include:

i) **Landscapes and small-world provocations** – These could include an arctic scene, prehistoric landscape or small-world farmyard, 'fields' of growing carrots, or a builder's tray of compost or soil, with plants, pots and trowels for children to use. A search for messy play activities on Pinterest or various Tuff Tray fora will reveal a wealth of provocations like these.

ii) **Themed provocations** – These elaborate set-ups are often focussed on **events** such as Christmas, Chinese New Year and Valentine's Day; **themes**, like growing and the seasons; and **interests** such as dinosaurs, farms and princesses. Far from uniform, some are enticingly realistic detailed creations which must have taken hours to create. Others have a much looser nod to a theme, like blue Gelli with floating pirate eye patches, or pink sand or gloop with hearts in it. Lacking added play value other than the Gelli, sand or gloop, adult-focussed set-ups like these are only included as the theme doesn't prevent children's play.

iii) **Sensory and focussed provocations** – Such as coloured ice cubes and paper; a selection of dried pulses, utensils and sorting trays; or a sink and float activity with water and objects.

Application – These may tie in with a theme or book; build upon the child's knowledge funds; extend thinking; model ways of using resources; spark seeds of inquiry, imagination or children's strategies for addressing situations.
Suitability – These could suit . . .

- Children who find free play challenging as they are not used to making decisions or responding freely and creatively to resources.

- Older children who need more opportunities for sensory engagement but may resist simpler sensory or immediately messy material engagements as being babyish.

- Situations where a more prescriptive set-up is needed to model ways of using and engaging with the resources.

- Using stories and special interests like dinosaurs or animals to incentivise children with sensory processing difficulties to engage with difficult resources.

This may not be appropriate for younger children who need to explore in an embodied, then projective way before being ready for role-play or a more limited and targeted interaction with the resources.

Although these provocations tend to be adult-initiated, contained and planned, this does not mean that child-led play is impossible. This, however, will be determined by the permissiveness of the adult for children to re-purpose, reject and ignore the adult's original intentions, like the Keralan boy able to pursue his own interests and needs with playdough (page 24).

1) Ice cube painting

In-between wet and sticky	Indoors	Contained	Planned	Adult-provided Child-led

PROVISION

A low table was attractively arranged with some fruit-shaped ice cube trays, each a different colour. The cubes contrasted with the colours of the trays, and lolly sticks had been set at an angle making them very inviting and easier to use. Each child stood wearing an apron selecting which cubes to use to dab onto their piece of paper. Several staff members sat with the 2-year-olds, supporting them in using the ice cubes. Initially some children were distracted and curious about my presence, but gradually enjoyed moments of discovery and joy. Despite the high adult ratio, children were free to choose the coloured ice cubes, touch and taste them and use with the paper as they wished. Several of the children tasted the 'lollies', potentially linking to their knowledge funds of ice lollies. One appeared to be testing whether each colour tasted different. Wellbeing and Involvement ranged from 3 to 4 (Leuven), depending upon the child and stage in observation. This might have increased with time and as the ice melted.

136 Creating enabling messy play environments

	Child	Adult
A	■ Children were free to explore the resources as wished. ■ Adults encouraged involvement by modelling, supporting sharing, mirroring children's discoveries, reflecting back to the children.	■ Although child-led the session felt contained by adult presence and protective aprons. ■ Adults were calm.
R	■ Adults supported the children in sharing the 'lollies' and followed their lead. ■ Children were able to experience the sensory ice cubes with their body and mouth. ■ The attractively arranged resources invited exploration.	■ I sensed that adults felt slightly uncomfortable about children tasting the cubes.
C	■ Children were able to use the lollies to make marks, explore cause-and-effect and sensory qualities.	■ The activity and adult ratio provided a reassuring sense of containment and control.

CONTINUITY IDEAS

- The food colouring could be replaced with herbs, spices or citrus fruit peelings to increase the sensory qualities and reduce mouthing concerns.
- A sprinkler of salt could extend or vary exploration.
- Different types of paper could be provided, e.g. tissue paper, crepe, kitchen towel, coloured sugar paper, or even plain fabric to explore if and how this changes the absorption of colour.
- Larger-sized ice shapes and pipettes of food colouring or watercolour would encourage children to use their whole hands and explore change.

Moderate mess – Joint ownership

> These adult-initiated but child-led activities include simple provocations, planned or discovered, that spark a child's investigation and inquiry, spiralling a journey of discovery. While certain uses and engagements may be suggested by the resources, children are able to choose how to explore and engage with them.

Examples include: Finding 'dinosaurs', 'creepy crawlies' or other unexpected provocations, such as herbs, gems or magnets (being aware of choking hazards) in frozen 'eggs'; discovering clues; finding a 'fossilised egg' in a sand pit.

Application – These may complement or spark a theme or seed of inquiry, build upon the child's knowledge funds; provide opportunities for challenging or extending thinking – particularly scientific investigations – and develop mastery of tools and physical development.

Suitability – This could suit . . .

- Children who need continued sensory experiences.
- Children who are beginning to formulate their own theories.
- Young children giving opportunities for sharing knowledge funds and testing thinking.

2) Citrus ice eggs

In-between texture	Indoors	Contained	Planned	Child-led

PROVISION

> For this session for babies to 4-and-a-half-year-olds a mixture of fruit peelings and herbs were put in the bottom of silicone egg moulds [or cheap plastic eggs], filled with water and frozen overnight.

> [I] pop the eggs in the centre of a tray with all the accessories around the outside [and] sprinkle salt onto the ice eggs before the children arrive. [To start] I always get the children to see what they can see and smell – it's a good way to get them to engage with myself as well as one another. Then the real fun begins as the children start to melt down the ice. There's lots of laughter and giggling at this point. One boy made me orange peel tea. We talked about where ice and oranges come from and where you might find ice around the world. A lot of the children suggested penguins live on ice. Once the ice had melted enough the children used the plastic tweezers to remove the hidden scents. There were a lot of 'ooohs' and 'ahhhs' at this point and some tasting from . . . younger children.
>
> I always like to turn the clean up . . . into a game, so for this we use[d] plastic nets to scoop out all the bits-and-pieces into a bowl to put onto the grass outside for the birds. The salt water gets put down the drain. I give each of the children a paper towel and let them dry down the tray.
>
> (Nikita Baldwin, 2018)

	Child	*Adult*
A	■ Children's interests, opinions and variety of foci are accepted and valued. ■ The clearing up process supports children's knowledge and understanding.	■ Adult is relaxed, in part due to minimum time and cost investment in preparing the session, joint responsibility for clearing up, **relatedness** and containment.
R	■ Adult plans for children's involvement and **relatedness** with a sensory focus at the start and clearing up activity at the end. ■ **Relatedness** to children's interests in planning future provocations. ■ **Relatedness** to the environment from knowledge of birds and waste.	■ Pre-warns parents to bring a spare set of clothes to minimise stress. ■ Saves fruit peelings and herb cuttings by freezing in a ziplock bag to save on cost and wastage. ■ Adult is attuned to the children and sensory affordances.
C	■ Sprinkling the eggs with salt and providing the right tools enables children to succeed. ■ Expectation that the children will take responsibility for clear up conveys trust.	■ Structure but freedom provides containment for both the adult and children.

CONTINUITY IDEAS

■ Let the children use the salt to develop **autonomy** and scientific understanding.

■ Introduce other surprises in ice eggs, such as magnets or penguins as suggested.

- Provide different-sized pots with frozen contents instead for extending thinking about how to 'free' the contents.

- Provide cups, metal teapots, a sugar bowl, water and more fruit peelings and herbs etc for extending the tea focus.

- Provide soil, trowels, pots, appropriate food waste (and optional spaghetti 'worms') for exploring growing and compost.

3) Clingfilm-covered paint

Wet but covered	Indoors	Contained	Planned	Child-led

PROVISION

An area measuring approximately 2 metres long and 1.5 metres wide was covered with a roll of plain paper, with squiggles of various coloured paint evenly distributed and then covered in clingfilm. When I joined the room the 19 to 22-month-olds were either sat or stood near the provocation or on practitioners' laps. Several of the children were tired and initially upset, but gradually began to touch the clingfilm and move the paint around with their finger, flat palms, feet or bottom. Several children experimented with moving toy vehicles over the clingfilm, some seemed surprised that they did not get paint on their body and then re-experienced surprise when the paint seeped under the edges, getting paint on them. Two children experimented with using pencils to poke the paint with. Noticing the hole they'd created in the clingfilm and paper beneath, they prodded and pulled this with their fingers. Wellbeing and Involvement developed to 4 (Leuven).

	Child	*Adult*
A	■ Children were not hurried into taking part. ■ Practitioners' calm acceptance and supporting presence enabled the children to take the lead. ■ Adults accepted babies' choice to use pencils and pens and the resulting exploration of holes in the clingfilm and paper! ■ Adults supported sharing and sustained interest by providing vehicles and mirroring children's movement of these.	■ Children were dressed in nursery clothes to minimise stresses and enable them to get as messy as they wanted. ■ Adults appeared calm and relaxed.

continued

... continued

	Child	Adult
R	■ Practitioners provided reassurance and nurture if needed. ■ Practitioners supported sharing between the children. ■ One child benefited from playful hand-on-foot support to help them engage. ■ The children experienced cause-and-effect when the colours mixed or paint left marks. ■ The toys provided an intermediary for touching the paint.	■ Adults were relaxed and unfazed by the holes in the clingfilm and resulting mess. ■ Adults seemed comfortable and unfazed at being observed.
C	■ The children engaged in their own unhurried way. ■ Children's curiosity was evident in their reactions to the paint spreading beneath the clingfilm and positive response to surprise – when they noticed paint on them and discovered gaps in the clingfilm and paper. ■ The children shared the toys and pencils. ■ The children explored mark-making with their fingers, feet, vehicles and pencils.	■ Adults modelled and supported approaches to exploring and sharing without stifling. ■ Practitioners were happy to be led by the children and seemed relaxed.

CONTINUITY IDEAS

- Offer a collection of sensory balls, natural treasures or rollers for exploring with the paint.
- Repeat activity outside.
- Offer paint in individual zip-locked bags.

4) Tea-making

Wet but covered	Indoors	Contained	Planned	Child-led

PROVISION

Four 22 to 36-month-olds sit at a table when they see an adult approaching with a tray, china cups, two teapots and a cafetiere. Containers are placed on the table for children to help themselves to sugar, coffee and tea bags. The adult sits nearby only helping, if needed, to lift the heavy teapots. Each child chooses what to add to their large china cup, pointing and using simple statements and questions, such as 'thank you', 'sugar now?', 'me one' and 'we stir it' to describe, check, request and thank. It feels natural, like real life rather than role-play. Several times the adult calmly reminds them that they can't drink their drinks. The activity continues after all the ingredients have been used up with level 4 wellbeing and level 5 involvement throughout.

	Child	**Adult**
A	■ Adult was available but very child-led and unhurried. ■ Adult reflected upon children's actions, sharing etc. ■ Authentic children's conversations.	■ The table was covered with a cloth to catch spillages and children freely remained seated at the table giving a sense of calm control.
R	■ Simple activity felt very natural, homely and authentic. ■ The adult/child engagement felt authentic and equal. Even when help was needed this remained child-led. ■ Real china and ingredients increased authenticity, sensory feedback and **relatedness**.	■ The adult appeared natural and at ease, only feeling the need to gently instruct when the children tried to drink their creations.
C	■ Mastery orientation of pouring from real heavy china pots. ■ Fine and gross motor strength and skills, hand–eye coordination. ■ Sensory awareness and tasting of creations. ■ Introduced some concepts re volume, capacity, more, less, empty within an appropriate context. ■ Turn-taking initiated by the children felt natural rather than an awkward wait.	■ Adult-modelled process. Demonstrated her genuine trust and sense of being at ease.

CONTINUITY IDEAS

■ Reappraise whether restricting children's tasting of their creations is an 'unnecessary' limit. Trying their drinks is a natural extension of this activity, which appeared 'real' to the children rather than a role-play. With limits on the types and quantity of ingredients offered and allergy checks, the coffee could be substituted for hot chocolate and warm pre-boiled water used.

■ Change sensory dimension with fruit tea bags for different smells and colours.

■ Vary fine and gross motor skills with loose tea and tea strainers, cocoa dusters and freebie sachets of sugar.

■ Increase science and maths dimension with measures, different-sized spoons, sugar lumps (solids, dissolving), sorting tray (like in hotels) for tea bags, cause-and-effect of trying creations.

■ Provide paper placemats for mark-making with fruit teabags in context.

■ Introduce a café role-play, incorporating similar resources?

■ Apply same approach to 'real eating/drinking' opportunities?

■ Offer the equivalent with perfume-making – continuity as involves similar process.

5) Mud pies

| Wet and sticky | Outdoors | Contained | Planned | Mix of adult and child-led |

PROVISION

A group of children were gathered around an elevated builder's tray upon which were arranged a selection of bun trays, a large mixing bowl, wooden spoon, paper bun cases and a variety of spices and glittery water in jars. Nearby a container of soil was available and another builder's tray was attractively set up with a selection of vegetables, plastic knives and olive wood chopping boards. To the side of this children could access pots and pans and use shelving as 'ovens'. The adult gave the spoon to one boy to mix and the remainder of the children added ingredients to the bowl. All the children actively explored the ingredients, looking at, smelling (and some feeling) the vegetables and spices to decide which to include. The mixture was spooned into trays of bun cases and collectively decorated with a plethora of ingredients. There were discussions about measures, how long the mixture would take to cook and what else needed to be added, including requests for more water. More children had an opportunity to mix the ingredients as more batches were created. The practitioner encouraged the children to use their hands, modelling this herself. Several of the children initially looked very uncomfortable and self-conscious, stood like rag dolls displaying their muddy hands. With time they became absorbed in exploring materials with their hands. Wellbeing and involvement level 4 and 5, respectively (Leuven).

	Child	Adult
A	■ Children worked together and individually, sharing resources and supporting each other. ■ Adult was available providing a mix of adult-led (original focus of making mud pies), child-led (individual and co-ownership. ■ One child experienced more **autonomy** from mixing and this may potentially have limited other children's ownership of the mixture, although pots were available so perhaps they found equally satisfying ways of exerting **autonomy**.	■ The adult was a key focus for several children so there was a sense of her being 'stretched' at times. ■ Perhaps the adult picked a child to lead on stirring to enable her to step back.
R	■ Wonderfully accessible and inviting area. Flexible storage repurposed by children as 'ovens'. ■ Lovely examples of children sharing spices etc. ■ Practitioner modelled getting her hands dirty, accepting and supporting children's discomfort.	■ The adult could relate to children's reaction to touching and exploring the mess, initially appearing uncomfortable.
C	■ Children used their senses, explored the resources collectively and individually, role-played, and drew upon their knowledge funds. ■ Relevant and authentic discussion re timings for cooking, amounts, colours, spices, processes, e.g. cutting, mixing, mashing, decorating, mathematical language of size, number, more, less, lots, only supported if needed by practitioner.	■ The adult was understandably conscious of being observed, but at ease with the children and unconcerned by mess.

CONTINUITY IDEAS

- Set up a store cupboard nearby, 'Masterchef style', so the children choose what they need to add, making repeated trips, if needed, thereby potentially minimising wastage. This could include an assortment of no-cost natural treasures too, collected by the children and attractively arranged in separate labelled containers, avoiding the need for glitter.
- Some empty pots, labels and pens would empower children to choose and collect their own contents from the garden.
- It's worth considering what might be an optimum number of resources (see Chapter 5) to minimise waste and mess.
- Plant herb pots with the children for them to use in their 'cooking' and save vegetable trimmings, carrot tops, cauliflower leaves, etc for use, instead of fresh ingredients.

- A range of measuring spoons, scales and a timer could extend children's focus on measures and time.
- An accessible water supply could extend play and scientific learning.
- Bringing the vegetables inside afterwards would enable children to watch their natural transformation and decay as occurs in Reggio settings.
- Create a science lab (see below) with labelled jars, lab coats, goggles and clipboards.
- Create a garden café serving mud pies and teas to provide a context for messy play.

Messiest provisions – Child ownership

> These open-ended and child-led examples include spontaneous or planned engagements that spark a child's investigation and inquiry and spiral a child-led journey of discovery. While certain uses and engagements may be suggested by the materials and sorts of complimentary resources introduced in Chapter 5, children are able to choose how to explore and engage with them. Adults provide attentive noticing and scaffolding where appropriate.

Examples include:

Spontaneous: Discovering a frozen puddle, mud pit, muddy slope.

Planned:
- **Introducing disequilibrium** – e.g. introducing a new resource such as yellow powder paint.
- **Resourcing a science, perfume or potion laboratory; playdough creation station; or mud kitchen.**
- **Establishing a workshop zone or space** – e.g. providing a variety of different types, sizes, weights, material composition and colours of paper for children to freely explore with a range of equipment such as light tables, overhead projectors, fans, magnifiers, mirrors, torches, etc (as in the Material Encounters project).

Application – These may complement or spark a theme or seed of inquiry, build upon the child's knowledge funds; provide opportunities for challenging or extending thinking – particularly scientific investigations – and develop mastery of tools and physical development.

Suitability – This could suit . . .
- Competent and **autonomous** learners.
- Children that might struggle with formalised learning.
- Children's growing confidence and **ARC** with materials.

6) Workshop and science lab

Range of textures	Indoors and outdoors	Contained and uncontained	Spontaneous and planned	Child-led

PROVISION

A 'hands-on' workshop environment offers opportunities to explore and investigate materials as well as an array of other investigations. This approach is certainly evident in the Science Room in this German kindergarten, set-up with a woodbench and stations, resourced (with wood, child-size tools, paper, jars, food colouring and shaving foam), and used for inquiry-based projects like this:

Big question	*Inquiry*
Recycling – How to be a superhero	
Discussion points: ■ Superheroes ■ Superheroes in our community ■ How could we help with our community?	■ What ways can we help save the earth? ■ What are we already doing at home? ■ What could we do in the Kindergarten?
Action – Scavenger Hunt	***Stations***
■ Give everyone a reusable cotton bag. ■ Ask them to take time going around the Kindergarten finding things they think we could recycle or re-use. ■ Sort findings into groups. ■ Set up stations for ongoing recycling. ■ Show examples of things collected.	■ Set up a station for making crayons from old and broken crayons collected. Baking tins and an oven needed (teacher-assisted activity). ■ Set up a station with collected plastic bottles and different materials, e.g. rice, pasta, broken sticks, sand or water to go inside to make instruments.

(Samuel Armstrong, 2018)

	Child	*Adult*
A	■ Children follow their interests and inquiries. ■ Children work cooperatively and individually.	■ Adults feel comfortable in role as co-investigators.
R	■ Children have shaped their focus of inquiry and feel empowered to take actions.	■ Adults trust in children's abilities.
C	■ Children are curious and engaged. ■ Children experience success and satisfaction in investigations.	■ Adults trust children's abilities and are competent in their own skills to extend thinking.

CONTINUITY IDEAS

- Involve children's wider microsystem (Bronfenbrenner), by extending projects and presenting findings to home and the community.

7) Powder paint

This example was the result of a hotly contested decision to replace ready-mixed paint with one coloured powder paint.

Range of textures	Outdoors	Contained and uncontained	Planned and Spontaneous	Child-led

PROVISION

> We put pots of powder paint, water and spoons in a builder's tray, provided small transparent containers for mixing-in, and set-up a range of types and sizes of brushes and paper on an adjacent table.
>
> The children, particularly boys were immediately attracted by this new resource, enthusiastic to find out what they could do with this new offer. They engaged with the powder, initially adding lots of water and creating 'yellow water', then adding more powder resulting in lumps of wet powder in the sea of yellow water. Over time (weeks) children discovered how to produce paint that when applied to paper covered it effectively. With an alternative colour introduced at staff's request . . .
>
> Children continued to be fascinated by the possibilities of the dry powder, they put it in trays on the floor and used to make hand and foot prints, one child even hopping round the room frog-like leaving powdery hand and footprints behind her. This process took most of the autumn term.
>
> In the summer term one of the boys asked me if he could 'do an experiment'. Together we collected the builder's tray. He asked for one colour of paint, some water and pipettes. Soon a crowd had gathered all keen to engage with this 'experiment' and another exploration began.
>
> (Menna Godfrey, 2018)

	Child	*Adult*
A	- Children followed their interests and inquiries. - Children worked cooperatively and individually. - Children owned their play and felt comfortable in asking for help if needed.	- Adults felt uncomfortable and insecure about limiting children's choices and rights. - Adults didn't feel in control and were uncertain of what would happen.

continued

... continued

	Child	Adult
R	■ Children were drawn to the interesting paint qualities and resources provided. ■ Children tested their thinking.	■ Adults were concerned about children's rights. ■ Adults trusted in children's abilities. ■ Adults missed colours.
C	■ Children were curious and engaged. ■ Children experienced success and satisfaction in investigations. ■ Children took control of their play.	■ Adults were unsure as unchartered territory and didn't feel in control. ■ Adults trusted children's abilities.

CONTINUITY IDEAS

■ Explore satisficing in relation to other materials too.

8) Muddy puddle

Range of textures	Outdoors	Uncontained	Spontaneous	Child-led

PROVISION

> [With] a field of mud ... as soon as there was any rain the puddles and mud became deeper and more intriguing. Children shouted out with glee as they got stuck in the squelchy mud and waded through the puddles. Alongside this play we noticed that children were always eager to use the various containers and utensils that we provided to mix mud, water and vegetation. This led-us to introduce a mud kitchen, which was soon busy daily. The variety of consistencies had many uses: Most frequently children described the mixture as soup. Sometimes the consistency was thicker, and the children formed 'patties' – palm-sized flattened lumps of mud, flattened between the hands. Once 'Susan' sang her own mud song as she passed the patty from one hand to the other, 'Mud, mud, mud, muddy mud ...
>
> (Menna Godfrey, 2018)

	Child	Adult
A	■ Children followed their wide-ranging interests and inquiries. ■ Children used the resources creatively, linking knowledge funds.	■ Adults felt comfortable and able to notice cross-curricular learning.
R	■ Children were drawn to the changing provision and its infinite qualities for supporting exploration and play.	■ Adults trusted in children's abilities.
C	■ Children were curious, engaged and in control of their own play.	■ Adults trusted their own abilities and children's learning.

CONTINUITY

■ Provide containers and labels to spark collections of natural treasures for children to incorporate into their creations, if wished.

Deciding where on the scale to begin

When adults are attuned to children's interests and needs (**relatedness**); trust their **competence** to access materials in a sensorimotor way; and provide the **autonomy** to build upon their knowledge funds, they can galvanise thinking and develop meaning. As these vignettes demonstrate, children's self-set inquiries reap rich rewards. Far from being a 'one-size-fits-all' approach, the framework provides a tool for getting the adult/child balance right and creating 'possibility spaces', as seedbeds for children's learning to flourish.

> **IN THIS CHAPTER WE HAVE:**
>
> Explored how the benefits of **ARC** can be realised and anxieties about mess minimised by considering:
>
> - Decisions about planning and ownership.
> - The composition, location, degree of containment and scale of material engagements.
> - The importance of continuity in enriching learning.

Notes

1 It is recognised that while locating messy play opportunities outside often increases mess, this doesn't typically increase the adult's stress. Conversely, messy play indoors increases the practitioner's (and potentially child's) anxieties and need for greater containment. In deciding where to position 'indoors' and 'outdoors' on this scale I have focussed on the child's experience, and extra freedom that messy play outdoors brings to both adult and child.
2 Resources identified by participants in a seminar at Childcare Expo (Gascoyne, 2018b).
3 Adult-set, product-focussed interactions are deliberately omitted from this scale as, although fun and sensory, these types of activities need re-badging as messy approaches to art or literacy, rather than messy play per se.

7 Material encounters and inquiry-based learning

> This chapter positions material encounters as inquiry-based thinking tools with much wider scope than narrowly defined 'school subjects'. Bringing satisfaction and wellbeing and a vitally important sensorimotor education, engagement with messy resources hardwires the brain for lifelong learning. Freed from the constraints of a narrowly defined curriculum, children's learning can be appreciated in its widest sense, with effortless links between messy play transformations and children's executive functions, scientific inquiry and a raft of other learning possibilities. The sliding scale introduced in Chapter 6 is extended with a focus on 'possibility planning' as a tool for embedding inquiry-based learning approaches and ensuring that the wonder of messy play is not lost in our eagerness to chart children's learning.

We began our theoretical tour in Chapter 2, with Bronfenbrenner's positioning of the child at the centre of a series of environmental, social, political and cultural systems. We now return to the importance of starting where children are when planning material engagements and the learning and benefits that this brings. For young children, 'life is not separated into times for "living in the world" and times for "learning about things" in the world' (Holzman, 2009: 47), but a seamless inquiry-led process where children naturally learn in a multi-sensory, active and naturalistic way. Messy play is ideally suited to enrich such inquiry-based provision.

Children's learning and curriculum silos

Two parallel processes are evident in the lifetime of learning:

1. We tend to move from being 'generalists to specialists' (Early Childhood Development Centre Cologne, 2018) and

2. Children's learning starts with the influences in the child's immediate environment or context, gradually widening to embrace wider beliefs and experiences.

Returning to the two faces (adult/child) of **Autonomy**, **Relatedness** and **Competence** (**ARC**) (Deci & Ryan, 2000) introduced in Figure 1.3 (page 11), this presents an anomaly between adults' and children's approaches to learning. Adults' understanding of the world tends to revolve around acquiring and instilling 'specialist subject knowledge [but] for very young children, there are no single subjects, they perceive everything as one' (Early Childhood Development Centre Cologne, 2018). Add to this the potentially narrow subject focus of a curriculum and practitioners can find themselves experiencing the uncomfortable disconnect between an emphasis upon school readiness, phonics and targets at Bronfenbrenner's Exo, Macro and Meso scales and the child's process of active discovery in the Microsystem (Figure 2.2, page 16).

Interpreting learning

'Children naturally blend and apply a range of understanding to each activity they engage with' (Gripton, 2017: 10) so with this disconnect between compartmentalised curriculum-based areas for learning and children's organic approaches comes the potential for different lenses on **competence**. Adults may feel compelled to identify specific learning milestones (the 'what' of children's learning), while children may find their interests and self-set inquiries thwarted or unappreciated (the 'how'), as these don't neatly translate into curricular tick-boxes. Both scenarios offer potential for practitioners and children to experience a lack of **ARC** and associated reduction in self-worth and morale. The challenges presented by this divide are tangible in this candid sharing by two experienced practitioners, as is the value of the Leuven Scales, as a tool for measuring involvement and wellbeing when practitioners struggle to define learning:

> **Menna Godfrey:** a 3-year-old . . . stood in a puddle for nearly one whole afternoon. It was probably about three or four inches deep and it was something that the children had dug [and] had been filled with water. [He] only came to us once a week for three hours and this particular afternoon he stood in the puddle. I was left thinking; do I get that child out and get him to do some 'proper' learning? Or do I do what my heart believes – that he was in the puddle for some reason that he understands . . . So I started looking more carefully at what he was doing . . . [wondering] what am I going to tell his dad when he picks him up? "He's been standing in a puddle for three hours?" I couldn't unpick exactly what his learning was but I'm convinced, when I go back to what the Leuven Scales tell us, that there was learning going on for him that afternoon.
>
> **Kathy Brodie:** You couldn't have a better definition of a level 5 involvement than somebody who stands in a puddle ALL afternoon . . .

> **Menna Godfrey:** The wellbeing and involvement scales show us so much about what's going on with the child and take away the necessity for me to unpick absolutely everything. Because it wasn't that he did that every time he was with us. It was this particular afternoon.
>
> **Kathy Brodie:** ... We might not know what their learning is but we know that gut feeling that ... there is learning going on because they are so involved ... WE might not be able to put our finger on what the learning is, but there IS learning going on there. So why would you disturb that?
>
> (Brodie & Godfrey, 2018)

By forcing play observations into curriculum tick-boxes, we risk losing the wonder and essence of children's unique learning journeys in the process, as well as implying that some outcomes and learning activities are deemed more important than others. If we can trust in our gut feeling and resist the pressure to compartmentalise children's learning, the Leuven Scales provide a useful barometer for measuring potential learning and valuing inquiries like these. Malaguzzi referred to the importance of practitioners 'becoming comfortable with the unknown' (1994: 3) and this is apparent in Menna Godfrey's honest reflection of self-doubt and inner critique of what she would say to the child's parent.

Planning, or perhaps, restricting learning?

When learning opportunities are planned with specific outcomes in mind, be it encouraging mark-making, supporting physical development, or inspiring creativity, practitioners are in danger of planning for the areas of learning rather than 'physical spaces for activity or resources' (Gripton, 2017: 10). Even just being aware of the need for a focus can act as a subconscious lens through which children's play is viewed. For example, if you, like me, believe we need to promote children's scientific inquiry, then you're more likely to be drawn to opportunities and spot missed 'teachable moments' for science.

An alternative approach

In many of the most enriching material engagements described in this book, the child takes centre stage, orchestrating their inquiry, with the adult in the wings, noticing and accepting children's explorations; supporting and facilitating their learning; and furnishing children with the resources and opportunities to develop skills and conceptual theories. Picture the deep rivulets on that upturned jelly in Chapter 2. Children's wellbeing and self-esteem are dependent upon their understanding and **relatedness** to the world (Deci & Ryan, 2000) so a natural starting place for child-led inquiry is a focus on topics such as: 'Who we are', 'Where we are in place and time', 'How we express ourselves', and 'How the world works' – key ingredients of a *transdisciplinary* approach.

The term transdisciplinary was introduced by Piaget in the 1970s when he noticed children's tendency for cross-discipline thinking. As much about the inquiry-led experience as the outcome, the prefix 'trans' conveys 'learning that has relevance across the subject areas and more importantly, learning that transcends the[se] to connect to what is real in the world' (International Baccalaureate, 2010: 1). Described by Nicolescu (2008, cited in Savage and Drake, 2016: 2) as 'not just an intellectual activity but involving the entire person: mind, body and emotions', the Institute for the Future has identified transdisciplinary thinking as a 'key and essential skill for the future workforce' (Levinson, 2016).

Throughout this book the three cornerstones of **ARC** have provided a framework for considering children's material encounters, and these are also essential for supporting transdisciplinary ways of thinking. With children now, more than ever, connected to global events via the media (**relatedness**), the global dimension of transdisciplinary approaches provides the tools for children to develop the **competencies** and **autonomy** to feel empowered that they can make a difference. An example of one such inquiry was the appearance of 'the last bucket of water in the world' in one school, creatively challenging children to find ways of saving this precious resource (Savage & Drake, 2016). Similarly, reusing waste was a focus for a German kindergarten's inquiry (see page 146).

Broad topics like these naturally give children opportunities to widen their focus, 'like the ripples when you drop a stone in a pond' (Grenier, 2018: 37) or the concentric circles in Bronfenbrenner's systems. For adults too, they are sufficiently broad and flexible to augment with specialist knowledge. With strong parallels to Reggio-inspired practice, an inquiry-based approach is particularly suited to young children as:

> teachers and students discover the curriculum together and document their learning as they experience it. Rather than delivering information to them, educators co-construct meaning with students and guide them to develop their own understandings ... High-quality interactions between adults and children are essential for a meaningful learning experience. Inquiry in the early years is intimately connected with the development of children's understanding of the world and acknowledges children's competencies to explore, discover and interact with the physical and social world around them. Through play, children become increasingly skilled at being group members, initiating and working through projects, asking questions and exploring possible worlds through imagination.
>
> (Vientiane International School, 2018)

Rather than narrowly defined subject areas which would be incongruent with our focus on open-ended resources, this chapter recognises the value of materials as 'bones' of curriculum (Carter & Curtis, 2007, cited in Paccini-Ketchabaw et al, 2017: 3), stripping back learning to a series of dispositions and key thinking skills, necessary to create an enabling climate for child-led inquiry with materials.

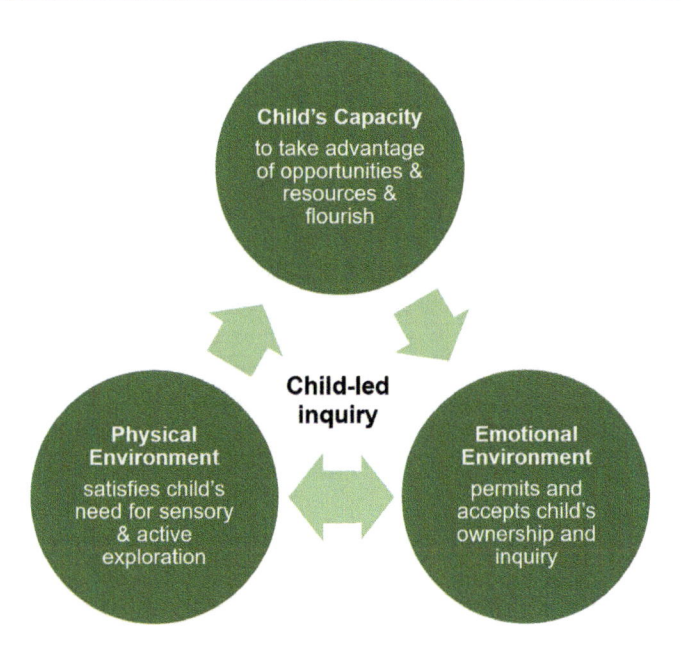

Figure 7.1 Foundations for inquiries

- Child's Capacity to take advantage of opportunities & resources & flourish
- Physical Environment satisfies child's need for sensory & active exploration
- Emotional Environment permits and accepts child's ownership and inquiry
- Child-led inquiry

Pre-requisites for inquiry-based learning

As we shall explore further in Chapter 8, genuinely child-led inquiry requires different types of physical spaces and ways of interacting to thrive. The pre-requisites shown in Figure 7.1 are essential.

Executive functions as cross-curricular thinking tools

Given the right environment, a child's capacity to flourish in self-set inquiries will be shaped by their Executive Functions (EF). A truly cross-curricular tool, EF are 'central to academic success [underpinning] attainment in all areas of learning' (Pascal et al, 2018: 36). Comprising:

- Cognitive flexibility (including creativity and flexibility),
- Inhibition (including self-control and self-regulation),
- Working memory, and
- More complex EF's of problem-solving, reasoning and planning.[1]

These 'shape children's ability to filter distractions, prioritise tasks, set and achieve goals, and control impulses as well as providing a sense of self-efficacy, agency and self-esteem' (Pascal et al, 2018: 36), core inquiry skills which we return to throughout this chapter. As is apparent from Table 7.1, the child's experience of **ARC** (Deci & Ryan, 2000) is key to their ability to capitalise upon material engagements.

With many of the areas in Table 7.1 already introduced, our focus now turns to the core skills identified in italics.

Table 7.1 Ingredients of inquiry-based learning

	Autonomy	*Relatedness*	*Competence*
CHILD's experience of ...	Permission Acceptance Choice	Acceptance Trust Permission Noticing connections in the environment. Creativity, flexibility, problem-solving, reasoning and planning through materials.	*Self-regulation* *Mastery orientation* Making a difference, e.g. cause-and-effect *Resilience.*
ADULT's provision of ...	Opportunities for children to make choices, joint-planning, receive support to pursue self-set inquiries and experience risk-taking.	*Modelling* and adult's own self-regulation. Equipping with necessary skills, e.g. using specialist tools or developing thinking tools. *Noticing* child's interests and inquiry.	Ongoing learning to develop their own thinking and better support and understand children's inquiries.

Supporting self-regulation

Self-regulation is an essential component of inquiry-based approaches and a pre-requisite for school readiness. It stems from children having consistent boundaries; opportunities for thinking time and slowing things down; practice in delaying gratification; a good balance between novel and familiar experiences; and space and opportunities to calm themselves down. With sustained periods of time for messy play, children can experience the familiarity of how liquids and solids work, and the disequilibrium of gloop; the calming benefits and thinking time of engaging with multi-sensory resources; the opportunities for developing focus; practising sequencing; delaying outcomes and managing disappointments when children are absorbed in their own scientific inquiries.

'Experiences that invite curiosity and exploration through the senses are great for promoting mindfulness' (Grace, 2018: 16), like this boy's investigation of water with a decorator's brush:

> He dipped a brush in a puddle of rainwater and proceeded to paint the sides of the nursery steps and wooden decking. As he 'painted' different surfaces with the broad brush, he momentarily paused, as if testing his ideas about whether the metal would look the same as the wood. There was a sense of serious investigation and curiosity, as he explored cause-and-effect and carefully noticed the effects of his actions.

Unperturbed (indeed potentially sparked) by the rain, this young boy's silent and steady investigations resonate with Kaplin and Kaplin's notions of 'fascination', 'compatibility' and 'immersion' (1989), a stark contrast to the immediacy of social media, television, electronic games and press-and-do toys.

Reflection

Consider how many of the material engagements and scientific provocations currently provided offer instant or dramatic gratification, like volcano experiments? What changes or other materials are needed to support children's executive functions, setting them up for life, not just for school?

Self-regulation is highly pertinent to messy play given the extremes of reaction reported in Chapter 1. 'For some adults, messy play can be a real challenge causing them to become dysregulated. Children are sensitive and will always be watching, listening and absorbing words as well as actions' (O'Neill, 2018). As an external regulator helping children to learn self-regulation skills, it is essential for the adult to manage their own feelings if the child is to enjoy positive experiences:

> Maisie was 5-years-old when referred to Play Therapy. Using messy play as a vehicle for transformation and fostering self-regulation, with the adult's presence, Maisie learnt to inhibit her impulsive behaviour and messiness of play. As she became more skilled in this, her behaviour at home and school also improved. Maisie had learnt to self-regulate and was able to manage her big feelings more appropriately.
>
> (Karen O'Neill, 2018)

In mainstream environments too, a skilled practitioner and 'authentic contexts . . . plann[ed] for endless possibilities' (Gripton, 2017: 12) enable children to self-regulate. As is apparent from this focus on leaves, in planning for possibilities 'we do not ask what it is but what it could be and what it can be used for' (Gripton, 2017: 12).

> Collect some leaves, being careful to avoid potential dangers from animal waste. Clean, if needed, with soapy water to remove bacteria. When dry, arrange in a huge pile. Children may burrow in to experience a wealth of sensory sensations, from the surprisingly loud rustling of the leaves, the darkness of being enveloped, the earthy smells of the forest floor and touch of soft or crisp leaves. Others may hide then burst out like an erupting volcano, or kick and throw the leaves excitedly trying to catch them, a challenging endeavour thanks to the laws of deterministic chaos! (Perceval, 1992). A story about hibernation may prompt a child to discover what this might feel like or a game of hide-and-seek could be elevated to a new level. Children may sort, classify, use creatively, or simply 'just be'.

Reflection

Notice children's responses and try for yourself! Discuss any surprises and compare with your expectations.

Resilience and mastery orientation

Competence stems from children feeling able to make a difference, and messy play resources provide rich opportunities for exploring transformation and cause-and-effect, as well as gratification delay if resources are picked wisely. In the presence of a supportive adult, messy play successes can 'build curiosity, bravery and adaptability, giving children strength and resilience to explore the world' (O'Neill, 2018).

> This was noticeable for 6-year-old Billy, who over eighteen Play Therapy sessions experimented with water, paints, cornflour and shaving foam. At first he tentatively used a wooden spoon to aid mixing. In later sessions, he became braver using his hands to immerse himself in the mess that he had created. Squeals of delight and laughter radiated from Billy as he experimented more and more with different media in the shallow tray. He stopped asking 'Am I allowed to do this' because the only permission he needed was from himself, not the adult who had contained him without judgement. Perseverance showed Billy that he could take risks in messy play. There was a sense that through these experiences, Billy had the capability to explore his world and adjust accordingly.
>
> (Karen O'Neill, 2018)

It was suggested in Chapter 6 that being too closely tied to objectives can detract from 'possibility planning'. Flexibility was certainly key in the following session (introduced in Chapter 6). As the practitioner didn't slavishly control consistency, and natural resources were available, children were free to experience many more learning opportunities including the science of cause-and-effect, sink and float, creativity and a range of motor skills.

> The children displayed enjoyment and critical thinking skills throughout the observation alongside personal, social and emotional skills. The sensory messy play gave children with SEND the opportunity to take part in an activity that was appealing to them, incorporating social skills at the same time.
>
> (Fiona Smith, 2018)

Self-expression

'Children need the resources and tools with which they can represent their ideas, understanding and feelings, [furthering] their interpretation of themselves and their world (Bruner, 1990, cited in Gripton, 2017: 12). As we discovered in Chapter 3, children's messy creations may serve as tools for self-expression (Gascoyne, 2016) and:

> play that incorporates rich textural experiences allows children to express their emotions through manipulating the materials. The richer the textural experiences, the richer their cognitive and language development will be – how can a nine-year-old grasp the concept of "slimy" if he has never touched anything "slimy"?
>
> (Parnell, 2018)

As we saw in Chapter 5, context is critical to children's learning (Paul-Smith & Barber, 2011) and self-expression. Tomasello (in Bakhurst & Shanker, 2001: 33) recognised its contribution to the 'nonlinguistic cognition of actions, objects and properties', a natural fit with messy play.

Modelling by the adult

O'Neill reminds us that some children can't make the most of open-ended opportunities (like exploring puddles, on the sliding scale of material engagements introduced in Chapter 6), without first experiencing appropriate modelling by an attuned adult. Interestingly for the detailed adult-planned provocations to the left of the scale, this direction appears to be provided (as Dewey envisaged) by the resources (i.e. context), with children benefitting from the possibilities being modelled and knowledge funds increased, in readiness for free play. Some children look to an adult for their reaction, which can be 'problematic given the negative associations of messy play' (2018). For 'Lily', a 6-year-old referred for Play Therapy, the benefits of positive modelling are evident.

> With change challenging, Lily's default position on messy play materials was avoidance, choosing not to engage with sand, clay or paint. Over several sessions with adult support she was able to engage increasingly with these creative media. Each messy play encounter was a small-step towards connecting with unstructured positive experiences as she made sense of her world and was able to participate uninhibited while having fun!
>
> (Karen O'Neill, 2018)

Instilling playful inquiry

Playfulness is influenced by our age, upbringing and disposition, shaping in turn our understanding of the allure of provocations and acceptance and **relatedness** to children's actions. By practising playfulness, it helps adults put themselves in a child's shoes when faced with a pile of sand or beckoning puddle, recognising their appeal to a sensory being, and not just a hassle for adults! Material engagements provide literally a wonder-full opportunity for adults to reconnect with their more playful selves. Similarly, Brookfield suggests that 'regularly experiencing what it feels like to learn something unfamiliar and difficult is the best way to help teachers empathise with the emotions and feelings of their own learners' (Brookfield, in Boud et al, 1993: 21).

Reflection

Consider how you can develop your own learning and playfulness to better understand children's material encounters.

Developing thinking tools

Here we look at two ways to help develop children's thinking tools:

1. Supporting scientific thinking, and

2. Tools for noticing

1) Supporting scientific thinking

It is often remarked that a child's play is reminiscent of a scientist at work, yet with science pigeon-holed as a distinct curriculum area it's easy to forget its cross-curricular relevance as a

Table 7.2 Messy play and phases of scientific thinking

PHASE	Objects floating in water[2]	Tea-making activity[3]
INQUIRY Noticing something establishes a goal for investigations	Playing in the water tray with an assortment of objects sparks the child's observation that the small objects float.	When warm water is added to coffee granules they disappear (dissolve) and the water changes colour. In cold water the granules float.
	↓	↓
ANALYSIS Comparisons are made between evidence from phenomena and the child's existing theories	Evidence that a small toy metal boat floats. The TV programme about the Titanic sinking may (wrongly) reinforce a relationship between buoyancy and size.	The tea leaves don't disappear in cold or warm water but the water changes colour. Mud changes the colour of warm bath water.
	↓	↓
INFERENCE Draws upon what information is known and whether this is sound	A large metal ship and metal ball sink but a cork, pine cone, and metal toy boat float. Knowledge funds – when I curl up in a ball in the sea I sink.	The temperature of the water is important for helping the coffee granules mix with the water.
	↓	↓
ARGUMENT Theoretical position	Changing the shape of an object (rather than its size) will affect whether it floats or sinks.	Changing the temperature of the water affects the rate at which some things dissolve.

thinking tool. David Hawkins makes the link between scientific thinking and playing or 'messing about' with materials and ideas. Noticing university students' difficulties with scientific concepts, Hawkins discovered that 'a style of laboratory work ... called "kindergarten revisited", dramatically liberated their intellectual powers' (1974: 1), proof positive of the importance of children's formative years. Similarly, Kuhn identified four phases of scientific thinking naturally occurring in children, of which the Inquiry and Analysis phases naturally align with 'messing about' (Kuhn, 2004, cited in Goswami, 2004: 378). An awareness of these phases of scientific thinking set out in Table 7.2 can inform early years practice.

As Table 7.2 demonstrates, an understanding of these naturally occurring phases in children's thinking helps practitioners provide an enabling physical and emotional environment for self-chosen inquiries. This entails: discovering alongside the child; following their interests;[4] furnishing them with the appropriate vocabulary (e.g. dissolve, displace) and skills, if needed, to scaffold thinking and make the links to their knowledge funds. As such the adult's role is not speeding up the connection of ideas and discovery of 'aha' moments (Gopnik, 2000), but rather providing the possibility space in which this can organically happen.

2) Tools for noticing

Noticing is a key ingredient of scientific inquiry as well as productive lifelong learning. Occurring naturally when children experience safety and **ARC**, it is something that children are typically much better at than adults!

Adults' noticing

Pacini-Ketchabaw et al (2017) emphasised the importance of attentive noticing as did Axline – as we shall explore in the next chapter. Sometimes this affords glimpses of cognitive reasoning in children's material engagements:

> Like the 28-month-old child playing with a collection of objects and dry sand who filled a container with powdery sand then pressed a plug into this, visibly surprised not to see a resulting imprint.

If we actively notice fleeting moments like these, they reveal a child's knowledge and understanding of cause-and-effect, use of tools for mark-making, experience of creating prints and knowledge of sand. How easily though could this have been missed, leaving this child's treasure trove of knowledge funds undiscovered?

Children's noticing

Not only are the opportunities for noticing (the Inquiry stage in Table 7.2) seemingly endless in messy play, but if appropriately resourced with open-ended familiar materials (as described in Chapters 4 and 5), children will also encounter these at home and in daily interactions

(Bronfenbenner), thereby rooting the child's noticing and investigations within the real world. An effective way of encouraging and valuing children's noticing is provided by the See/Think/Wonder tool (Harvard Graduate School of Education), used in transdisciplinary approaches:

SEE/THINK/WONDER QUESTIONS

What do you see – This subtly shifts the focus from knowledge, right or wrong answers and a knowledge deficit, to children's individual interests and experiences which all hold equal value so children experience a sense of self-worth and **ARC**. Rather than artificially closing off avenues of thinking through questions like: *'Who can tell me?'*, which only play to the most confident children's strengths and stifle contributions for fear of getting things wrong, this opens up possibilities for shared deliberation and valuing of creative thinking.

What do you think? – Again, subtly different to traditional knowledge acquisition, this values the child's noticing and invites them to draw upon their interests and knowledge funds to share their thoughts about the phenomenon. As with the noticing stage, by positioning these as knowledge-informed views, children feel empowered to contribute and a richer diversity of ideas, viewpoints and therefore fields of inquiry emerge.

What do you wonder? – This stage helps children formulate individual and shared 'questions worth asking' (Rich et al, 2006, cited in Woods, 2017a: 16), a stark contrast to the contrived and inauthentic questions that we can find ourselves asking children, which they know we know the answer to! 'Challenging and interesting, these big questions promote creative thinking, encourage connection-making and involve issues of generality and conceptual thinking' (Gripton 2017: 16). They draw upon children's broad, randomised and richly interconnected knowledge, not just linear lines of inquiry.

Creating possibility spaces

With these learning dispositions and thinking strategies in place, we now revisit the sliding scale introduced in Chapter 6. Our aim is to explore what different levels of adult/child ownership and planning might look like in relation to children's learning outcomes and how best to put this into practice in the varied landscape of early childhood environments.

At one end of this scale are the exciting workshop environments and physical science laboratory spaces created and resourced by and with children. Their associated culture of permission, acceptance of the child as leading inquiry, and the adult positioned as co-investigator are key. At the other end of the spectrum lies existing good-quality practice, which if reviewed through a 'possibility finding' lens (Craft, 2002) can be modified and tweaked to offer children possibilities for even more meaningful material engagements.

Like a tender green shoot in early Spring, still vulnerable to a sharp frost, so an adult's response can stunt a child's inquiry, sparking guilt, shame or incompetence, or nurture it with scaffolding and support. With this in mind a range of 'planting schemes' (or levels of inquiry) are offered from which practitioners can pick, to best harmonise with the culture of the setting, adult and child capacity:

'**Wooden stakes and netting**' – Small-scale physical actions for enhancing existing activities and approaches can help encourage and protect developing seeds of inquiry, giving the young seedling a better chance of bearing fruit. Actions may focus on increasing the authenticity of children's encounters and widening their **autonomy** and possibilities.

'**A mini cloche in the garden**' – A valued bubble of space and time enables the introduction of Big Questions – self-contained inquiries born from the big issues, potentially with global significance, that children identify for investigation.

'**The provision of a greenhouse**' – Affording greater protection from curriculum intrusion and a more stable foundation for investigation rooted in daily interactions, project-based working blends the physical and emotional essentials to deeply satisfying material engagements, to create a micro-climate for inquiry.

'**The creation of an arboretum**' – A climate of inquiry is well established in this 'all-singing' gardener's dream. Including the science laboratories and open workshop spaces described in Chapter 6 together with children's unfettered access to outdoors, children are confident and competent investigators, assured in the importance of their material engagements and adults' recognition of these.

With each stage of increased affordance (offered by the sustaining emotional and physical environment) comes increased opportunities for self-regulation, mastery orientation and wellbeing in the child. It stands to reason that inquiry in an 'arboretum', where children can freely follow their threads of thinking and happen upon chance encounters or moments of disequilibrium, is going to deliver more impactful learning than a discrete bubble of inquiry-based thinking (the 'cloche'). Our attention now turns to a single resource, the humble oat, exploring its potential to be used creatively in all four levels of inquiry or 'planting schemes' from 'wooden stakes and netting' to 'mini cloche', 'greenhouse' or 'arboretum'!

The possibilities of porridge

What porridge oats (or any open-ended resource) offer is the opportunity to:

- Showcase a range of creative possibilities, challenging us to think outside the box.

- Demonstrate the variety of cross-curricular learning afforded by a single resource.

- Reinforce the importance of continuity, as the oats provide a common thread in a series of disparate activities and processes.[5]

- Offer a variety of opportunities for embedding inquiry-based approaches and laying stepping stones towards that 'arboretum' of inquiry.

> We've been focussing on *Goldilocks and the Three Bears* this week, so put dry porridge oats in our tuff spot with three spoons of different sizes. The children, (many of whom have very little English) were spontaneously retelling the story. I heard so many

> "Who's been eating my porridge?" After a couple of days, the children watched as we added water to the porridge oats to make a really messy, gooey porridge mixture. I was sat reading a story in the book corner yesterday when I was brought a lovely bowl of overflowing, dripping, messy porridge for my breakfast!
>
> (Jackie A, posted May 19, 2007; Foundation Stage Forum)

This wonderful example demonstrates the benefits when children can return to their messy play (**relatedness**) and have the **autonomy** and **competence** to follow their interests. It also highlights a wealth of learning.

Table 7.3 Possibilities and porridge oats

Level of inquiry	Activities	Possibility-widening actions
Wooden stakes and netting	As above, share a story e.g. The Magic Porridge Pot before children's sensory and physical exploration and role-play.	Enjoy a real bowl of creamy porridge first to root children's investigations and link with knowledge funds. Plan exciting provocations at a range of scales.
Wooden stakes and netting	Offer dry oats and a range of different-sized containers, sieves, tea strainers and spoons.	Provide different-sized porridge oats – finely milled through to jumbo oats for comparisons, exploring size, and investigating how these properties affect the end-result, when water or milk is added (Drake, 2005). Offer a range of fit-for-purpose spoons including measuring spoons and different sizes to hone physical strengths and skills and spark STEM.[6] Add a wow factor with a spurtle, a special porridge stirrer. Invite personal preferences and build on knowledge funds with a tiny salt spoon or sugar shaker.
Mini cloche	Big Question	What's the optimum porridge consistency for eating/building with? How few oats could feed a family?
Greenhouse	Projects and 'problem spaces'	One Year 1 teacher set up a breakfast crime scene complete with police tape, an empty bowl, props and clues for children to crack (Kingsley, 2015). Less elaborate provocations will similarly develop children's EF.
Arboretum	Science lab/The Outdoors Workshop	Provide porridge oats (and other resources) with containers, pipettes, funnels etc for children's own investigations indoors and out.

We will now briefly explore each of these levels of inquiry, starting with 'Enhancing existing provision', where we consider two play scenarios with a view to highlighting possibilities.

'Wooden stakes and netting' – Enhancing existing provision

If we have a particular focus in mind this can cloud our awareness of other learning. The lens through which we view children's explorations will be a product of our own interests, skills and knowledge (or lack of these, particularly when it comes to science and maths) as well as those of the child. This is how it's possible for two practitioners to view the same play session and draw different conclusions. The effect can be doubly powerful where the adult plans provision to meet specific targets as well as interpreting a child's actions as evidence of these, when the child's real seed of inquiry or focus may be very different.

Session 1 – Tea-making

Reading a practitioner's observation of a tea-making session that I had been privileged to observe (introduced in Chapter 6) crystallised the potential power of the adult, as both facilitator and interpreter of a child's play. This wonderful session was so authentically rooted in children's interests and knowledge funds (Bronfenbrenner's Microsystem) that apart from the children not being able to taste their creations, it felt to me like 'real life' rather than pretend play. The activity had been set up to support *Understanding the World*: '*In pretend play imitates everyday actions and events from own family*' (UW22-36, Development Matters) but unaware of this I was able to watch this session unfettered by any expectations or assumptions. The adult recorded the children's role-play and '*Communication and Language: 16-26 – Beginning to put two words together*' (Development Matters) but if asked to pinpoint all the learning this could have included:

- **Physical development** – fine and gross motor skills (from pouring the heavy tea pots).

- **Personal, social and emotional development** – turn-taking, sharing, resilience, independence, expressing choices, self-regulation and self-care (as the children potentially did not view this as role-play but the real world and so kept trying to drink the tea!).

- **Science** – discovering what happens if liquid is added to powder; heat, and cause-and-effect as additions generated change.

- **Communication** – asking for help, commenting on their actions and creations and communicating with each other.

- **Mathematics** – an exploration of capacity, size, volume and sequencing.
- **Creativity** – experimenting with creating their own concoctions.

This practitioner recognised the links to, and children's interests in, mathematical development, planning a follow-up activity. But in distilling children's cross-curricular learning into narrowly defined goals, there is a risk that the adult's intention provides a lens not only shaping what resources children are provided with, but also potentially how their play is documented. With material encounters so conducive to scientific and mathematical investigation and research showing that these are areas in which many practitioners lack confidence and knowledge (see page 172), it is apparent how easily opportunities for inspiring and developing scientific thinking might be lost.

A 'science of curiosity'

A curriculum focus changes our start and end positions, and even the resources available for in-between! For the 22 to 36-month-olds so absorbed in tea-making, opportunities to experience similar sensory experiences, as described by Grace in Chapter 2, might look very different to provision for a linear progression of specific skills. Woods uses the term a 'science of curiosity' (2017b: 96), which perfectly describes children's natural inclination to probe and discover and the creativity that consequently flourishes. With few changes or additional resources, this activity could effortlessly support a raft of further mathematical, scientific, emotional and creative thinking, offering opportunities for extending children's own inquiries in an authentic context, as seen in Table 7.4.

Being receptive to using messy play materials for scientific investigation is key to optimising possibilities. For some practitioners this may involve developing their own confidence in STEM, (an example of which is provided on page 172), rather than defaulting to a sensory, role-play or creativity focus which may feel more comfortable.

Reflection

Pick some examples of messy play and consider:

- What areas of learning you intended the play to meet?
- What learning actually arose?
- Were scientific and mathematical thinking opportunities maximised?
- What changes, if any, could increase children's possibilities?
- What knowledge and skills do you need to support children's mathematical and science investigations?

Table 7.4 Possibilities and tea-making

Possibility-widening actions	Potential benefits
Providing milk (check allergies) and taking steps suggested in Chapter 6 to enable children to taste their creations.	■ Cause-and-effect, science, sequencing as children choose to add first the teabag and then the milk and water – depending upon personal preference! ■ **Autonomy**, self-esteem, resilience, self-efficacy, self-regulation. ■ Hand–eye coordination. ■ Creativity. ■ Taste, smell, tactile, visual, awareness of thermic (temperature), proprioceptive (spatial awareness) and vestibular (balance).
Adding teaspoons, tablespoons and measures or sugar cubes.	■ Measure, number, volume, sorting, classification. ■ Dissolve, cause-and-effect. ■ Fine motor skills. ■ Self-regulation, concentration, gratification delay. ■ Tactile, taste, smell, visual, proprioceptive and vestibular.
Providing fruit teabags and a sorting container; sugar cubes or sachets; and measuring spoons for measuring ingredients.	■ Maths, sorting, sequencing, science. ■ Fine motor skills. ■ Mark-making and creativity. ■ Visual, smell, taste, proprioceptive and vestibular.
Providing coffee filter papers.	■ Absorption and capillary action, time, sequences. ■ Visual, tactile.
Providing similar provision but with bottles, flower heads and mixing bowls or pestle and mortars and jugs for perfume-making.	■ Cause-and-effect, science. ■ **Autonomy**, satisfaction. ■ Visual, smell and tactile.
Providing similar provision but bowls or cauldrons, assortment of ingredients and bottles for potion-making.	■ Cause-and-effect, science. ■ **Autonomy**, satisfaction. ■ Visual, smell and tactile.
Water activity with different-sized jugs and funnels for pouring and filling.	■ Cause-and-effect, science. ■ **Autonomy**, satisfaction, calming. ■ Visual, sound, tactile, proprioceptive and kinaesthetic (muscle/joint movement) senses.

Session 2 – Playdough creating

In Chapter 6, the accidental addition of a large bottle of oil and containers of flour transformed involvement and play in a pre-school room (see page 131). As Table 7.5 demonstrates, several simple steps could potentially further broaden appeal and widen learning possibilities:

Table 7.5 Possibilities and playdough making

Possibility-widening actions	*Potential benefits*
Situating the 'home corner' next to the 'playdough station'.	Added value to both areas of provision from incorporating and transferring materials and associations.
Making available extra ingredients and containers.	Changed the emphasis in favour of more open-ended scientific investigations, attracting boys and girls.
Replace predominantly pink and plastic tools with wooden and metal, gender-neutral, alternatives.	Widened appeal, introducing more sensory qualities. Potentially generated a different form of investigation and tool usage, drawing on knowledge funds due to similarity with home.
Provide playdough ingredients in labelled containers.	Increase interest, mastery orientation, self-efficacy, fine and gross motor strength from opening and closing containers. Spark interest and language.
Optimise shelving by arranging resources for children to select themselves, or set up as a science lab, complete with goggles, clipboards and lab coats.	Increase flexibility and legibility. Establish a context for scientific thinking. Increase self-esteem and convey to children adults' trust in their abilities. Develop gross and fine motor skills. Introduce excitement and a sense of theatre to elevate investigations.
Provide other ingredients, such as spices, herbs and natural treasures in containers.	Add further textural, scent and visual interest. Introduce opportunities for exploring change. Positions the children as agents of change. Provides opportunities for creative approaches and customisation.
Offer a range of explorative opportunities at different times, such as playdough, Play-Doh, bread and salt dough.	Provides consistency and continuity, (supporting scientific thinking[7]) as they're all manipulatives, so invites comparison of their smell, colour, texture, malleability, smoothness, stretchiness, stickiness, etc.
Provide a range of containers for collecting natural treasures in and access to an outdoors area rich with natural seedpods, twigs, stones, grass and herbs (that children are permitted to use).	Increased play possibilities from combining 'loose parts' with playdough. Encourages ownership over ingredients and more creative play. Invites writing in context.
Adapt area with the addition of a draped black sheet, to create a witch's den/lair, complete with cauldron and potion bottles for mixing and perhaps torches and UV lighting for exploring light and opacity.	Introduce excitement, awe and wonder. Attract children not normally using this resource.
An adult could sit alongside the children and resources, etc.	Supports inquiry, **relatedness**, children's sense of value. Values area of resource provision by adult's presence.

'Mini cloche' – Big questions

Some practitioners have reflected upon their overuse of 'I wonder' terminology, to the extent that this is becoming as intrusive as the narrowly defined questions they were seeking to avoid! An alternative is the use of broad guiding questions which can help frame investigations and reduce the need for so many adult wonderings. A 'Big' guiding question identifies a general 'conceptual terrain' (Palincsar & Magnusson, 2000). Key to its success is ensuring that this is rooted in children's interests or seeds of inquiry, and **autonomy** is assured by children having ample time for free-flowing investigations of materials.

Drawing upon Chin's research into the use of questions with 5-year-olds, Tunnicliffe urges practitioners to 'utilise free exploring in the learning environment' and be flexible, encouraging children to 'use their existing knowledge, skills and experience in solving problems and meeting challenges' (2015: 9), a sentiment which chimes with 'messing about' and knowledge funds.

'Greenhouse' – Projects and problem spaces

One approach for introducing scientific thinking and encouraging an inquiry focus (essential for later *analysis*) is setting this within a particular 'problem space'. This could be a Big Question as outlined above, a provocation, such as the crime scene described in Table 7.3, or discovering ice in a container outdoors. Examples of guiding questions could be: 'why do some things sink and others float?', 'what changes water into ice?' or 'why are magnets attracted to metal?'. Inquiry then proceeds through cycles of investigation guided by specific questions (e.g. 'What metals are magnets attracted to?') or phenomena (e.g. observing ice melt).

Integral to this approach is envisioning the classroom or early years setting as a 'community of inquiry' (Palincsar & Magnusson, 2000) with children's scientific investigations taking place alongside opportunities for secondary instruction from practitioners and knowledge sources. In such 'a "hybrid" teaching approach, blending adult instruction with play-based, child-led' inquiry (Pascal et al, 2018: 36), the adult supports the child in framing the focus of their inquiry (essentially what distinguishes it from random exploration), by asking the sorts of questions used in the see/think/wonder approach to establish what we want to know. The following project reinforces the value of continuity, offering an approach for increasing practitioner confidence:

> Children were offered compact discs, then soap bubbles and finally water and mirrors on different occasions with torches. These seemingly disparate and unrelated resources all had light as a unifying factor, a focus enjoyed by the children over a five-month period through discovery and joint-learning. By concretising activities and focussing on simple resources, practitioners felt empowered to delimit, tune-in and pare-back daunting topics such as light and density. With a focus on just the fundamental ideas of the topic instead of feeling the need to cover everything, adult-initiated activities provided opportunities for child-led exploration and enrichment. So density was explored using water in three states. As water is a familiar resource to young children they were able to draw upon their own knowledge funds and explore density in an unhurried iterative process of revisiting and extending thinking.
>
> (Elm, 2017)

Arboretum – Science lab or workshop

'Small children are natural scientists, driven by an innate desire to explore, question and understand the way things are' (Goddard, 2018b: 42). As we discovered in Chapter 6, the creation of a science room has been applied with considerable success in Rainbowtrekkers – a German kindergarten. 'Hands-on' workshop environments offer children opportunities to explore, investigate and transform a range of wet and dry materials and follow seeds of inquiry (Skinner et al, 2008: 20). The provision of laboratory coats, clipboards and protective goggles enriches a selection of different-sized containers; measuring cups, spoons, pipettes sieves and magnifying glasses; and assortment of 'ingredients' in labelled jars or containers. Such an approach strongly signals to children the seriousness of their playful explorations. With an adult on-hand to engage with the child's inquiry, this has the potential for sustained shared thinking.

The outdoors 'workshop' – Arboretum

A natural and sensory-rich environment and children's **autonomy** to change and re-purpose resources provide a rich hot-house for authentic inquiries. This landscape doesn't need to be pristine, in fact all the better for resembling the richly affording wastelands of some of our childhood memories! From a puddle to a mound of earth, nature's store cupboard and the elements provide plentiful opportunities for children's enriching material engagements without the need for specialist provision. For five 4-to-5-year-olds, a mound of post-construction earth and a hosepipe became the focus for their physical enquiries. As Ben Kingston-Hughes' account of this spontaneous play episode highlights, these young children experienced and explored flow, not to mention the potentialities of mud!

Mud-sliding

> Initially children were running up and down the mound. Inevitably this led to rolling. They then decided to take the hosepipe, generally available year-round, and made a waterfall by pouring water down the mound. One child climbed the wet mound and promptly slipped on his face. The look of horror soon gave way to enjoyment as the other children started sliding down on their bottoms. After about 10 minutes the children were more mud than child.
>
> The collecting of the hose was initially problematic as it was slightly further away than we would normally unwind it. It requires a degree of strength and coordination to unreel the hose. Four of the children worked together on this task while another stood on top of the mound directing them. She then grabbed the hose and pulled it the remainder of the way, while another child ran back and turned on the tap. Once the mud-sliding was underway, the mound became extremely slippery and the children began to help each other up. Often [they] seemed to deliberately let go or "fall" adding to the fun.
>
> (Ben Kingston-Hughes, 2018)

For these children drawn to the potentialities of mud, physical development was not their focus, yet an abundance of benefits was evident from their rolling, sliding, climbing, physical coordination, balance and cross-lateral movement, not to mention handling the hose. The experience hadn't been planned by an adult, but its learning benefits are clear. Negotiating the difficult terrain, self-esteem is apparent with high levels of wellbeing and engagement etched on their faces. Problem-solving, self-regulation and resilience were essential to manoeuvre the hose (and handle the shock of those bumps), as were social interaction and negotiation. Children's experience of gravity and forces (from the water flow, hose and their own bodies) will also forge memories and assist future inquiries.

A focus on movement and flow

We began this chapter with the assertion that children's free-flowing thinking (cognitively and physically) is incompatible with the glass boxes of curricular-based subjects. We now come full circle with a focus on flow, both in Csikszentmihalyi's sense of deep-level engagement but also how children learn naturally when free to physically engage with materials. We know the value of flexible environments for accommodating changing interests and giving children **autonomy** to use, move and re-purpose resources for further investigations. Those mud-caked children amplify the benefits and appeal of large-scale provisions which facilitate movement and forge a repertoire of physical strengths and skills rather than a narrowly defined focus on fine and gross motor skills. But, as a 'one-size-fits-all' approach is unnecessarily limiting, we end this chapter with some simple ideas for increasing the flow of possibilities, in and outdoors.

If allowed, messy play materials, whether wet, dry or in-between consistencies, naturally lend themselves to a focus on movement and flow. As children follow their instincts and exercise choice over their messy play movements and what to use in conjunction with other provision, they develop their sense of self-efficacy and self-esteem. With little time or investment, environments can be adapted so that they don't just accommodate movement and flow but actively encourage this:

- Remove unnecessary tables and chairs to discover children's desire-lines and broaden their repertoire of movements.
- Encourage different forms and tempos of movement, through exploration of resources, with different parts of the body, at different scales and through clearing up, to evoke different energies.
- Provide opportunities for transforming, diverting and containing water and other flowing media.
- Focus on flow in materials, e.g. paper, paint, clay, driftwood and water as opposed to more fixed resources like wooden blocks; and lifecycles, e.g. gloop.
- Provide a range of different-sized tools and containers (see Chapter 5) to support diverse and repetitive movements.

Given a genuine reason to do so, such as filling bags with sand or gravel to create a barricade, or 4-year-olds pulling their friends out of waist-deep mud, as I witnessed in a Forest School session, 'if the physical environment is attuned authentically to the nature of learning and the unique nature of childhood . . . endless possibilities' occur (Gripton, 2017: 10). We've seen how children are drawn to different gradients, textures and levels to navigate, discover how materials behave and develop gross motor skills. The addition of lengths of guttering and tubes to sand or water add interest and challenge as well as encouraging gross motor skills and strength, a necessary precursor for fine motor development. Even making small changes to resources can introduce flow, novelty and challenge functional fixedness (Brown & Kane, 1989).

> Like the mother who propped a builder's tray on its side so that her toddler could paint and discover the appeal of running paint.
>
> (Sarah Duffield, 2018)

Movement and flow were similarly encouraged both in and outdoors in one Reggio Emilia setting:

> An eclectic mix of floor tiles, wooden blocks, material, ribbon, natural treasures, rope and railway track were invitingly laid out in flowing arcs on the floor. Thoughtfully placed baskets of animals, cars, mosaic pieces and chalk actively encouraged children to move as they interacted with the materials. Not only did the attractive arrangement inspire children's connectivity and flow but it was sufficiently free-flowing to facilitate change too. This same focus on movement and flow was also apparent in the positioning of a huge roll of paper outdoors. Invitingly draped from a height and ripe for scrunching and moving, a circle of small carefully positioned pots of paint on a cable drum, each a slightly different tone of green to the next, beckoned children's use to explore gravity and flow in action.
>
> (Robinson Pre-School, Reggio Emilia)

Reflection

Consider if and how the existing environment and practices influence children's freedom to move.

- Can children freely access outdoors where they can be messier?
- Can they make associations by bringing natural treasures indoors to explore in the water tray, make a meal with, or take utensils, toy diggers and mini people outside for role-play and larger-scale material engagements?
- Does containing mess restrict children's movement and flow?

- Are there opportunities to work on different scales to activate gross and fine motor muscles?

- Can children easily move between resources, a water supply and the outdoors?

Conclusion

In trying to pinpoint specific learning areas, we are in danger of doing what Montessori urged against, 'pinning down the butterfly's wings'. As the examples throughout this book so richly convey, children's meaningful material engagements shouldn't neatly slot into single curriculum areas, but rather weave between and across these. With 'openture' and 'immersion in experience' (Bogost, 2016: 223), material encounters bring opportunities for fascination, wonder, interest and understanding as children's inquiries roam free.

IN THIS CHAPTER WE HAVE:

- Considered the significance of supporting the development of children's executive functions, inquiry skills and flow to facilitate fruitful inquiries and learning.

- Offered a range of levels of inquiry and approaches for increasing possibilities.

Notes

1. Diamond and Lee (2011).
2. Thornton and Brunton (2006).
3. This tea-making vignette was introduced in Chapter 6.
4. Where adults follow, rather than lead children's interests and enjoy joint attention on objects and phenomena, children's learning is enhanced (Bakhurst & Shanker, 2001: 37–38).
5. Learning is more effective when children can explore a chosen science concept using a range of related examples because this enables them to progress from applying their knowledge in familiar contexts to developing more widely applicable ideas (Harlen & Qualter, 2009).
6. Science, Technology, Engineering and Maths.
7. Keeping one element as a constant simulates scientific experiments.

8 Agency and messy play

> This chapter explores the interplay between adult and child, unpicking the myriad of influences which determine the quality and ownership of material engagements. Using Virginia Axline's principles as a cornerstone, an approach is offered for supporting and enriching children's messy play. We are reminded of the importance of children's and adults' need for **Autonomy**, **Relatedness** and **Competence** (**ARC**) (Deci & Ryan, 2000) to be met and the role of resources as agents in children's encounters. With suggestions for getting the delicate balance between adult and child right, minimising stress and increasing children's agency, this chapter ends with a focus on the importance of adults engaging first-hand with messy play!

If our intention is to offer child-led material encounters, it is obviously important to recognise the impact of adults, whether direct and intentional or unconscious and subtle. Like it or not, an adult's view of messy play will impact upon the quality of a child's experience, affecting the:

- Frequency, types and locations of resources and opportunities offered (Chapter 3);

- Stage at which children are involved, e.g. planning for, creating, clearing up and saving (Chapter 5);

- Open-endedness or degree of agency and control afforded to the child (Chapter 6 and 7);

- Child's positive acceptance or rejection and guilt; and

- Child's ability to change resources, re-purpose environments and become masterful agents of their own play.

This was evident in Chapter 6 when we explored five different play scenarios with playdough indoors, discovering just how different the quality and outcomes can be for children, depending upon the degree of adult involvement, the resources provided and the extent to which children felt able to deviate from adult objectives. Throughout this book a plethora of approaches have been suggested for consciously supporting children's material encounters using Deci and Ryan's SDT as a guiding framework (2000). But we will only create that 'arboretum of inquiry', introduced in Chapter 7, if encounters are sustainable and not at the expense of adults' own sense of **ARC**.

Adults or children as agents of play?

'If our methods make the world in particular ways [and] the nature of the attention that we give to things shapes that which we are considering … then the ways that we attend to things matter' (Law, 2004: 1, cited in Kind, 2017: 1). Children's material engagements rarely, if ever, take place without the adults' presence or involvement in some form and it's important for us to recognise this so that we make informed choices. When messy play encounters are honestly and authentically reviewed, 'warts and all', we get to see where the balance of agency and control lies and the extent to which child-led activities and processes really are child-led. The framework provided in Chapter 6 serves as a useful tool for considering the types of actions which increase or limit children's **ARC** as well as those which extend or challenge adults' **ARC**.

The impact of adults' decisions

While the provision of complementary resources doesn't dictate usage (resonating with Dewey), it certainly hints at their possible use. Examples include:

- Utensils and containers near sand – encourage filling, pouring and mixing.
- Collections of unusual eggs and spoons – promote transporting, problem-solving and fine and gross motor skills as children are drawn to trying out different spoon and egg combinations.
- A cauldron and selection of bottles and containers – inspire potion-making.
- Conkers and tubing – spark transporting, social interaction, problem-solving and fine and gross motor skills, as we discovered in Chapter 4.

Watts invites us to consider the resourced environments that we provide and children's interactions with them, looking beneath the surface, at the decisions which have been made to shape these encounters.

> Taking the example of a nearly 2-year-old child (his own son) painting outdoors at an easel, he highlights the multitude of choices involved. Several decisions stemmed from a desire to 'make the experience easier and more enjoyable' for his son, but he also wanted him to 'develop his confidence in using brushes to mix and apply paint' on a large scale so to encourage this he carefully established the environment in such a way as to facilitate these outcomes:
>
> - Carefully sorted two palettes of paint with colours separated – to delay colour mixing.
> - Set up the easel outdoors – inviting mess.
> - Offered the A2 paper portrait rather than landscape – requiring full-stretch movements.
> - Provided two brushes, one large and one small – introducing scale.
> - Chose when to photograph his child's creation – documenting learning.

His son did make decisions about 'composition, mark-making, colour and tone' (Watts, 2011: 41) but each of these choices was influenced by the adult's prior decisions and the physical environment provided. While achieving key deliverables, Watts readily acknowledged that his decisions restricted his son's outcomes, potentially impoverishing his learning.

> **Reflection**
>
> Think about a specific activity you've initiated with a child and write down all the decisions, consciously or sub-consciously involved.
> For each of these consider:
>
> - who was responsible for them?
> - what might have happened if these decisions hadn't been made?

Selecting resources – Watts drew our attention to the myriad of decisions which underpin resource provision and the intentionality behind enhanced provision. From the materials themselves to how and where these are arranged, types of containers or tools offered as accompaniments, and time made available, all these factors and more influence the play and exploration which emerges. As the following attuned practitioner demonstrates, our influence also extends to the environment in which materials are offered:

> I didn't want to limit children's gross motor movements so had removed the chairs. Some of the children collected chairs to sit at the table. The children that stood up were more physically active than those who chose to sit. This included pushing down into the mixtures and stirring at a harder pace.
>
> (Fiona Smith, 2018)

This simple action was a conscious choice not to limit children's opportunities. The children were free (and as importantly, felt able) to get chairs. Some chose to do so, and still others exercised their right to choose not to use them!

Deciding what to document – As we discovered in Chapter 7, even decisions about what and when to document children's processes reflect the adult's judgement and conscious decision-making. 'While we treasure the products of children's work, children themselves are more likely to value the process' (Watts, 2011: 38). In Watt's case he chose to photograph his son's progress before the brown paint 'obliterated' earlier stages! This dilemma was also highlighted by Pacini-Ketchabaw et al (2017) when grappling with the challenge of what, when and how best to document children's learning in a free-flowing, objective-free environment. As children encounter materials, they bring to bear their existing knowledge funds, skills and interests which, if permitted, influence the nature of their engagements.

In deciding what to photograph and document, practitioners also determine what remains unnoticed, undocumented and potentially undervalued, unhelpfully introducing a two-tier valuing of children's inquiries. 'Every encounter with materials involves decisions about what, and in what way, to notice' (Pacini-Ketchabaw, Kind & Kocher, 2017: 81). Every decision about what to photograph or jot down will be informed by the adult's own knowledge funds and lens on learning. 'Right from when the camera is turned on, decisions are made about what to attend to, what view to take, what will matter, and what further understandings the video [or photograph] might generate' (Kind, 2017: 2–3).

So how can we be sure to notice and document children's most important instances of learning or insight, rather than simply our assumptions of these? With fewer interruptions and stress points in the day and an inquiry-based approach, practitioners can engage in attentive noticing, potentially spotting 'lightbulb' moments. But sometimes as Menna Godfrey discovered, we just need to trust children to know that they are doing something with such focus and intent that it must be beneficial – like the boy stood in a puddle in Chapter 7.

Reviewing engagement and outcomes

It's only with attentive noticing, a key ingredient of inquiry, that we discover whether resources are being used as we expected (Hutt et al, 1989). An awareness of this is key to providing for children's unmet needs or considering how resources are offered to broaden or deepen use. Children's engagement is fundamental to planning in the moment with young children. Seen by Ephgrave (2018: 9) as the primary indicator of quality early childhood education and care, engagement indicates the child's sense of wellbeing and readiness to explore and learn.

If Laevers' Wellbeing and Involvement Scales help us monitor and evaluate the suitability or otherwise of the physical environment for children's deeply focussed play and interactions, reflective practice can help us consider the practitioner's role in shaping the emotional environment. By focussing on: 'what we do, how we do it, why we do it that way and whether we should do it that way in the future' (Newstead & Isles-Buck, 2012: 18), we can ensure that children are deeply engaged and have agency over their play and learning. Using the five-point model of Intention, Experience, Actions, Outcome and Development (Newstead & Isles-Buck, 2012: 22), adults can check whether what they hope and believe an area of provision or material engagement will achieve, actually does!

So, for the unfortunate practitioner whose cereal brick creation was destroyed (Chapter 5), no analysis is needed to know that the practitioner's *intentions* were not realised. Reflecting on the *experience* – the children smashed the structure with their hands – no adults were present to model engagement. The *outcome*, although not as envisaged, potentially demonstrated high levels of engagement. As they pounded the cereal bricks experimenting with which parts of the hand make the best demolition tools, they were discovering about cause-and-effect; experiencing embodiment and projection; expressing a trajectory schema; and developing fine and gross motor skills and strength. With the addition of water, it would have been interesting to see if and how children's exploration might have developed into creating something out of the chaos of crumbs. In the *development* stage the practitioner was able to put bruised feelings aside and share what didn't work and why. Exploring the gap between expectations and outcomes enabled her to put the personal disappointment behind her and conclude what needed to happen differently at each of the stages.

Getting the adult/child balance right

A key focus of this book has been on getting the balance right between adult and child agency, actual rather than intended. Practitioners working in the Toy Free Kindergarten in Munich took the bold step to remove all toys and equipment from the setting, after concerns that addictive habits start in the early years (Schubert & Strick, 1996). Practitioners found that the resulting child-led inquiry required new ways of engaging with children founded on attentive trust. Borrowing from Play Therapy, the following eight Axline's principles (1964) helped practitioners provide the support needed for children's play.

1. Warm and friendly relationship
2. Accepting the child as is
3. Establishes feeling of permission
4. Reflect back so child gains insight
5. Child's responsibility to make choices
6. Child leads – adult follows
7. Adult does not hurry
8. Few limitations, anchor to reality

As will become apparent from our tour of these principles, many neatly dovetail with mainstream practice, while others challenge us to view children and our role differently.

Principle 1 – Warm and friendly relationship

Warm and friendly relationships are a pre-requisite in early childcare settings. Thanks to the work of early educationalists, we understand the importance of a foundation of strong attachment, security and wellbeing for children to develop agency and mastery and give them the confidence to explore seeds of inquiry. The materials provided by adults can further enhance the quality of adult/child relationships, as is evident in this therapeutic interaction:

> When invited by a child to put my hands in a tray of cool Gelli I willingly accepted. We played with the Gelli, talking about what it felt like. With both of his hands semi-immersed I asked whether he would like me to bury his hands. He nodded happily. I gently scooped and patted the Gelli until it was mounded-up over his hands, being careful not to touch him. With a good layer now covering his hands I gently pressed down on his fingers and palms, watching him closely for signs as to whether to continue. After several minutes of pressing down, watching the Gelli ooze into the tray then re-covering his hands, I withdrew my hands, so he could explore alone.

> I was surprised when he asked if he could bury my hands, then repeated the pressing down action, giving me a taste of just how relaxing and calming it was.

Principle 2 – Accepting the child as is

Practitioners shape both the physical and emotional environment through the resources, space and time made available and permissiveness. This casts adults in a leading role in ensuring that we have the optimum attitude towards material engagements. Accepting a child's messy play can manifest in a variety of ways, whether supporting a reticent or tactile-defensive child, understanding a child's need to move and explore, welcoming a child's mess or suspending our own expectations. The adult's response is key.

Adult's attitude to and perceptions of mess – The emotional environment that we cultivate through our body language, relationships, modelling and the physical environment we provide signal our unconditional acceptance or disappointment and shame, as this girl with new leather shoes unwittingly discovered.

> I remember the exhilarating feeling as I stepped into the cold slightly slimy water which spilled over the top of my shoes, soaking into my socks ... the peculiar but blissful feeling ... and how indignant I felt [at being] thoroughly ticked off.
> (Crowe, 1983: 30)

And there is the rub because as was reflected in the social media discussions (Chapter 2), messy play materials tend to evoke strong and often extreme reactions, some of which can be involuntary or spontaneous, and children are expert readers of even subtle mismatches between our body language and words. With many children and adults negatively associating mess with 'being naughty', the ability to be messy in front of another person is highly significant and founded on safe and trusting relationships. Adults have a huge responsibility as their response can determine whether they reinforce shame, negativity and rejection (remember Erikson's stages in Chapter 2), or conversely, the child experiences complete acceptance.

Of course, this applies to everything that we do with children, not just material engagements, but it is particularly relevant to messy play as i) adult and child views and experiences are potentially polar opposites, and ii) adults' **autonomy** and control are likely to be more bounded than other areas of provision. This can unhelpfully position adults' and children's **autonomy** as oppositional, like the negative influences in Bronfenbrenner's systems.

Active exploration – We know that children intuitively learn in a whole-bodied way and yet in the Western world, young children are 'mainly authorised to use sight ... to explore the world' (Irigaray, 2017: 19). Cries of 'Do not touch!' introduce a disconnect between what some adults might expect or want (whether motivated by concerns over safety, lack of time or an adult's lens on children's actions), and what children intuitively need and are hard-wired to do. For very young children, acceptance involves understanding their need to be constantly on the move, touching things and discovering the world with all their senses. This is an important process not to be rushed (see the seventh principle).

While an adult may choose to distance themselves from the sensory experience of paint by using a paintbrush (or looking instead of touching), children need to physically engage with it to try to understand the wet silky-smooth paint. Expecting a child to only touch an invitingly sticky medium with the tip of one finger, or better-still none, is unrealistic and setting children up to fail. Yet many home-based art and craft activities do take place within such a bubble of constraint.

Embodied sensory engagement – As practitioners, we may be working with children who are experiencing trauma and may not therefore be ready to learn. For these children judgement-free sensory provision can literally change their world.

> One 7-year-old boy's immersion in sensory resources like sand, dried rice and shredded paper physically and emotionally prepared him for engaging in formal learning.

Inclusion – Conversely, for a child who is resistant to touching messy resources due to sensory or emotionally learnt behaviour, they may need gentle support, recognition of their concerns and opportunities to become involved through intermediary resources such as utensils and tools, ziplock bags, water or orbies in a plastic glove or clingfilm over paint.

Reflection

It's important to consider where on Jenning's EPR stages (1990, 2011, Chapter 2) the child is, irrespective of their age, to consciously decide whether tools should be made available as an interface with the messy materials, or if the child will benefit more from using their body instead.

Sometimes children may be reticent to touch a material because it is out of their comfort zone, they're unsure of what it will feel like or are simply not in the mood. It is important to accept and respect this, as was the case in this baby room:

A 19-month-old child was reticent to engage with a tempting provocation of swirled paint covered by a layer of clingfilm. Knelt next to the clingfilm with the child sat on her lap, the attuned practitioner provided comforting reassurance, an unfazed, unhurried manner and an acceptance of the child as is, all that was needed to boost their confidence to tentatively explore the paint with their toes.

In Chapter 3 we discovered how adults' perceptions of mess may be shaped not just by the actual spread of mess (Hastings, 2012) but a range of changeable and at times personal factors. Recognising these can be key to accepting a child's mess without introducing shame.

> **Reflection**
>
> Think back to a childhood memory when your 'mess' was greeted with negativity or a time when you wish you'd responded differently to a child's mess. Can you think of how a different reaction to a child's process or mess might have conveyed a more positive view of self?

Principle 3 – Establishes feeling of permission

The emotional environment – Adults are central to a child's feeling of permission to make mess. It was clear from Ben Kingston-Hughes' account of mud-sliding (in Chapter 1) that acceptance of getting muddy was conveyed through modelling with his own sliding! For the 4-year-old's spontaneous encounter with mud following a fortuitous accident (Chapter 7), key to sustaining this was the adult 'not giving instructions but giving appropriate resources and tacit permission for these experiences to continue' (Kingston-Hughes, 2018).

As I discovered, despite our best intentions, such acceptance is not always easy:

> As a Play Therapy client explored mess, I became uncomfortable with the amount of paint being used. With school budgets stretched, creating a culture of permission and supporting their messy play explorations in an authentic and accepting way was proving challenging. I discovered the importance of setting limits and offering smaller containers of paint to contain the child, both practices as relevant to a mainstream environment.

The physical environment – The resources made available and choice of environment in which to engage sends powerful signals of an adult's expectations, permission or otherwise.

> Take the example of Lego presented in a beautifully designed circular container in a Denmark nursery. With each colour arranged in a different segment, this probably looked very appealing, but unhelpfully conveyed adult's expectations that the Lego colours should not be mixed, resulting in the area being under used! (Skreland, 2014).

When supporting children's material engagements, we might not always get it right but what is important is that we recognise that play with materials is influenced by the relationship between them, the adult and child.

> When attending an arts workshop with my children I found myself drawn to a 9-month-old's unfolding encounter with paint. With his twin unsettled, he sat happily on his mum's lap evidently enjoying not just the colour and feel of the paint but his firm possession of a long-handled paintbrush too! His relaxed mum gave him space and permission to explore the paint and brush. Attuned to his needs she noted his intent on holding the brush (which was quickly becoming weaponised) and sensitively substituted this with a shorter brush without compromising his **autonomy**.
>
> I sensed from his partial absorption (and now fractious twin) that his focus may be short-lived, so, with his mum's permission, I squirted pools of different-coloured paint into an A3 sealable bag and laid it out flat for them to explore together. He moved his fingers back and forth clearly surprised by the fact that he was spreading the paint but his hands were not wet! At times I sensed a flicker of frustration at this barrier to the paint (although the paint, brush and paper were still within reach). I also noticed synchronicity between mother and child as she sensitively mirrored his pushing of the paint in the bag by rhythmically moving her fingers so that the colours began to mix, swirl and merge. The infant seemed calm and relaxed as he stretched out his arms to move the paint, watching the paint spread and move. At times he dipped his head gazing elsewhere while continuing to feel the bag with his fingers.

Reflecting upon my intervention, I am unsure whether this was well judged, extending this baby's explorations, or a frustrating barrier to more fulfilling sensory play. Recognising the impact of our actions, particularly on infants, is fundamental to offering children true **autonomy** with materials and establishing a feeling of permission.

Principle 4 – Reflects back so child gains an insight

In recent years there has been a shift from practitioners asking open or closed questions, to using noticing and wondering comments (a cornerstone of inquiry). Many practitioners have shared their concern that these also are in danger of becoming overworked, sounding staged rather than 'in the moment'. This is especially true of messy engagements which have so much potential for noticing and wonderment! Borrowing from the world of Play Therapy, sometimes it is enough to simply reflect or repeat **some** of a child's words, naturally not robotically of course. This is because hearing our own words and thoughts said by another can increase personal insight and boost self-esteem.

> While using Gelli in a therapeutic session, one child shared how much they hated the sticky substance. They tried to avoid touching it but were compelled to experiment with what happened when things were dropped in it (some sank and others unexpectedly floated). Retrieving the items and uttering 'yuck' when their hands were covered in the sticky residue, they wiped them clean before repeating the process again. A combination of approaches helped support this child's difficult engagement with materials, including reflecting back, noticing and wondering, with some open and closed questions and silent observations.

For the young child on the beach in Chapter 1, their realisation of the uncomfortable feeling of sand in their shoes could have been sensitively acknowledged, supporting their growing insight. A good starting point is always valuing and acknowledging the child (or indeed adult's) concerns. A playful yet empathetic 'You don't like the feel of the scratchy sand?' or 'Yes that scratchy sand doesn't feel nice' can work wonders as simply acknowledging and reflecting this back can help a child feel listened to and regulate their emotions. With the problem restated there is an opportunity to distract from the negative (e.g. 'Let's see who can get to the beach hut quickest to take their shoes off') or positively suggest actions to support their management of the situation, (such as 'Do you want to take your shoes off so they don't scratch?' or 'Let's put our stuff down so that you can take your shoes off'). This mindful approach validates a child's feeling of distress and supports them in managing a resolution to the situation, leaving them feeling empowered and in control. The three dimensions of Deci and Ryan's SDT (2000) are evident as the child experiences a sense of **ARC** (with no negative impact upon the adult), and the resulting material engagement and adult/child **relatedness** are supported and enriched.

Principle 5 – Child's responsibility to make choices

Giving children responsibility to make choices sounds in keeping with child-led practice, but honest reflection may reveal that this is not always the case. As Watts (2011) highlighted, sometimes without even realising it, we may consciously or inadvertently limit children's potential for making choices. Of course, this may be important for safety reasons, although lots of evidence points to children's ability to carry out risk assessments, if empowered and enabled to do so.

Reflection

Consider your practice to see whether the child …

- Would have played for longer if their investigations hadn't been interrupted by a timetabled activity?

- Would have returned to their investigations if these hadn't been discarded or cleared away?
- Might have discovered a phenomenon in the indoor sand tray and immediately tried it out on a larger scale outdoors, if access had allowed this?
- Would have mixed and served up gloop for 'dinner' in the home corner, if this wasn't 'off limits'?
- Might have persevered with touching a substance that they didn't like, had they been able to wash their hands or had tools or gloves provided?
- Might have stayed outside longer to watch ice melting in a puddle, or powder paint spreading on the rain-spattered ground, had the system offered free flow rather than organising as a group?
- Would have developed knowledge and agency from exploring the transformational qualities of resources like cornflour, had they been involved in preparing resources?
- May have received a calming sensory workout and mastery orientation as they created their own playdough, coloured and scented to their own specifications?
- Could have benefited from divergent thinking rather than functional fixedness?

Principle 6 – Child leads – adult follows

Although this lies at the heart of planning in the moment, honest reflection can reveal surprising results. Notwithstanding their intention to support children's discoveries, an experienced practitioner discovered that 'in our efforts to teach we were often eroding children's opportunity to learn' (Buckler, 2013). This was happening in subtle ways as instead of letting children make their own links from what they were seeing, practitioners were unwittingly 'stealing the thinking from the learner' (Buckler, 2013). By noticing and changing adult/child interactions (the emotional environment) and planning physical environments which support a consolidation of thinking and learning, as children revisit and reinvent their creations, practitioners found they were better able to scaffold (Vygotsky) children's thinking. To flexibly scaffold children's unhurried move from 'hmm' to 'aha' moments (Gopnik, 2000), the rigid bolted-together structures of Western scaffolding are inappropriate. Instead, practitioners need to draw inspiration from the seemingly organic bamboo structures of Asia, which provide only as much support as is needed. This is a key priority for practitioners and closely linked to Axline's seventh principle.

Principle 7 – Adult does not hurry

Time – We have already witnessed the positive effect of an attuned practitioner not rushing an infant's interaction with paint (on page 185). With many children's lives over-scheduled and potentially stressed, the value of space, time and permission not to rush can contribute significantly to children's sense of wellbeing and readiness to learn. Kaplin and Kaplin elucidated the benefits to the brain of children becoming absorbed in environments and resources which fascinate, give opportunities for 'being away', and whose compatibility with the child's interests and emotions enable immersion and absorption (1989). If allowed, messy play resources can calm and captivate, supporting deep engagement and flow (Csikszentmihalyi, 2008).

Patience – Once children are absorbed in material engagements a sense of timelessness often pervades, which can bring them into conflict with adults wanting to speed up or truncate processes to suit timetables. Sometimes practitioners and parents can feel pressured to move children onto the next milestone rather than affording children more opportunities to explore and understand more of the same. At other times we can inadvertently steal a child's 'aha' moment or fail to spot the wonder of discovering something for the first time. Hawkins (1974) emphasised the importance of children having ample time for 'messing about' with materials and for adults not to rush to link their discoveries or try to move them on.

Interestingly, in several material engagements it was the adult and not the child that wanted to introduce new paint colours, materials or water to children's engagements! It's important to be aware of whose need we are satisfying by introducing actions, resources and change.

> ### Reflection
>
> Next time you start to wonder if you need to supplement or change provision, consider what the Leuven Scales tell you about children's experience of the resource to see if changes are really needed?

Stress – If we're conscious of the need to work at a pace, then even the most pleasurable activity can quickly become a chore. The timescale shifts our focus from being in the now of sensory beings, to the pressures of planning for the next stage, making for a much less satisfying experience all round. Factor in the contribution of heightened stress levels in the child's home, and children's inability to focus on learning can be the net result. With the stresses of tidying up identified as one of the biggest barriers to messy play (Gascoyne, 2018a), it's important to take steps (like those outlined in Chapter 5 and 6) to minimise stress wherever possible.

Interruptions – 'Even with good wellbeing and a superb environment, one of the main aspects of practice that causes stress and tension is the timetable and. . . interruptions' (Ephgrave, 2018: 25). For adults to sensitively support children's material engagements, they really need to understand, through first-hand experience, just how absorbing it is to draw a finger through gloop or try to squeeze it into a solid ball before it tumbles free as a liquid, or the capillary action of paint working its way across a pane of ice, or the rainbow projected onto a puddle. Until we re-live mesmerising moments like these it is difficult for even the most sensitive and attuned adult to appreciate the importance of going slow, or what Jan White terms 'slowliness' (2014: 6). Csikszentmihalyi (2008) highlighted the importance of flow in play and exploration, but if we keep interrupting and rushing children we are training them to not focus on anything for sustained periods of time. Conversely, if we plan for children's need to explore, focus and move about, by minimising unnecessary interventions, then we (and children) are rewarded with high levels of engagement and wellbeing, and an associated reduction in behavioural problems.

> ### Reflection
>
> Cast your mind back to the activity on page 44. How did you feel when the process of 'getting to know the resource' was interrupted? How many times can you be interrupted without losing your flow?

Facilitating deep-level engagement – When urging practitioners to give plentiful time to children's engagements Di Chilvers used the evocative term 'wallowing'. Given our focus on messy materials it would be remiss not to dwell on its meaning as 'an act of wallowing' or 'depression containing mud or shallow water'. With the verb 'to wallow in' associated with 'a person indulg[ing] in an unrestrained way in (something that one finds pleasurable)' or '(chiefly of large mammals) roll[ing] about or [laying] in mud or water' (Oxford English Dictionary, accessed 15 February 2018), the parallels with children's material encounters are evident. With few focussed activities to timetable, practitioners are free to observe and play alongside children, optimising teachable moments whose real context and child-initiated inquiry make them far more productive than unconnected curricular activities unrooted from a meaningful context.

Deciding whether to intervene – Having noticed a potential teachable moment, how do we decide what to do? An 8-month-old:

> starts spooning sand using the teaspoon. She puts the handle end in her mouth and discovers that the sand is stuck to the wet part of the spoon and continues spooning sand and putting the handle end in her mouth.
>
> (Gascoyne, 2012: 91)
>
> Observing this child's discovery, the practitioner subtly placed a selection of brushes within reach of the child. She momentarily glanced at these before resuming her exploration with the teaspoon.

Noticing a potential opportunity for extending this child's repertoire of interactions, the attuned practitioner's subtle actions gave this child **autonomy** over her play. To intervene verbally would have irrevocably burst the bubble of the moment, artificially truncating the child's focus, which as it turns out was on the 'sticking' sand rather than exploration with tools. Noticing this interest, the practitioner could provide water or moist sand in a future play episode for her to explore, if she wished.

Principle 8 – Few limitations, anchor to reality

Minimising timetabled interruptions – As suggested already, the removal of artificial breaks (or shifting these to the beginning or end of the day) affords several benefits for messy play. With stresses minimised, staff are better able to provide a positive emotional environment; children can engage for longer and more deeply; and behaviour generally improves, freeing practitioners up to play and interact with the children instead of managing behaviour. Borrowing from Wolfgang and Glickman's (1986) power continuum of teacher action, this moves away from the rules and consequences of maximum teaching power (Sahin-Sak et al, 2016), to an environment founded on listening and quality relationships, conducive to maximising teachable moments that come from children's curiosity. By planning in the moment practitioners are free to trust children to be able to find what interests them and share sustained moments of genuine learning, vested in and driven by children's interests.

This is not to denigrate 'coming together occasions [whose significance is amplified] as times for sharing, reflection and interaction about what children have discovered or drawing upon their knowledge funds from home experiences' (Ephgrave, 2018: 25). Put simply, a day with fewer interruptions and a more flexible, yet still contained structure, is better suited to children developing flow.

Structure, limits and responsibility – Structure and limits are vitally important for children's and adults' sense of safety and containment, especially if we want to avoid increasing children's **ARC** at the expense of adults' (Deci & Ryan, 2000). Montessorian practice instils responsibility for children's own actions by giving them the tools, instruction and trust that they are competent. In mainstream settings too, children can be empowered to take responsibility for their actions and mess, a process which, as we discovered in Chapter 5, delivers valuable learning opportunities, increased resilience and mastery orientation, mindfulness and self-regulation.

With changes to how the day is planned, practitioners can provide the necessary containment and stability of structure without endless disparate activities and interruptions. With fewer limitations and pinch points to contend with, no restrictive timescales on clearing up materials, and confidence in as few restrictions as needed, many of the stresses of messy play can be instantly eliminated, freeing adults to enjoy the experience. While structure and limits are essential, flexibility is also needed. As Godfrey's reflection on the challenges of dressing for mud play demonstrate, given that each child, moment and encounter are unique, hard-and-fast rules are inappropriate. 'Consistency' [is paramount] as are the weather conditions and the consent of the child to be involved in the activity' (2018).

Adult expectations – Our expectations for an activity, material, space or child are inextricably related to the limits that we impose. For the practitioner who invested so heavily in the creation of a cereal city, it would have been difficult for her to accept the children's reactions without a glimmer of frustration. Even where we haven't invested considerable time or expense in establishing experiences, we are not immune from a certain disappointment when this feels 'sabotaged!'

> While washing-up some resources my son discovered how liquid tends to flow in circles[1] and that when different-coloured paints converge, they mix in swirling patterns to create a new colour. Using a turkey baster and powder paint in some conveniently shaped plastic packaging, he experimented with moving overflowing liquid from one compartment to another. It was fascinating to watch his self-set exploration of water and the affordance of paint, waste packaging and clearing up! I decided to share this vignette with training practitioners, keen to highlight the sense of awe and wonder of self-led discoveries and reinforce that costly resources are not necessary for sustained shared thinking. A small group of practitioners gathered round trying to recreate the effect as I explained my son's experience. Their focus was abruptly interrupted when a practitioner joined the group and immediately started adding pipettes of different-coloured paint to each compartment.

Although an interesting effect was created, it was not our shared focus, serving as a reminder that we do not necessarily view the same resources through the same opportunity lens! Instead, we bring with us our own interests, knowledge and objectives, which will shape how we respond to moments. Similarly, a disconnect can occur between the adult's and child's vision or priorities, like when an adult sees a puddle as an opportunity to look at reflections or symmetry, and a child wants to see what happens when they toss a stone or poke a finger or toe in the puddle!

We discovered in Chapter 3 and 4 just how wide-ranging the affordances of materials are when married with children's own unique interests and needs. Situations like these remind us how frustrating it can be when someone redirects our attention, imposes their own agenda, or holds a different value set. It's also worth considering the potential for ill-judged interruptions of 'what colour', or 'how many', to detract from children's infinitely richer focus on their seed of inquiry.

Coping with discomfort – Relationships are key in supporting children's transition towards Vygotsky's ZPD (Goldstein, 1999: 651), which makes it essential for adults' experience of discomfort to be sensitively managed if it is to avoid constraining experiences. What is interesting about Godfrey's experience of limiting paint and the inquiry-based approach of the *Encounters with Materials* project (Pacini-Ketchabaw, Kind & Kocher, 2017) was the discomfort of being in unchartered territory. As adults didn't know where inquiry was going, they needed to sit with the 'chaos and controversy inherent in the adults' interpretation of play and its value' (Bruce 1991, cited in Woods, 2017a: 2) and trust in children and the process.

Materials as agents – Pacini-Ketchabaw, Kind and Kocher's documentation of children's material encounters suggest we position materials as equals in shaping children's (and adults') explorations, a conclusion supported by resource use in a therapeutic context (Gascoyne, 2016). If we view materials as agents, influencing and inspiring children's (and adults') material engagements, then not necessarily all the structure and boundaries fall to adults to provide, as often resources themselves set limits. Materials can influence what to play with, how, when and why. When added to children's and adults' influence, this creates a complex inter-weaving of 'intra-actions' (Pacini-Ketchabaw, Kind & Kocher, 2017).

Ongoing investigations – As well as minimising tidying up and enabling children to enjoy the lifecycle of messy play interactions introduced in Chapter 5, establishing areas for ongoing investigation can bear fruitful thinking. By giving ourselves the luxury of time to consider children's process and creations, we can also spot learning milestones, areas for future support and extension, and resources or provocations that might otherwise be missed in our rush to tidy up. This doesn't need to be elaborate. The removal of unnecessary tables, re-purposing of a cupboard or under-used space, and introduction of creative storage like attaching metal shopping baskets to a wall, can create a mini science lab, workshop or studio for storing children's ongoing work in a freely accessible and visible way.

Familiarity breeds ... competence – The practitioner's and child's lens on messy play determine how fluid or tightly reigned activities might feel or need to be, to provide **ARC** (Deci & Ryan, 2000) for both adult and child, but familiarity also plays a part:

> When reflecting upon the five 4-to-5-year olds' engagement with their accidental mud-slide, Kingston-Hughes (2018) was surprised by 'the lack of tears! I firmly believe that if we had introduced this to a setting where this kind of outdoor experience was not commonplace the children would have reacted completely differently. I think the same can be said of all messy play that the more commonplace it is for young children to experience this type of play the more they respond to it and take it to new levels'.

Children's familiarity with mud potentially increased their resilience and ability to face challenges, not to mention discomfort, and the same is potentially true of adults' messy play journey:

When I first started I hated messy play as I found it too much to clean up. However, as time went on I learnt ways to deal with these worries ... and so I feel more accepting of mess and I feel the clients can sense this.

(Survey respondent, Gascoyne, 2015)

If we can support practitioners and parents who are not natural advocates of messy play to access, become familiar with, and enjoy successes using the framework offered in Chapter 6, their confidence and mindset can be transformed:

> after a paint splatting session recently, I felt excited and fired-up, rather than worried about the mess.
>
> (Survey respondent, Gascoyne, 2015)

Being able to tap into our own experiences of clay, mud, sand or gloop makes us much better placed to plan and respond effectively to children's investigations, as well as valuing and appreciating their awe and wonder. On a messy play training day that I ran:

> One practitioner couldn't resist a mountain of multi-coloured torn-up tissue paper, choosing to lay on the floor amidst the mound. As the other adults gently cocooned her in the delicate paper, she experienced **relatedness**, safe touch and nurture, gaining a new perspective on material engagements.

Reflection

Try if you can to experience the calming and liberating sense of embodiment that only comes from large-scale material engagements like this. Put aside your inner critic telling you 'grow up!', 'adults don't behave like this' and 'don't make a mess!' and enjoy the cocooning sensation of large-scale play with materials.

Insights such as these help us better understand children's urges and needs and equip us to plan for the myriad of potential experiences that, depending upon their scale and degree of containment, materials can provide.

Getting the adult/child balance right

Quality and sustainable material engagements depend upon delivering **autonomy**, **relatedness** and **competence** for both adults and children. Drawing upon Axline's principles, the interplay between adult and child can be strengthened in pursuit of a 'culture of encouragement' (Bayley & Broadbent, 2008) and possibilities – pre-requisites for satisfying child-led material inquiries.

IN THIS CHAPTER WE HAVE:

- Explored the plethora of decisions involved in shaping the agency, control and quality of material encounters.
- Considered the value of Axline's principles in supporting messy play.
- Introduced the pre-requisites for achieving an adult/child balance.
- Unpicked adults' attitude to and perceptions of mess.
- Emphasised the importance of practitioners engaging in first-hand experiences.

Note

1   Water particles move in a circular path because of the energy from kinetic movement.

9 Misadventure or mess adventures?

Messy play is 'the kind of play that is self-chosen, experimental, often uncontained and full of sensory feedback that helps us to understand how we fit into the physical world around us' (Chown, 2010: 66).

> When training as a Play Therapist I was given the opportunity to experience sand on a huge scale, no mean feat for adults. A tarpaulin was spread over a carpeted hotel floor with a pile of sand spanning a couple of metres in diameter and half a metre high. The minute I saw it I knew exactly what I wanted, indeed needed to do. But being an adult, I first gained permission before lying prone and carving out an angel in the sand with my arms! I was quickly joined by a peer and could easily have lingered, had it not been for the adults waiting.

Finding time for our own material engagements is key to supporting children's. It reminds us what it's like to experience the world as a sensory being and encounter, perhaps for the first time, the sheer joy, fascination and wonder of such self-set material engagements. Equipped with this insight we can understand the significance and thrill of many sensory experiences and better support and respect children's absorption and compulsion to continue exploring, when we might otherwise deem an activity to have come to an end!

With Deci and Ryan's Self-Determination Theory (2000) to hand as an essential travel companion, this book has plotted a course through the intricacies of understanding, choosing, planning and facilitating an enriching balance between adult and child-led messy play. Equipped with practical tools for minimising stress, ideas for improving our **relatedness** to children and materials, and a spotlight on the plethora of decisions shaping children's messy play, we can take up the mantle of 'planning for endless possibilities' (Gripton, 2017: 10). While the child takes centre stage in orchestrating their own inquiries, the adult's role is central in carefully providing for, noticing and valuing children's whole-bodied messy play.

When practitioners and parents join children in their investigations we send a powerful signal to children that such material engagements are not just child's play but the serious work of budding scientists, engineers, architects, adventurers or pedagogues, perhaps. The case for child-led material encounters is clear. As we reach the end of our messy play journey, I urge you to begin your own adventure across the full breadth and depth of material encounters. With time to linger, I wonder, will you choose to dip your toe in, or jump in with abandon?

References

Books

Athey, C., 2007. *Extending Thought in Young Children: A Parent-Teacher Partnership.* London. PCP.
Axline, V. M. (1964) *Dibs: In Search of Self.* New York: Ballatine.
Bakhurst, D., & Shanker, S. G., 2001. *Jerome Bruner – Language, Culture, Self.* London: Sage Publications.
Baldwin, J. M., 1894. *Mental Development of the Child and the Race.* New York: Macmillan, p. 23.
Baldwin, J. M., 1906. Thought and Things: A Study of the Meaning of Thought (Vol. 1). Swan Sonnenschein & Co., Ltd, p. 88. In Russell, J. 1996. *Agency: Its Role in Mental Development.* Hove: Erlbaum (UK) Taylor & Francis Ltd, p. 172.
Beckerleg, T., 2009. *Fun with Messy Play: Ideas and Activities for Children with Special Needs.* London: Jessica Kingsley Pub.
Bettelheim, B., 1977. *The Uses of Enchantment – The Meaning and Importance of Fairy Tales.* New York: Vintage Books.
Bodrova, E., & Leong, D., 2017. The Vygotskian and post-Vygotskian approach: Focussing on "the future child". In L. E. Cohen & S. Waite-Stupiansky (Eds.), *Theories of Early Childhood Education: Developmental, Behaviorist, and Critical.* New York. Routledge, pp 58–70.
Bogost, I., 2016. *Play Anything: The Pleasure of Limits, the Uses of Boredom, and the Secret of Games.* New York: Basic Books.
Brookfield, S., 1993. Through the lens of learning: How the visceral experience of learning reframes teaching. In D. Boud, R. Cohen, & D. Walker (Eds.), *Using Experience for Learning.* Buckingham: Open University Press, pp.21–33.
Case, C., 1990. Reflections and shadows: An exploration of the world of the rejected girl. In Case, C., & Dalley, T. (Eds.), *Working with Children in Art Therapy.* London: Routledge, pp. 131–161.
Citro, A., 2015. *The Curious Kid's Science Book: 100+ Creative Hands-On Activities for Ages 4–8.* Woodinville, WA: The Innovation Press.
Cobb, E., 1977. *The Ecology of Imagination in Childhood.* London: Routledge.
Cohen, A., & Garner, N., 1967. *Readings in the History of Educational Thought.* London: University of London Press Ltd.
Cohen, L. E, & Waite-Stupiansky, S., 2017. *Theories of Early Childhood Education: Developmental, Behaviorist, and Critical.* New York: Routledge.
Crowe, B., 1983. *Play is a Feeling.* Hemel Hempstead: Unwin.
Cunningham, D. D., & Breault, D. A. (2017). Educative experiences in early childhood: Lessons from Dewey. In L. Cohen & S. Waite Stupiansky (Eds.), *Developmental to Critical Theories of Early Childhood Education.* New York: Long Island Press, pp 149–164.
Craft, A., 2002. *Creativity and Early Years Education.* London: Continuum.

Dalley, T. (Ed.), 1984. *Art as Therapy: An Introduction to the Use of Art as a Therapeutic Technique.* London: Routledge.

Dalley, T., 2008. 'I wonder if I exist?': A multi-family approach to the treatment of anorexia in adolescence. In Case, C. & Dalley, T. (Eds.), *Art Therapy with Children: From Infancy to Adolescence.* London: Routledge, pp. 215-231.

Dewey, J. 1966. *Democracy and Education: An Introduction to the Philosophy of Education.* New York: Free Press.

Dewey, J., 1968. *The Child and the Curriculum and the School and Society.* Chicago. IL: The University of Chicago Press.

Dixon, P., 2005. *Let Me Be: I Am a Child – a Book for Parents and Teachers.* 1st ed. United Kingdom: Peche Luna Publishers.

Donaldson, J., 2010. *Cave Baby.* London: Macmillan Children's Books.

Ephgrave, A., 2018. *Planning in the Moment with Young Children: A Practical Guide for Early Years Practitioners and Parents.* Oxon: Routledge.

Featherstone, S., 2016. *50 Fantastic Ideas for Messy Play.* London: Featherstone Education.

Fraser, S., & Gestwicki, C. 2002. *Authentic Childhood: Exploring Reggio Emilia in the Classroom.* Albany, NY: Delmar – Thomson Learning, p. 113.

Gascoyne, S., 2012. *Treasure Baskets and Beyond.* Maidenhead: Open University Press.

Gelb, M. J., 1995. *Thinking for a Change.* London: Harmony Books.

Gettman, D., 1987. *Basic Montessori: A Manual to the Teaching Methods and Theory.* Bromley: Christopher Helm Publishers Ltd.

Gibson, J. J. 1979. *The Ecological Approach to Visual Perception.* Mahwah, NJ: Lawrence Erlbaum Associates.

Goldschmied, E., & Jackson, S.,1994. *People Under Three.* London: Routledge.

Gopnik, A., 2000. 'Explanation as orgasm and the drive for causal understanding: The evolution, function and phenomenology of the theory-formation system'. In F. Keil & R. Wilson (Eds.), *Cognition and Explanation.* Cambridge, MA: MIT Press, pp. 299–323.

Goswami, U., 2004. *Blackwell Handbook of Childhood Cognitive Development.* Malden, MA: Blackwell Publishing.

Grace, J., 2018. *Sensory-Being for Sensory Beings: Creating Entrancing Sensory Experiences.* Oxon: Routledge.

Grossmann, K., Grossmann, K. E., Kindler, H., & Zimmermann, P. 2008. A wider view of attachment and exploration: The influence of mothers and fathers on the development of psychological security from infancy to young adulthood. In J. Cassidy & P. R. Shaver (Eds.), *Handbook of attachment: Theory, research, and clinical applications* (2nd ed.). New York: Guilford, pp. 348–365.

Hall, N., 1992. *The New Scientist Gide to Chaos.* London: Penguin Books.

Harlen, W., & Qualter, A., 2009. *The Teaching of Science in Primary Schools.* (5th ed.). Abingdon, Oxon: David Fulton Publishers.

Hawkins, D., 1974. Messing about in science (1965). In *The Informed Vision: Some Essays on Learning and Human Nature*, 1. New York: Agathon Press, pp. 1–6.

Hodgman, L., 2011. *Enabling Environments in the Early Years.* London. MA Education.

Higashida, N., 2014. *The Reason I Jump: One Boy's Voice from the Silence of Autism.* London: Sceptre.

Holzman, L., 2009. *Vygotsky at Work and Play.* New York: Routledge.

Howard, J., & McInnes, K., 2013. *The Essence of Play: A Practice Companion for Professionals Working with Children and Young People.* Oxon: Routledge.

Hutt, S. J., Tyler, S., Hutt, C., & Christopherson, H., 1989. *Play, Exploration, and Learning: A Natural History of the Pre-School.* London: Routledge.

Irigaray, L., 2017. *To Be Born: Genesis of a New Human Being.* Cham, Switzerland: Palgrave Macmillan.

James, O'D. O., 1997. *Play Therapy: A Comprehensive Guide.* Northvale, NJ: Jason Aronson Inc.

Jeffs, T., & Ord, J., 2018. *Rethinking Outdoor, Experiential and Informal Education.* Oxon: Routledge.

Jennings, S., 1990. *Dramatherapy with Families, Groups and Individuals.* London: Jessica Kingsley.

Jennings, S. 2011. *Healthy Attachments and Neuro-Dramatic-Play.* London: Jessica Kingsley.

Jennings, S., 2014. Applying an Embodiment-Projection-Role framework in groupwork with children. In Prendiville, E., & Howard, J. (Eds.), *Play Therapy Today.* Abingdon, Oxon: Routledge, pp. 81–96.

Jones, L. A., & Lederman, S. J., 2006. *Human Hand Function.* 1st ed. New York: Oxford University Press.

Jung, C., 1959. *The Collected Works*. Vol. 9, Part 1. London: Routledge.

Kaplin, S., & Kaplin, R., 1989. *The Experience of Nature – A Psychological Perspective*. New York: Cambridge University Press.

Kelly, L., & Stead, D., 2015. *Inspiring Science in the Early Years: Exploring Good Practice (UK Higher Education OUP Humanities & Social Sciences Education)*. Maidenhead: Open University Press.

Kiese-Himmel, C., 2008. Haptic perception in infancy and first acquisition of object words: Developmental and clinical approach. In M. Grunwald (Ed.), *Human Haptic Perception*, Basel: Birkhäuser, pp. 321–333.

Kuhn, D., 2004. What is scientific thinking, and how does it develop? In U. Goswami (Ed.), *Blackwell Handbook of Childhood Cognitive Development*. Malden: Blackwell Publishing, pp. 371–393.

Landreth, G. L., 2012. *Play Therapy: The Art of the Relationship*. Hove: Routledge.

Laevers, F., 1994. (Ed.) *The Leuven Involvement Scale for Young Children LIS-YC Manual*. Leuven, Belgium: Centre for Experiential Education.

Laevers, F., & Declercq, B. (Eds.), 1997. *A Process-Oriented Monitoring System for the Early Years*, revised edition. CEGO Publishers.

Law, J., 2004. *After Method: Mess in Social Science Research*. New York: Routledge.

McMahon, L., 2012. *The Handbook of Play Therapy and Therapeutic Play*. Hove: Routledge.

Mooney, C. G., 2000. *Theories of Childhood*. St Paul, MN: Redleaf Press.

Morris, K., 2015. *Promoting Positive Behaviour in the Early Years*. Maidenhead: Open University Press.

Newstead, S., & Isles-Buck, E., 2012. *Essential Skills for Managers of Child-Centred Settings*. 2nd ed. Oxon: David Fulton.

Norman, D.A., 1988. *The Design of Everyday Things*. New York: Basic Books.

Oaklander, V. 1978. *Windows to our Children*. Moab, Utah: Real People Press.

Pacini-Ketchabaw, V., Kind, S., & Kocher, L. L. M, 2017. *Encounters with Materials in Early Childhood Education (Changing Images of Early Childhood)*. New York: Routledge.

Pagliano, P., 1999. *Multisensory Environments*. London: David Fulton Publishers.

Paul-Smith, S., & Barber, J., 2011. *The Purpose of Planning and Observation*. Practical Pre-School Books. London: MA Education Ltd.

Percival, I., 1992. Chaos: A science for the real world. In Hall, N. (Ed.), *The New Scientist Guide to Chaos*. London: Penguin Books, pp 11–21.

Phillips, A., 2007. *Winnicott*. St Ives: Penguin Books.

Povell, P., 2017. Maria Montessori: Yesterday, today, and tomorrow. In Cohen, L. E, & Waite-Stupiansky, S. (Eds.), *Theories of Early Childhood Education: Developmental, Behaviorist, and Critical*. Abingdon, Oxon: Routledge, pp. 18–31.

Ramsey, P. G., 2015. *Teaching and Learning in a Diverse World: Multicultural Education* (4th ed.) New York: Teachers College Press, p.125.

Rinaldi, C., 2006. *In Dialogue with Reggio Emilia: Listening, Researching and Learning*. Oxon: Routledge.

Ritson, L., 2016. *Adventure Education: Fun Games and Activities for Children and Young People*. Oxon: Routledge.

Rosen, M., 1989. *We're Going on a Bear Hunt*. London: Walker Books.

RNIB. May 2014 *Understanding Complex Needs – Effective Practice Guide*. p.8.

Sagar, C., 1990. Working with cases of child sexual abuse. In C. Case & T. Dalley (Eds.), *Working with Children in Art Therapy*. New York: Routledge, pp. 89–114.

Seus, Dr., 1949. *Bartholomew and the Oobleck*. New York: Random House.

Swim, T. J., 2017. *Infants, Toddlers and Caregivers: Caregiving and Responsive Curriculum Development*. 9th ed. Boston: Cengage Learning, p. 196.

Szekely, G., 2015. *Play and Creativity in Art Teaching*. Routledge: New York.

Thornton, L., & Brunton, P., 2015. *Understanding the Reggio Approach: Reflections on the Early Childhood Experience of Reggio Emilia*. 3rd ed. Abingdon, Oxon: Routledge.

Tudge, J, R, H., Mercon-Varga, E. A., Liang, Y., & Payir, A., 2017. The importance of Urie Bronfenbrenner's bioecological theory for early childhood education. In Cohen, L. E, & Waite-Stupiansky, S. (Eds.), *Theories of Early Childhood Education: Developmental, Behaviorist, and Critical*. New York. Routledge, pp 45–57.

Tunnicliffe, S. D., 2016. *Starting Inquiry-based Science in the Early Years*. 1st ed. Oxon: Routledge.
West, J., 1992. *Child-Centred Play Therapy*. Sevenoaks: Hodder & Stoughton Limited.
White, J., 2014. Exploring appropriate outdoor provision for babies and toddlers. In Maynard, T. & Waters, J. (Eds.), *Exploring Outdoor Play in the Early Years*. Maidenhead: Open University Press, pp. 42–54.
White, J., & Edwards, E. 2012. *Making a Mud Kitchen*. Sheffield: Muddyfaces.
Wolfgang, C. H., & Glickman, C. D., 1986. *Solving Discipline Problems: Strategies for Classroom Teachers*. 2nd ed. New York: Allyn and Bacon, Inc.
Woods, A., 2017a. *Child-Initiated Play and Learning*. 2nd ed. Abingdon, Oxon: Routledge.
Woods, A., 2017b. *Elemental Play and Outdoor Learning: Young Children's Playful Connections with People, Places and Things*. Abingdon, Oxon: Routledge.

Articles/journals/research papers etc

Bayley, R., & Broadbent, L., 2008. Like bees, not butterflies. *Nursery World*, 8 January 2008, pp. 16–17.
Bell, K. W., 1997. *The Relationship between Perceived Physical Competence and the Physical Activity Patterns of Fifth and Seventh Grade Children*. [Thesis]. Virginia Polytechnic Institute and State University, p. 133.
Chown, A., 2010. Making a mess of things! *SEN Magazine*, issue 46, pp. 66–67. senmagazine.co.uk.
Brodie, K., & Godfrey, M., 2018. *The 2018 Spring Summit on Children's Outdoor Play and Learning: Puddle Play, Mud Kitchens and* Spirituality. Available from: www.earlyyearssummit.com [Accessed 5 June 2018].
Csikszentmihalyi, M., 2008. *Flow: The Psychology of Optimal Experience*. New York: Harper Perennial.
Deci, E. L., & Ryan, R. M., 2000. The "what" and "why" of goal pursuits: Human needs and the self-determination of behaviour. *Psychological Inquiry*, 11(4): 227–268.
Diamond, A., & Lee, K., 2011. Interventions shown to aid executive function development in children 4-12 years old. *Science*, 19 August.
Duffy, B., 2007. *All about Messy Play*. The Early Years Foundation Stage Primary National Strategy.
Elm, A., 2017. Less is more – Early childhood teachers' pedagogical content knowledge in science and technology. In *27th Early Childhood Education Beyond the Crisis*. EECERA.
Gascoyne, S., 2009. *Introducing Treasure Baskets. Training Handout*. Available from: www.playtoz.co.uk. [Accessed 12 May 2012].
Gascoyne, S., 2015. *The Special Qualities, Benefits and Application of Messy Play in Special Time*. (Diploma essay).
Gascoyne, S., 2017. Patterns and attributes in vulnerable children's messy play. *European Early Childhood Education Research Journal*, 25(2): 272–291. doi:10.1080/1350293X.2017.1288019.
Goddard, C., 2018a. Fit for purpose. *Nursery World*, 30 April–13 May, pp. 32–33.
Goddard, C., 2018b. Fizz, bang... *Nursery World*, 30 April–13 May, pp. 42–43.
Goldstein, L., S. (1999) The relational zone: The role of caring relationships in the co-construction of mind. *American Educational Research Journal*, 36: 647–673.
Goodman, R., Renfrew, D., & Mullick, M., 2000. *European Child & Adolescent Psychiatry*, 9: 129. doi:10.1007/s007870050008.
Grenier, J., 2018. In Jones Russel, M., Go public. *Nursery World*, 30 April–13 May, p. 37.
Gripton, C., 2017. Planning for endless possibilities. In Woods, A. (Ed.), *Child-initiated Play and Learning*. Abingdon, Oxon: Routledge, pp 8–22.
Hastings, C., 2012. *Containing the Chaos and Mess*. Theoretical essay. Canterbury Christ Church University.
Hastings, C. 2013. *Messy Play – An Evaluation of the Therapeutic Messy Play of Looked After Children and Their Changing Emotional Needs*. [unpublished MA thesis.] APAC/Christchurch Canterbury University.
International Baccalaureate, 2010. *The Primary Years Programme as a Model of Transdisciplinary Learning*. Cardiff, p. 1.

Laevers, F., 2005. *Deep-level-learning and the Experiential Approach in Early Childhood and Primary Education*. Katholieke Universiteit Leuven Research Centre for Early Childhood and Primary Education, p. 5. Available from: https://vorming.cego.be/images/downloads/BO_DP_Deep-levelLearning.pdf [Accessed 20 June 2018].

Laevers, F., & Declercq, B., 1997. *A Process-Oriented Monitoring System for the Early Years*. Revised Edition. Averbode, Belgium: Centre for Experiential Education.

Lederman, S. J., & Klatzky, R. L., 1987. The intelligent hand. In Bower, G. (Ed.), *Psychology of Learning and Motivation: Advances in Research and Theory* (Vol. 21). New York. Academic Press, pp. 121–151.

Marlen, D., 2014. Faster is not better. *Teach Nursery*, 4(8): 38–39.

Mickelburgh, J., 2010. Educational pioneers: John Dewey, 1859-1952. Available at: https://eyfs.info/articles.html/teaching-and-learning/educational-pioneers-john-dewey-1859-1952-r42/ [Accessed 19 June 2018].

Moll, L., Amanti, C., Neff, D., & Gonzales, N., 1992. Funds of knowledge for teaching: Using a qualitative approach to connect homes and classrooms. *Theory into Practice*, 31(2): 132: 132–141.

Papatheodorou, T., 2009. *Sensory Play*. Pilot Research Project. Anglia Ruskin University.

Palincsar, A. S., & Magnusson, S. J., 2000. *The Interplay of Firsthand and Text-Based Investigations in Science Education*. University of Michigan. CIERA Report.

Pascal, C., Bertram, T., & Peckham, K., 2018. Speaking up. *Nursery World*, 30 April–13 May, pp. 34–36.

Perry, L. K., Samuelson, L. K., & Burdinie, J. B., 2013. Highchair philosophers: The impact of seating context on young children's naming biases. *Developmental Science*. doi:10.1111/desc.12147.

Powell, M., 2006. *Containers That Hold Alchemy in Play Therapy*. Unpublished essay. Post Graduate Diploma in Play Therapy. London: APAC.

Rice, J. 2013. *The Benefits of 'Messy Play' as Part of the Play Therapy Tool-kit*. [Unpublished theoretical essay.] Postgraduate Diploma in Practice Based Play Therapy.

Sak, S., & Sak, R., 2016. Developmentally appropriate behaviour management: Turkish Preschool teachers' practices. *International Journal on New Trends in Education and Their Implications*, 7(4): Article: 07. Available from: www.ijonte.org. [Accessed 26 August 2018].

Saunders, E. 2013. 'Containing the Mess' workshop, Gloucestershire. In Rice, J. (Ed.), *The Benefits of 'Messy Play' as Part of the Play Therapy Tool-kit*. [Unpublished theoretical essay.] Postgraduate Diploma in Practice Based Play Therapy.

Savage, M. J., & Drake, S. M., 2016. Living transdisciplinary curriculum: Teachers' experiences with the International Baccalaureate's primary years programme. *International Electronic Journal of Elementary Education*, 9(1): 1–20.

Sebba, R., 1991. The landscapes of childhood: The reflections of childhood's environment in adult memories and in children's attitudes. *Environment & Behavior*, 23: 395–422.

Sigman, A., 2011. Close encounters of the green kind. *Montessori International*, April–June: 40.

Skinner, Mosley & Ebbutt, 23 October 2008. Let's explore... Wet and dry. *Nursery World*, pp. 19–22.

Thornton, L., & Brunton, P., 2006. Water ways. *Nursery World*, pp.12–13.

Tomkins, S., & Dale Tunnicliffe, S., 2007 Nature tables: Stimulating children's interest in natural objects. *JBE*, 41(4), 150–155.

Veilleux, C. M., 2017. *The Implementation of a Silence Area into the Environment and how it Impacts the Social-Emotional Behaviour of the Students*. [MA Thesis.] University of Wisconsin – River Falls. Available from: https://thisonebreath.wordpress.com/tag/children/.

Waite, S., 2010. Losing our way? The downward path for outdoor learning for children aged 2-11 years. *Journal of Adventure Education and Outdoor Learning*, 10(2), 111–124. Available from: www.tandfonline.com/loi/raol20.

Watts, R., 2011. The choice is theirs. *Teach Nursery*, 1(5), 38–41.

Weinstein, N., 2016. Break the mould. *Nursery World*, 18 April–1 May, p. 30.

Wells, N. M., 2000. At home with nature: The effects of nearby nature on children's cognitive functioning. *Environment & Behavior*, 32: 775–795.

Wells, N. M., & Evans, G. W., 2003. Nearby nature: A buffer of life stress among rural children, *Environment & Behaviour*, 35(3): 311–330.

Whipple, N., Bernier, A., & Mageau, G. A., 2009. Attending to the Exploration Side of Infant Attachment: Contributions From Self-Determination Theory, *Canadian Psychology*, Vol. 50, No. 4, 219–229.

Presentations

Buckler, L., 2013 *The Inspired Child – A Creative Journey*. MSA National Conference, University of London.
Kind, S., 2017. *The Poetics and Possibilities of Video in Pedagogical Narration*. EECERA.
Skreland, L., 2014. *Kindergarten Rules and Space*. EECERA.

Online/Electronic

Aldridge, F., 1998. Chocolate or shit aesthetics and cultural poverty in art therapy with children. *Inscape* [online], 3(1): 2–9. Available from: http://arttherapybrighton.co.uk/wp-content/uploads/2010/09/Chocolate-or-shit-aesthetics-and-cultural-poverty-in-art-therapy-with-children.pdf [Accessed 27 August 2018].

Bruce, T., & Dyke, J., May 2017 EYFS Best Practice: Learning from Froebel… Nurture, family and community. Available from: www.nurseryworld.co.uk/nursery-world/feature/1161180/eyfs-best-practice-learning-from-froebel-nurture-family-and-community. [Accessed 20 June 2018].

Development matters in the EYFS. Available from: www.foundationyears.org.uk/files/2012/03/Development-Matters-FINAL-PRINT-AMENDED.pdf [Accessed 16 June 2018].

Drake, J., 20 July 2005. *Water ways*. Nursery World. Available from: www.nurseryworld.co.uk/nursery-world/news/1080663/water [Accessed 10 June 2018]. .

Early Childhood Development Centre Cologne. Available from: www.rainbowtrekkers.de/en/home/index.html. [Accessed 15 June 2018].

Early Education, 2018. About Froebel. Available from: www.early-education.org.uk/about-froebel. [Accessed 16 March 2018].

Ellington, V. *Philosophy of Education*. Froebel Web. Available from: www.froebelweb.org/web2002.html. [Accessed 20 June 2018].

Foundation Stage Forum. Available from: Eyfs.info>forums>topic>9498.html. [Accessed 25 April 2018].

Gees, S., 2018. *New research drives home how crazy it is that triclosan is still in hundreds of everyday products*. Quartz Media. Available from: https://qz.com. [Accessed 10 June 2018].

Gburczyk, K. (2012) *The Role of Messy Play*. 9 July [Online blog]. Available from: www.childrenstherapies.co.ik/the-role-of-messy-play [Accessed March 2015].

Harvard Graduate School of Education, *Project Zero*. Available from: www.pz.harvard.edu/ [Accessed 16 June 2018].

Institute for the Future. Available from: www.iftf.org/home/ [Accessed 20 May 2018].

Kingsley, A., 12 February 2015. *'How to catch a porridge thief': Hooking Year One into Traditional Tales*. Innovate my schools. Available at: www.innovatemyschool.com [Accessed 28 May 2018].

Kuhl, P. K., 2011 Sept. 9. *Brain Mechanisms in Early Language Acquisition*. PMC. Available from: www.ncbi.nlm.nih.gov/pmc/articles/PMC2947444/ [Accessed 10 June 2018].

Levinson, M., January 21, 2016 *Transdisciplinarity: Thinking Inside and Outside the Box*. Available from: www.edutopia.org/blog/transdiciplinarity-thinking-inside-outside-box-matt-levinson. www.edutopia.org website [Accessed 10 June 2018].

Lil Bebe Academy, 2018. Available from: www.lilbebeacademy.net/ [Accessed 28 May 2018].

Marti, G., in Jewell, S., 1999. The nursery that took all the children's toys. *The Independent*. Available from: www.independent.co.uk/news/education/education-news/the-nursery-that-took-all-the-childrens-toys-away-1125048. [Accessed 21 June 2018].

Mickleburgh, J., 2010. Educational pioneers: Friedrich Froebel. *Early Years Foundation Stage Forum*. Available from: https://eyfs.info/articles.html/teaching-and-learning/educational-pioneers-friedrich-froebel-1782-1852-r44/. [Accessed 28 May 2018].

Oxford English Dictionary. Available from: https://en.oxforddictionaries.com/definition/gloop [Accessed 1 February 2018].

Pacini-Ketchabaw, V., Kind, S., & Kocher, L. L. M., 2017. *Encounters with Materials*, podcast. Available from: www. encounterswithmaterials.com/ [Accessed 3 October 2017].

Parnell, L., 2018. The importance of messy play. *Natural Child Magazine*. Available from: www.natural childmagazine.com/0808/messy-play.htm. [Accessed 16 June 2018].

Running Past. *The McMillan Sisters and their Open Air Nursery*. Available from: https://runner500.wordpress.com/2015/12/02/the-mcmillan-sisters-and-their-open-air-nursery/. [Accessed 11 June 2018].

Schubert, E., & Strick, R., 1996. *Toy-free Kindergarten – A Project to Prevent Addiction for Children and with Children*. Munchen: AktionJugendschutz.

Sheehan, B., 2015 'When is mess just a mess?', *Play Therapy, BACP Children and Young People*. Available from: www.eqe-ltd.com/downloads/When is a mess just a mess.pdf. [Accessed 20 June 2018].

Sonnier, A., 2012. Available from: www.learnplayimagine.com/2012/06/childs-play-101-fun-with-food.html. [Accessed 21 May 2018].

Swift, J. 2016. Available from: www.campaignlive.co.uk/article/prisoners-spend-time-outside-todays-children-claims-persil-campaign/1388344 [Accessed 28 March 2018].

Vientiane International School (VIS), 2018. Available from: www.vislao.com/learning/primary/early-years. [Accessed 27 May 2018].

Surveys

Gascoyne, S., 2015. *Messy Play Survey*. Survey Monkey.
Gascoyne, S., 2018a. *Messy Play Experiences Survey*, Survey Monkey.
Gascoyne, S., 2018b. *Childcare Expo Seminar*, London.

Index

Page numbers in italics refer to figures. Page numbers in bold refer to tables.

"accepting the child as is" principle 183–5
active exploration 183–4
"adult does not hurry" principle 190–3; facilitating deep-level engagement 191–2; interruptions 191; patience 190; stress 191; time 190
adults: adult-initiated activity 5; attentive noticing 29; as curators of emotional environment 29–31; decisions, impact 178–81; as 'directors of environment' 26–7; giving children responsibility 28; role in supporting children's material encounters 26; self-awareness 51; *see also* minimal mess – maximum adult control
affordance 43, 46–7, 56–7, 62, 65–68, 71–2, 92–94, 96, 98, 101–2, 104, 106–109, 113, 123, 128, 138, 164, 194
agency, of children 11, 47, 81, 115, 177, 182; balancing with agency of adults 182, 197
agents of play 178
Ainsworth, M. 18
arboretums 164, **165**; outdoor 'workshops' 173; science lab/workshops 172–3
ARC *see* autonomy, relatedness and competence (ARC)
attachment: containment and 47–9; relevance 19; secure 18, 19; strong foundation of 18–19
attention restoration 46
attentive noticing 29–31, 57, 67, 98, 101, 108, 117, 121, 145, 153, 156, 161–2, 180–1, 187, 199
autonomy 10, 17–18, 29–30, 37–8, 46, 49, 52–3, 55, 59, 61, 83, 87–8, 90, 97–8, 100, 114, 125, 127, 138, **144**, 149, 164, 169, 171, 173–4, 183, 187, 193 and *see* autonomy, relatedness and competence (ARC)
autonomy, relatedness and competence (ARC) 9–10, 11, *11*, 29, 37–8, 40, 57, 60, 94, 100–1, 117, 120, 122, 124, 127, 132–3, 152, 154, 156, 165, 177, 197
Axline, V. 29, 30
Axline's principles: "accepting the child as is" principle 183–5; "adult does not hurry" principle 190–3; "child leads – adult follows" principle 189; "child's responsibility to make choices" principle 188–9; "establishes feeling of permission" principle 186–7; "few limitations, anchor to reality" principle 193–7; "reflect back so child gains an insight" principle 187–8; "warm and friendly relationship" principle 182–3

Baldwin, N. 138
Beckerleg, T. 6, 124, 125
Bender 47
Bogost, I. 109, 111, 125
Bowlby, J. 18, 19
Brodie, K. 152, 153
Bronfenbrenner, U. 16, 27, 31, 107, 151–2, 154, 163, 167, 183

Case, C. 55
childhood, microsystem of 17
"child leads – adult follows" principle 189
"child's responsibility to make choices" principle 188–9

children: engagement of 181; explorations of 37–8; taking outdoors 26; responsibility 28; see also agency, of children; messiest provisions – child ownership
citrus ice eggs 137–9
clay 89–90; benefits 89; challenges 89; characteristics 89; sensory qualities and vocabulary 89
clearing up 59; benefits of tidying 115; positioning tidying as an essential part of activities 116–17; preparing for mess 114; routine, development 115; self-cleansing and care 117–20
cognitive disequilibrium 6–7, 27, 32, 87, 90, 104
colours: and appearance of mess 54–6; see also dark colours
communication: and self-expression 47; tool 55–6
competence 10–11, 38, 48, 51–3, 55, 59, 61, 83, 97, 149, 152, 158, 163, 196 and see autonomy, relatedness and competence (ARC)
compost: benefits 92; challenges 92; characteristics 91; sensory qualities and vocabulary 92
containing stage 59; learning potential 113; legibility and function 111–13; material properties 109; quantity 111; shaping affordance 113; size 110–11; variety and shape 109–10
containment: and attachment 47–9; continuum of 48
coping with discomfort (adult) 37, 126, 194, (child) 6, 144, 196
cross-curricular thinking tools, executive functions as 30, 120, 155, 157
Crowe, B. 34, 45, 183
Csikszentmihalyi, M. 174, 190–1
curiosity 31; 'science of' 168
curriculum silos, learning and 151–2

dark colours: appeal of 54; creation of 55
Deci, E. L. 9, 37, 178, 199
deep-level thinking 68
Dewey, J. 26, 29, 31
discarding stage, of messy play 60, 120
discomfort, coping with 37, 126, 194
Di Stead 36
dry textures, in messy play 71–6
Duffield, S. 175
Duffy, B. 5–7

ecological systems model (Bronfenbrenner) 16, *16*
EF see executive functions (EF)
embodied sensory engagement 184

embodiment stage, of messy play 22–4
Emilia, R. 25
emotional environment 122, 186; adults as curators of 29–31; relevance 18; stages of development 17–18; strong foundation of attachment 18–19
enabling environments, creation of 122; balanced approach 125–6; messy play encounters *123*, 123–4; setting objectives 124–5
engagement, of children 181
enriching, messy play as 49–50
environments *see specific types*
Ephgrave, A. 181
Erikson, E. 17–19
"establishes feeling of permission" principle 186–7
executive functions (EF) 30, 120, 155, 157
explorations, of children 37–8
exploring and experimenting stage *58*, 58–60; as complementing and contrasting 107–8; as culturally representative 107; as exploring and experimenting 104; as novelty 106–7; protective equipment 104; scale 106; utensils and tools 104

fear of mess, management of 43, 61
"few limitations, anchor to reality" principle 193–7
festivals, international 4
flow see Csikszentmihalyi
foodstuffs, in messy play 66
forest schools 26
Froebel, F. 20, 27, 29
funds of knowledge 17, 38 and see knowledge funds
fun, messy play as 49–50
functional fixedness 71–2, 107, 175, 189
funnels, metal jam-making 104

Gascoyne, S. 25, 43, 46, 55–7, 105
Gburczyk, K. 41, 43
gelli baff/gelli play 87–8; benefits 87; challenge 87; characteristics 87; sensory qualities and vocabulary 87
Gifts (Froebel) 20, 27
Glickman, C. D. 193
gloop/oobleck 90–1; benefits 90; characteristics 90; sensory qualities and vocabulary 90
Godfrey, M. 17, 99, 100, 104, 126, 147, 152, 153, 181, 193
Goldschmied, E. 25
Grace, J. 4, 32–36, 124, 125, 156, 168
grains 72–4
greenhouses 164, **165**, 172

harnessing stage, of messy play 59, 113–14
Hastings, C. 46, 55, 56
Hawkins, D. 6, 162, 190
herbs 72–4
heuristic play 25
Hodgman, L. 109
Holi Festival, India 4
Hutt, C. 67, 100

ice cubes, painting with 134–7
in-between textures: playdough/play-doh 76–7; water 79–81; water beads 77–9
inquiry-based learning: ingredients of 156, **156**; pre-requisites for *155*, 155–60
Isaccs, S. 27, 28

Jennings, S. 3, 22, 32, 46, 48, 62
Jung, C. 21

Kaplin, R. 46, 54, 56, 97, 114, 118, 157, 190
Kaplin, S. 46, 54 56, 97, 114, 118, 157, 190
Kindergartens 20, 146, 162; Nature 26; Toy Free 30, 182
Kingston-Hughes, B. 173, 186, 196
knowledge funds 36, 65, 73, 80, 92, 102, 107–8, 116, 124, 126, 134–5, 137, 144–5, 149, 160–163, 165, 167, 170–172, 180–1, 193

Latham, L. 62
learning: and curriculum silos 151–2; interpreting 152–3; neuroscience, sensory experience and 32–7; planning/perhaps, restricting 153; potential containing stage 113; sensory experience and 32–7; thinking and 31–7; *see also* inquiry-based learning
Leuven Scales 49, 129–31, 135, 139, 143, 152–3
linguistic being 32
Loose Parts Play (Nicholson) 25

macrolevel 122, 124, 127, 133
macroscale (Bronfenbrenner) 17
Malaguzzi, L. 25, 153
Maslow's hierarchy of needs 15
mastery orientation, resilience and 158–9
materials encounters 4, 7, 17, 23,-28, 38, 40, 64, 96, 112, 120–1, 123–4, 145, 151, 154, 160, 168, 176–8, 192, 195, 198, 200
material engagement, messy play as 12
materials: affordances 46, *56*, 65–7, *66*, *67*; as agents 195; continuum of resources 70–1; natural 66; spectrum of resources 93

McMillan, M. 26
mess: colour and appearance of 54–6; defined 7–8; as emotional barometer and communication tool 55–6; management of fear of 43; preparing for 114; *see also* minimal mess – maximum adult control; moderate mess – joint ownership
messiest provisions – child ownership 145–6; muddy puddle 148–9; powder paint 147–8; workshop and science lab 146–7
Messiness Scale 50
messy play: attention restoration qualities and 46; benefits of 49, *49*; definition 7–9; encounters, framework for planning *123*, 123–4; engagements, framework 9, *10*; enjoyment of 94; experiences *126*; as fun and enriching 49–50; extremes of *9*; as 'just good fun' 5; as material engagements 12; materials 65–7, *66*, *67*; materials, open-ended affordance 46; myths 1–6; needs and concerns *11*; and phases of scientific thinking **161**; planning and preparation 94–5; preparation time management 95–103; provision, sliding scale *127*, 127–32; restoring and calming 44–6; themes 64–5, *65*; triangle and theoretical context *15*; use, patterns 43, 64–93
messy play, provocations of 126–7; framework in action 133; messiest provisions – child ownership 145–9; minimal mess – maximum adult control 133–7; moderate mess – joint ownership 137–45
messy play, quantifying: emotional and material patterns 53–7; spatial patterns 50–1; temporal patterns 51–3
messy play resources 96; choice 99–102; context 97–8; continuity 102; legibility and affordance 98; safety 103; time, boundaries and space 103; types 40–1, **41**; types, problems accessing resources 41–2
messy play stages *58*, 58–62, *61*; clearing up 59, 114–20; containing 59, 108–13; discarding 60, 120; exploring and experimenting *58*, 58–60, 104–8; harnessing 59, 113–14; and implications for preparation 103–20; saving 59, 114
Messy Pots (Saunders) 49
microlevel 122, 124, 127–8
microsystems, childhood 17
mini cloche 164, **165**, 171
minimal mess – maximum adult control 133–4; ice cube painting 134–7
modelling 29, 115, 136, 143, 156, 160, 183, 186

moderate mess – joint ownership 137–45; citrus ice eggs 137–9; clingfilm-covered paint 139–41; mud pies 143–5; tea-making 141–2
Montessori, M. 20, 21, 26, 27, 28, 29, 104, 115, 176, 193
moods, changing 56–7
Mood Scale 49
Morris, K. 10, 37, 38, 99
movement and flow, focus on 174–5
mud 2–3, 8, 91–2, 104, 145, 186, 196: benefits 92; challenges 92; characteristics 91; 'clean' 71; kitchens 26, 106; pies 143–5; puddles 34, 104, 148–9; sensory qualities and vocabulary 92; slides/sliding 6–7, 9, 98, 114, 173–4
myths xx

natural environments 48; nature indoors with natural treasures 24–6; relevance 25–6; taking children outdoors 26
natural materials 66
Nature Kindergartens 26
Nature Tables 24
neuroscience, sensory experience and learning 32–7
New Year Songkran festival, Thailand 4
Nicholson, S. 25
Nicolescu 154
Norman, D. A. 98
noticing *see* attentive noticing

oats 72–4
occupations (Froebel) 20, 27
O'Neill, K. 158–60
'one-size-fits-all' approach 12, 127
oobleck *see* gloop/oobleck
Open Air Nursery 26
outcomes, of messy play 181

Pacini-Ketchabaw, V. 31, 162, 180
paint/painting 85; benefits 84; challenges 84; characteristics 84; clingfilm-covered 139–41; ice cube 134–7; powder 147–8; sensory qualities and vocabulary 84
paper, dry textures: benefits 71; challenges 71–2; characteristics 71; sensory qualities and vocabulary 71
pasta 72–4
patterns, in messy play 43–50; emotional and material 53–7; spatial 50–1; temporal 51–3; in use 57–8, 64–93
physical environments 19–20, 186–7
Piaget, J. 21, 32, 154

Pikler movement 21; approach 22
playdough/play-doh 54; benefits 76; challenges 77; characteristics 76; creation 169; making **170**; sensory qualities and vocabulary 77
playful inquiry 160
playfulness 160
Play Therapists 51
Play Therapy 30, 50, 56, 57, 110, 158, 160, 182, 187
POMS *see* Process Oriented Monitoring System (POMS)
porridge 164–6, **165**
possibility finding 163
possibility spaces 109, 149, 162–3
powder paints 147–8
practitioners 17, 171, 181, 182, 189, 191–4; attentive noticing and 29; defining learning 152–3; hybrid teaching approach 172; planning messy play 124; raising self-awareness of 51
Process Oriented Monitoring System (POMS) 50
projection stage 22, 23, 95
provocations 19, 74, 83, 95–6, 107, 113, 126–7, 133–4, 137–9, 157, 160, 165, 172, 185, 195
pulses 72–4, 135

questions 98, 154, 163–4, 171–2, 187–8

Rajan, A. 24, 83, 112, 130
"reflect back so child gains an insight" principle 187–8
relatedness 10, 11, 37–8, 53, 59, 61, 83, 97, 117, 124, 138, 142, 152–4, 160, 170, 188, 197, 199 and *see* autonomy, relatedness and competence (ARC)
resilience, and mastery orientation 158–9
resources, affordance and use of 67
responsibility, children 28
role-play **61**, 83, 92, 95, 142, 167
role stage 22, 23
Ryan, R. M. 9, 37, 178, 199

Sagar, C. 55
sand 8, 24, 25, 44, 54, 67, 75–6, 98, 100–1, 110–11, 188, 192–3; benefits 75; challenges 75; characteristics 75; sensory qualities and vocabulary 75
satisficing 111, 115, 148
Saunders, E. 49
saving stage 59, 114
scaffolding 30–1, 145, 162–3, 189
scale, importance of 68–70

science: 'of curiosity' 168; labs, and workshops 172–3; *see also* neuroscience, sensory experience and learning
scientific thinking **161**, 161–2
scoops 104
SDT *see* self-determination theory (SDT)
security of exploration 10
secure attachment 18
self-awareness 51
self-determination theory (SDT) 9, 30, 37, 117, 178, 188, 199
self-expression 159–60; communication and 47
self-regulation 112, 115, 155–8, 164, 167, 169, 174, 193
'sensory being' 4, 32, 124, 160, 191, 199
sensory engagement, embodied 184
sensory experience 15; and learning 32–7
sensory interaction 32, **32**
sensory play continuum 25
sensory-rich environments 32; active discovery 21–2; embodiment stage 22–4; movement and senses 21–4; projection stage 22, 23; relevance 20–1, 23; role stage 22, 23
sensory stimulation 4, 7, 16, 19, 27, 61, 80
shaving foam: benefits 82–3; challenges 83; characteristics 82; sensory qualities and vocabulary 83
Smith, F. 131, 159, 180
soil 91–2; benefits 92; challenges 92; characteristics 91; sensory qualities and vocabulary 92
Sonnier, A. 74
spaces, creation of 163–4
spices 72–4
spoons 41, 52, 75, 88, 98, 100–1, 104, 106–7, 110, 117, 142, 145, 147, 164–5, 169, 173, 179
Steiner, R. 20, 28
sticky textures *see* wet and sticky textures
Strengths and Difficulties Questionnaire (SDQ) data 55
sultanas 72–4
Szekely, G. 106

tactile defensiveness 8, 183
tea-making 141–2, 167–8; possibilities and **169**
textures *see specific types*

thinking: deep-level 68; and learning 31–7
thinking tools, development of: supporting scientific thinking **161**, 161–2; tools for noticing 162–3
Tomkins, S. 24
tools, utensils and 104
Toy Free Kindergartens 30, 182
transdisciplinary thinking 154
transformation levels 46–7
treasure baskets 25
Tunnicliffe, S. 24

utensils, and tools 104

Vygotsky, L. 29–31, 47, 189, 194

"warm and friendly relationship" principle 182–3
water 36–7, 44, 47–8, 56, 70–2, 79–81, 97, 110–11, 113, 172; benefits 80; challenges 80; characteristics 79; sensory qualities and vocabulary 80; soapy 117–18
water beads 77–9: benefits 78; challenges 79; characteristics 77; sensory qualities and vocabulary 78
Wellbeing 10, 16, 19, 30, 38
Wellbeing scale: Leuven 49, 67–8, 120, 131, 135, 139, 141, 143, 152–3, 173, 181, 191
West, J. 54
wet and sticky textures: clay 88–90; gelli baff/gelli play 87–8; gloop/oobleck 90–1; homemade natural yoghurt 86–7; mud, soil and compost 91–2; paint 84–5; shaving foam 82–3
Winnicott, D. 19
Wolfgang, C. H. 193
Woltmann 47
wooden stakes and netting 164, **165**, 166
workshops, and science labs 146–7

yoghurt, homemade natural: benefits 86; challenges 86–7; characteristics 86; sensory qualities and vocabulary 86

zone of proximal development (ZPD) 30, 31, 38